# YOURS TRULY
## HARVEY DONALDSON

Edited by David R. Wolfe

**Wolfe Publishing Co., Inc.**
138 North Montezuma Street
Prescott, Arizona 86301

Copyright © 1980 by Wolfe Publishing Co., Inc.

All rights reserved. No portion of this book may be reproduced without written permission from the publisher, except by a reviewer who may quote brief passages in connection with a review.

Manufactured in the United States of America

**Library of Congress Cataloging in Publication Data**

Catalog Card Number: 79-055916

ISBN: 0-935632-00-X   Deluxe Bound
      0-935632-01-8   Hard Bound

*Harvey A. Donaldson, had it not been for your efforts, there would not have been any bench rest shooting.*

*Townsend Whelen*

*August 29, 1954*

## Acknowledgments

John T. Amber, renowned for his superb editing of *Gun Digest* and *Handloader's Digest*, for contributing the Preface to this book as a "heartfelt tribute to old Harve."

Fred T. Huntington, for earning Harvey's longtime respect and helping him in the design of reamers for some Donaldson cartridges.

Mr. Joyce Hornady, for sending the Donaldson letter "Twenty-Shot Nickel-Size Group," even if he was sort of bragging about whose bullets were used.

Dr. Roger Wolfe, for driving his brother to Fultonville when he could have sat by a cozy fireplace listening to a Beethoven trio.

Robert Bump, a gun enthusiast who lived not far from Harvey, for helping us trace down some old magazines and letters, and for his continued encouragement.

George Martin, NRA Director of Publications, for granting us permission to reprint the articles and photos from *The American Rifleman*.

Barbara "Charlie" Pickering, Production Supervisor for Wolfe Publishing Company, for slaving at the typesetting machine many nights and weekends and infrequently exhibiting minor fits of rage.

Mrs. George Donaldson, for patiently helping us go through the boxes of letters and photographs on a wet, chilly day in 1977.

# Contents

| | |
|---|---|
| Preface | x |
| Introduction | xii |

## 1935-1936

| | |
|---|---|
| Rest-Shooting<br>Reprinted from July, 1935 *American Rifleman* | 1 |
| Rest Shooting and Schuetzen Loading<br>Reprinted from May, 1936 *American Rifleman* | 9 |
| Rest Shooting and Schuetzen Loading<br>Reprinted from September, 1936 *American Rifleman* | 17 |

## 1965

| | |
|---|---|
| Twenty-Shot Nickel-Size Group | 23 |
| It's A Tricky Business | 25 |

## 1966

| | |
|---|---|
| A Few 'Cutting' Remarks | 27 |
| Finding the Cause of 'Flyers' | 30 |
| Origin of the .25-20 Single Shot | 34 |
| On .30 Caliber Cast Bullets | 41 |
| Experiments in .25 Caliber | 43 |
| Those Flat Nose Bullets | 46 |

## 1967

| | |
|---|---|
| Secrets of Schuetzen Shooting | 51 |
| Favorite Hunting Calibers | 57 |
| Letter from Harry Pope, 1903 | 62 |
| An Insight into Primers | 69 |
| Mann-Niedner 'Hamburg' Rifle | 72 |
| Question of Proper Lubrication | 76 |

## 1968

| | |
|---|---|
| Tale from a Bird Hunter | 81 |
| Early Varmint Cartridges | 84 |
| More on Early Case Design | 90 |
| Black Powder & Cast Bullets | 94 |
| Bottleneck Case Controversy | 104 |
| My First Chuck Rifle | 111 |
| Bullet Casting Is An ART | 117 |
| Graphite Wads (Reprint) | 123 |

## 1969

| | |
|---|---|
| A 'Master' Crow Hunter | 130 |
| 6mm Cast Bullets on 'Chucks | 133 |
| Point Shape vs. Accuracy | 136 |
| Behind the .220 Swift Design | 140 |
| Barrel Life in the .220 Swift | 143 |
| Col. Whelen & the .257 Roberts | 147 |

# 1970

| | |
|---|---|
| *The Bigger, the Better?* | *150* |
| *A Good Gunstock Finish* | *154* |
| *It's the Primer that Counts* | *160* |
| *A Look Back at the .25's* | *167* |
| *Case Life Is Up To You* | *172* |
| *Expert Tips on Reloading* | *177* |
| *More on Beloved .25's* | *186* |
| *The Importance of Twist* | *191* |

# 1971

| | |
|---|---|
| *Loads for Schuetzen Rifles* | *201* |
| *A History of Bench Rest* | *207* |
| *Understanding Trajectory* | *215* |
| *Ramblings on the Past* | *218* |
| *A Visit to Pope's Shop* | *224* |

# 1972

| | |
|---|---|
| *Shooting A Pope Rifle* | *227* |
| *Loads for .225 Winchester* | *233* |
| *Ideas on Handloading* | *241* |
| *'Left the Range Forever'* | *244* |
| *The Harvey A. Donaldson Story* | *265* |

# *Preface*

I FIRST MET Harvey Donaldson in the 1950s, though we had corresponded for years before that meeting — which took place at the Pine Tree Club of Johnstown, New York.

I had been a handloader since the middle 1920s, yet Harve's deep knowledge, as revealed in his letters to me, impressed me greatly. He was particularly well informed about lead bullet reloading at the turn of the century and later, but his inquisitive and probing mind had kept him alert and interested in any and all later developments — the more modern the better, as long as newer directions in the art and science of making one's own cartridges were valid and worthwhile. Donaldson, in fact, had begun making swaged metal-jacketed bullets as early as 1903, so it was predictable that he would — and did — embrace modern benchrest shooting with the enthusiasm and delight that were so characteristic of the old man.

It was Harve's great verve and unremitting curiosity that endeared him to me — and to many others. I saw in him, if I may say so, a kindred spirit — a man anxious to learn and go on learning. His recurring excitement over this new find or that was infectious.

Nor was his devotion to shooting and handloading confined to those activities. He was, in his 80s, a dedicated sports car owner-driver, which struck another responsive chord in me! I had been a member of the Sports Car Club of America since 1950, owning a few MG's and an XK Jaguar.

I can see Harvey Donaldson now, on a bright Johnstown weekend in 1966, dashing around in his scarlet-colored Corvette, the top down, waving and shouting to his friends.

Harvey had known most, if not all, of shooting's great men of his time — Townsend Whelen, Adolph Niedner (then at Malden, Massachusetts), Franklin Mann, Ned Roberts, Wm. V. Lowe, Phil Sharpe, Harry M. Pope, W. Milton Farrow and many others. Harve had shot with and against these men, either at rest shooting or Schuetzen (offhand) shooting, the latter sport his chief interest from 1900 to 1915 or so. That shooting was done mostly at two hundred yards.

He had aided and assisted Niedner and Mann on the vast experimentation that preceded publication of Mann's book *The Bullet's Flight, From Muzzle to Target.* Earlier he had been instrumental in getting Col. Whelen (then a civilian) to take up handloading.

Harvey Donaldson's letters and articles, as published in *Handloader* and earlier in *The American Rifleman*, among others, have been a source of interest and instruction to many thousands of people. I'm grateful for the opportunity to write this preface to *Yours truly, Harvey Donaldson*, a book I feel sure you'll enjoy and profit from. To old Harve, somewhere up on the Big Range now, I offer this heartfelt tribute.

John T. Amber<br>
Editor Emeritus<br>
*Gun Digest*<br>
*& Handloader's Digest*

# Introduction

ON THE LAST page of the first edition of *Handloader* magazine (May-June, 1966) a "letter" appeared under the column heading "Yours truly, Harvey A. Donaldson." This was the beginning of an extremely popular series of columns (forty in all) by one of the fathers of modern handloading, the founder of organized benchrest shooting, and probably the last of the old-time Schuetzen shooters.

The Donaldson name is connected to some fifteen wildcat cartridges. And the venerable firearms experimenter is credited with the development of several well known commercial cases.

Harvey, a toolmaker, was working, shooting, and writing up to a few weeks before he died on November 6, 1972. He was eighty-nine years old and proudly proclaimed that he'd been shooting for eighty years. Much of that experience, going back to slug-gun and Schuetzen days, and later in the refinement of modern commercial and wildcat cartridges, is revealed in the six years of "Yours truly" columns.

In the seven years since Harvey's death, Wolfe Publishing Company has received hundreds of letters requesting that the old columns be offered in a book. We apologize for the delay. Our procrastination, however, may have been a blessing in disguise. Here's why:

In the fall of 1977, the wife of Harvey's nephew, Mrs. George Donaldson, contacted us; she was trying to dispose of the final contents in Harvey's shop. The tools, machinery, and supplies were all long gone. What remained, it seemed, were old books, magazines, and notebooks. Were we interested? You bet!

In the course of our conversation, I learned that there were also a few boxes of old correspondence in the barn. (Harvey's shop was the second floor of a barn-like building, with his deceased brother's print shop on the ground level.) Mrs. Donaldson said that many of the letters had been taken by interested parties over the last few years but "there's a lot left."

A few weeks later, on a cold and rainy morning, my brother, Roger, and I drove from New York City to

Fultonville. We found Harvey's shop so cluttered with boxes and debris, it was difficult to move around. The roof leaked badly in spots, and several windows were broken. Mrs. Donaldson apologized for the condition of the place, explaining that several collectors and interested parties had recently rummaged through the shop. She then said that she had thrown away several large boxes of old letters, and pointed to the ones that remained.

We later discovered that all of the correspondence with Pope, Niedner, Mann, Lowe, and many others had been either destroyed or taken by collectors. One man, Mrs. Donaldson recalled, had gone through the letters of the 1930s and bought the ones from Major Ned Roberts.

Harvey always kept a carbon copy of his correspondence. Hence we were able to put together nearly all of the communication between the old shooter and the people at Wolfe Publishing Company from 1965 to mid-1972. This book is the result. Included are several articles Harvey wrote for the *American Rifleman* in the Thirties. And his forty columns that appeared in *Handloader* are tagged "Yours truly."

In selecting and editing material for this book, we decided to include many letters that have little or nothing to do with guns. However, they contribute to the continuity and show the humor, wit, and broad knowledge of the man. Readers will find some repetition — especially in the articles concerning Harvey's youth. If we had eliminated some of the references to his mother and his "shooting uncle," Harve's true personality would have been shadowed. For in later years he *did* repeat himself — especially on subjects that were dear to him.

We regret the poor quality in photos for which the originals could not be found. In these instances, we are reprinting pictures from the magazines, and the reproduction suffers. But again, we decided that even a poor photo is better than none if it adds to the overall flavor of the book.

If Harvey were still with us, he'd have penned a dedication of this work, and you can bet it would have gone something like this: "To shooters young and old, who constantly strive for better accuracy through the knowledge of handloading, their equipment, and unlimited hours of practice."

Dave Wolfe

Author's early type of bench rest. Note that the recoil comes on upper arm and not on shoulder. There is a half-inch thickness of sponge rubber under barrel in V-rest.

The improved model of bench rest in use. Note that both forearms lie flat on table top, with buttplate against upper arm and left hand under toe of stock.

# Rest-Shooting

## By HARVEY A. DONALDSON

**Reprinted from July, 1935**
*American Rifleman*

In the December issue of *The American Rifleman* my friend Ned Roberts used two of my ten-shot one hundred-yard rest groups to illustrate the accuracy of the .22 Niedner Magnum cartridge. Ever since the appearance of this article I have had numerous inquiries as to how it was possible to do such shooting, and I shall therefore try to explain the methods that I am using. But if one were to turn back to the older copies of *Shooting and Fishing* — from 1895 to 1905 — he would find many such groups shown in nearly every issue — and very few inquiries as to how it was done, for the reason that most other well-informed shooters were doing as well, or better.

My own experimenting as a Schuetzen shooter began back in 1895, and by 1898 I had taken part in a number of our local two hundred-yard offhand matches; and I have continued this shooting and experimenting up to the present time. I have in my gun-room more than a dozen of the finest Schuetzen rifles that were ever made. They came from the hands of such experts as Harry M. Pope, George C. Schoyen, A.O. Zischang, O.M. Bremer, and others. Most of them are equipped with false muzzles and used with ball-starters; and each particular rifle has its own complete outfit housed in a separate box made especially for the purpose. Some of these rifles were owned and used by the best Schuetzen riflemen this country ever produced. One rifle in particular, in the hands of Mr. L.P. Ittel (now living in Pittsburgh, Pennsylvania) back in 1906 made a record of ten shots offhand at two hundred yards that has never been beaten. It has taken me years to acquire some of the best specimens of these Schuetzen rifles.

While looking over my collection on one of his frequent visits, Mr. N.H. Roberts remarked that he knew of no one else in the country who had so many especially fine specimens of this particular type.

Perhaps I was more fortunate than many of the riflemen of today, for I had as instructor an uncle who was a very expert old-time rifleman; he being, in fact, one of the Horace Warner Riflemen. This latter may not mean anything to the modern shooter, for whose information I will say that back in the Seventies and Eighties Horace Warner, of Syracuse, New York, and William V. Lowe, of Vermont, gathered together a small group of expert rest-shooters that were known as the Warner Riflemen. J.V. Perry, of Jamestown, New York, also had his group of experts, as did Norman S. Brockway, of Bellows Falls, Vermont. It is a matter of record that the Warner Riflemen were the most expert of them all, and won most of the matches.

My own rest-shooting began with an old heavy percussion muzzle-loading match rifle; and this same fine old rifle, together with the complete outfit, is still in my possession, and in perfect condition. I well remember one of the first things I was taught in rifle-shooting, which was to pay special and particular attention to all the little details in preparing the components used in loading, and this holds good to this day. The idea was that no rifle would shoot better than the loads prepared for it; and this may be the reason why so many modern shooters fail when they try to make some of the old percussion muzzle-loaders perform.

Another thing this uncle told me, years ago, that I have never forgotten. He said that whenever I was looking for information pertaining to rifle-shooting, to lose no time in getting in touch with the real rifle experts, as they were the only ones able to help me. That marked the beginning of an extensive correspondence with shooters, which has continued up to the present time. There must have been some very obliging shooters in this country back in those days, for while my letters were long and full of questions, so far as I can recall they always received an answer. I kept all these replies, and it gives me pleasure even today to read over some of them. As I write this I can see more than one shooter smile at the thought of keeping a lot of old letters all these years, but I was brought up that way, my uncle explaining that the one rule of a careful rifleman was to keep a record of everything.

In my files I have letters from such fine old riflemen as Rube Harwood, W. Milton Farrow, E.A. Leopold, Dr. W.G. Hudson, Harry M. Pope, Dr. Skinner, Tom Martin — the fine sight-maker, F.J. Rabbeth, John D. Kelley, Dr. Baker, and a host of others. Even to this day I hear from L.P. Ittel, V.R. Olmstead, and C.W. Rowland about once a month; and they, with Harry M. Pope, are about all that are left of that large number of fine riflemen of thirty years or so ago.

From Leopold I learned how to prepare and use the proper bullet lubricant — which was far more important back in the black-powder days than it is today. He also showed me how to catch lead bullets without mutilation, by firing them into a box filled with oiled sawdust.

Rube Harwood showed me how to prepare loads for the .25-21 S.S. Stevens rifle. And who can forget the fine articles on squirrel hunting with the rifle that he wrote in the old magazines, under the name of "Iron Ramrod!"

Dr. Baker and E.A. Leopold were also interested in the .25-caliber rifles, and both wrote very entertainingly on how to prepare loads for them; while I learned all about aperture sights from Thomas Martin ("Trim Nat" was his pen name), and I am using his sights to this day on some of my Schuetzen rifles.

I learned the principles of fine rest shooting from data received from F.J. Rabbeth, John D. Kelley, William Hayes, and C.W. Rowland, whom the old records show to have been the finest rest shooters this country ever produced.

C.W. Rowland, of Boulder, Colorado, can today, after nearly sixty years of active rifle shooting, go out on his two hundred-yard range and make some rest groups that would surprise the modern rifleman. I have before me a ten-shot group fired at my request by Mr. Rowland on his 75th birthday, at two hundred yards from bench rest, when he had to go to his range and shoot under conditions existing at the time, on November 16th, 1934. There is only a 3/4-inch vertical error in these ten shots, and my forefinger will completely cover the entire group. I have prints of a number of Mr. Rowland's two hundred-yard groups, made years ago, in which the ten shots cut into one ragged hole. I consider Mr. Rowland the most expert rifleman, in both offhand and rest-shooting, that this country has ever produced. Incidentally, some of you fellows that think you are pretty good might go out and try to duplicate this shooting.

From Doctor Hudson I learned how to prepare Schuetzen loads with smokeless powders, at times using Cream of Wheat to fill up the case. Doctor Hudson also had a fine formula for cleaning the old fired cases. I have his little Blue Book on rifle-shooting, and am sorry now that I neglected to have him autograph it for me. Some of his Schuetzen friends, by the way, never forgave him for leaving the

Schuetzen rifle and taking up the .30-40 Krag, which he used almost entirely during the latter part of his shooting career. When I look through some of my old files I feel certain that I have stored away enough data acquired through this extended correspondence with active shooters — which has continued right up to the present time — to fill several good-sized volumes on rifle-shooting. Also, I have continued my own experimenting and shooting without let-up, and am daily storing away more data for future use. And I might here remark that most of the things we learned in using the old black powder, semi-smokeless, and early brands of smokeless powders, are often useful even today.

Many shooters have written me that they were unable to find in any book on rifle-shooting the proper answers to problems that turn up now and then in preparing ammunition. This is a rather large subject, and I doubt if a single book could be written that would properly cover it. Just as an example, only a short time ago in a letter to a friend — who by the way is one of the country's most expert handloaders — I mentioned using a charge of 26½ grains of Pyro D.G. in the .22 Magnum case. This charge, I might mention, if poured directly into the shell, will overflow. Soon I received a letter from this friend saying that such a powder charge could not be gotten into that case. But we had had this same problem back in 1900 when using Semi-Smokeless, and this is how Rube Harwood told me to do it: You use a funnel having a straight stem that fits down snugly over the *outside* of the case-neck. A piece of steel rod three or four inches long is then placed upright on the powder in the shell, and the *shell* given several sharp raps to settle the powder. The follower thus used holds the powder down firmly, yet does not give any compression.

This is just one instance of an old-time method of loading that applies with equal force to one of our most modern cases; and so it is with most of the problems that come up in our modern shooting. And experience is the thing that counts the most. Furthermore, there are so many little details that enter into fine rest-shooting that unless one is willing to spend a great deal of

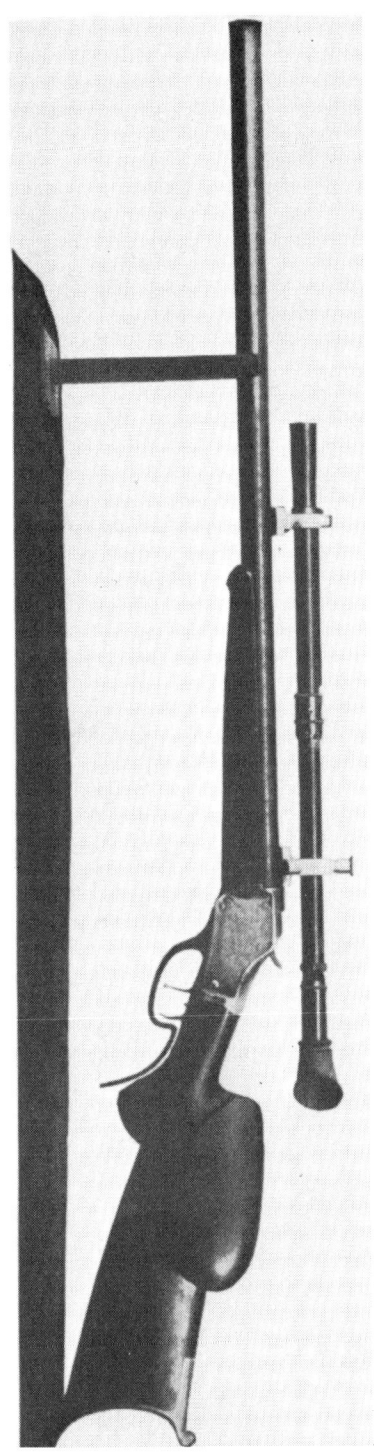

*Author's .22 Niedner Magnum Winchester S.S. rifle, with eight-power Fecker scope in quarter-minute click precision mounts set on 10.8-inch centers. Weight with scope, twelve pounds.*

time and exercise much patience, fine results will be difficult or impossible to obtain. I might go so far as to say that it is close attention to all the necessary little details that makes for small groups.

Now let us consider the rifles used in rest-shooting — and let no one think that it is possible to go out and buy such rifles ready-made. A good rest-rifle always was and probably always will be a more or less hand-made affair. This applies with equal force to the .30-caliber heavy bull-gun or free rifle, the Schuetzen rifle, and the modern vermin rifle built on a single-shot action. In rest-shooting a heavy barrel is required, as it is less influenced by changes in temperature, vibration, position, the way it is held in the rest, etc. Other things being equal, the heavier the barrel, the more accurate a rifle will always be. Such a barrel is also less apt to change its zero from day to day, which is a great advantage when the rest-rifle is used for chuck hunting.

Most well informed riflemen know that if the .30-'06 Springfield is to shoot well, the barrel and action must be properly bedded in the stock. With the old heavy single-shot rifles such as the Winchester, Ballard, and Stevens, the fit of the stock is of vital importance, and a loose-fitting stock will cause the group to open up. No shooting for groups should ever be attempted with a rifle having a loose or poorly fitting stock. The long pull-rod through the entire length of the stock of the Ballard rifle was the idea of W. Milton Farrow, and was one of the principal reasons why the Ballard was for years such a favorite with Schuetzen shooters.

I employ this same system of pull-rod with the Winchester Single-Shot action, brazing a short block to the under side of the upper tang. The block is then drilled and tapped for a long quarter-inch rod that goes entirely through the stock, this rod having a flat head with slot for a heavy screwdriver. I have corrected in this manner many loose-fitting Winchester and Stevens stocks on rifles that were brought to me because of their poor grouping; and invariably the trouble was cured by this treatment. All of my own Schuetzen stocks are attached in this manner; for a Schuetzen rifle especially must be rigidly held together, because of the heavy barrel and the fact that it is often balanced on a palm-rest in holding, which puts a severe strain on the stock-fastening.

The next thing is to have the barrel fitted tight to the action. The shoulder on the barrel that comes in contact with the receiver should fit tight all the way around. A close-fitting taper pin through the receiver and barrel was a device long used by Harry Pope and A.O. Zischang as an added assurance of a tight-fitting barrel. It may be that some of our readers have had occasion to remove the barrel from one of the old single-shot Schuetzen actions, in which case they will understand what a tight-fitting barrel is.

In order to have quicker ignition it is necessary to speed-up the lock time. This is done, in the case of the Winchester action, by drilling a number of holes through the hammer to make it lighter. Then both half- and full-cock notches are removed by grinding, and a new notch cut in only a short distance from where the half-cock notch had been. This will more than double the speed of hammer-fall if a stronger mainspring is used. I might add that anyone desiring to have such a job done can confidently entrust the work to M.S. Risley, of Hubbardsville, New York.

If the rifle is to be used with modern high-pressure loads, look well to your firing-pin. It is usually best to have the old firing-pin hole bushed, and a new, small pin fitted. My own Winchester breechlocks for magnum loads are all fitted with Mann-Niedner firing pins.

Now we come to set-triggers, and a whole book could be written on the subject and still not cover it properly. Here is where the final touch comes in that makes or breaks a good group. A set-trigger as used on a rest-rifle in fine group-shooting is a far different proposition from one used in offhand shooting. During a lifetime of active rifle-shooting, I have used, as well as examined, a goodly number of fine rifles, but in all this time I have seen only two set-triggers that were good enough for the finest rest-shooting.

#1 Target. Nov. 18, 1934.
22. N. Magnum.

*Last 6 Shots*

Date **Sunday P.M. 11/18/34**
Rifle **22 N. Magnum**
Shell **Winchester**
Primer **9½ Rem Non-M.**
Powder **Pyro D.G.**
Charge **26 Grains**
Wad **None**
Bullet **55 Gr. Sisk .224"**
Temper **R. Nose Soft Pt.**
Grease **L. over all 2 7/32"**
Air space shell **None**
Air space barrel **None**
Weather **Fair 50° above**

Distance **100 yards**
Shots **Ten**
Score **120**
Group **5/8" x 1"**
Position **Muzzle & Elbow Rest.**
Aiming point **Center**
Sights **8x Fecker "Scope".**
Aperture **Medium x hairs**
R. Scope **Same.**
Elevation **26**
Windage **138**
Light **Good 4:15 P.M.**
Wind **None.**

Witness **Arnold Flood spotted the shots.**
Remarks: Note after bbl. had warmed up last 6 shots cut into 1 hole 3/8" x 3/8". Note also how rifle holds its zero, first shooting today since Sept 10th when I made a 11/16" Group, with same sighting.

**H. A. Donaldson**

One of these — and the best one — was the work of Mr. Rowland. He first designed the trigger, and then made it up. The other was made by "Old Man" Bremer, of San Francisco, and he used to charge $30 apiece for them. I have one of these Bremer triggers which can be adjusted so fine that the mere weight of the trigger itself will fire the rifle if the barrel is pointed upward. Mr. Rowland's set-trigger is even more sensitive than this, for he can actually fire the rifle by blowing on it. It requires years of constant practice to acquire proper control over a finely adjusted set-trigger. When I turn to the finely adjusted trigger after using the ordinary double-set with which most of my vermin rifles are equipped, it is necessary for me to rub my trigger-finger with sandpaper until the blood starts, in order to have the finger as sensitive as the trigger.

Perhaps this is a good time to say that, after having used every type of single-shot action available, I am partial to the heavy Winchester action, on which all of my vermin rifles are built. Harry Pope remarked years ago that no other action could equal this one, and I have never had reason to question his judgment in the matter. If my readers could examine a Winchester action after it had left Pope's hands, they would know what I mean; for Pope could do things to that action that would have to be seen to be appreciated.

Readers will doubtless be interested in a description of the .22 Niedner Magnum rifle used in making the groups shown with this article, this being the same rifle that shot the two groups shown with the Roberts article in the December 1934 issue of this magazine. The barrel of this rifle was made by the Savage Arms Co. It is 28 inches long, 1 1/16 inches in diameter for its entire length, has a groove diameter of .222 inch, and is cut with four grooves on a sixteen-inch twist. This is a selected barrel, and required no straightening. There are no sight-slots or holes in the barrel, and the outside is in the rough just as it came from the rolls. The barrel was fitted tight to a heavy Winchester Single-Shot action by Mr. Niedner, who also did the chambering. The chamber is rather close, with hardly .001 clearance, and the throat is just right for the 55-grain Sisk bullet; all of which is conducive to fine accuracy. The bullets are a snug fit in the fired cases, which makes unnecessary any resizing of case-necks, and gives greater uniformity of bullet-pull.

I seat the 55-grain round-nosed soft-point Sisk bullet in the case to give this cartridge an overall length of 2-7/32 inches, it fitting snug in the chamber, with the bullet centered in the bore by the chamber throat. If an unfired cartridge is removed from the chamber there will be found a faint mark entirely around the bullet, showing that the bullet centers exactly in the bore. I have never seen a better chambering job, and Mr. Niedner evidently has this chambering business down to a science.

I use a 3/4-inch Fecker scope on this rifle. It has both the 4½X and 8X eyepieces, and is held in quarter-click precision mounts set 10-8/10 inches apart to permit very fine adjustment. I use the 4.5 eyepiece for offhand chuck-shooting or when using my chuck rest, and the 8X eyepiece for rest-shooting. This makes a fine combination, and is the best outfit for the money that I have ever used. I feel that much of the credit for the fine accuracy shown by this rifle is really due to this scope.

The action of this rifle is equipped with a special speed-lock having a stronger mainspring than standard. It has a small firing-pin and the breech-block is fitted up so close that it rubs on the head of the case. The set-triggers are of my own design, and are made over from the Winchester Schuetzen double-set. They allow such fine and sensitive adjustment that I have to change the adjustment when going from rest-shooting to chuck-hunting.

The stock is one I made over from an old Winchester stock, by fitting a higher comb and a cheekpiece. I bent the lower tang, added a pistol grip to the stock, and altered the lever to conform to the curve of the tang. The stock is securely fastened to the action by a long pull-rod, as previously described. Before attaching the stock, I applied cement to both wood and metal, where they come together; and when the bolt was drawn up tight I had the

#2 Target.   Nov. 18, 1934.
             22. N. Magnum.

```
        12
      11
```

Date *Sunday P.M. 11/18/34*  Distance *100 Yards.*
Rifle *22 N. Magnum.*   Shots *Ten*
Shell *Winchester*   Score *7/16" x 1/2"*
Primer *9½ Rem Non-M*  Group ⟶
Powder *Pyro D. G.*   Position *Muzzle & Elbow Rest*
Charge *26 Grains*   Aiming point *Center*
Wad *none.*   Sights *8x Fecker Scope*
Bullet *55 Gr Sisk .224"*   Aperture *Medium x hairs*
Temper *R. Nose Soft Pt*   R. Scope *Same.*
Grease *None*   Elevation *26*
Air space shell *None*   Windage *138*
Air space barrel *None*   Light *Good. 4.³⁰ P.M.*
Weather *Fair 50° above.*   Wind *None*
Witness *Arnold H Good*
Remarks: *This is about the best group I ever made at 100 yds with any rifle. I felt confident after noting last 6 shots on #1 Target that shots were going O.K. These two targets show really a 20 shot group.*

                            *H. A. Donaldson*

7

satisfaction of knowing that I had a tight job. It can readily be seen, therefore, that no little detail escaped careful attention.

The rifle, with scope and mounts, weighs twelve pounds.

The cases used for the .22 Magnum are hand-drawn by Mr. Niedner from Remington .25-35 rimmed cases. While they are still in the die the necks are reamed out carefully to insure the same thickness of metal all around, which is necessary in this special chamber. It also serves to center the bullet truly in the bore. I have no way of knowing how long these cases will last, for I have not yet had to discard any of them.

I am ready to believe that the fine accuracy shown with this remarkable cartridge is due entirely to the design of the case, together with the carefully made 55-grain round-nose bullets as furnished me by R.B. Sisk, of Iowa Park, Texas. After all, it is the bullet that makes the group. Mr. Sisk has a method of checking his cores for weight. I have checked up on his fine bullets with a powerful glass, a sensitive balance, micrometers, etc., and find that for uniformity and all-around excellence they are superior to any other .22-caliber bullets I have ever used. In a recent letter Mr. Sisk states that if there is a sufficient demand, he will place upon the market a .25-caliber bullet for the .25-20 Super-Speed loads.

For the benefit of the shooters who are demanding sharper-pointed bullets from Mr. Sisk, I will say that after having tried out every possible shape, including even the true pencil-point bullet, I have found the round-pointed bullet as now furnished by Mr. Sisk to be far the most accurate. Furthermore, with this shape of point the 45, 55, and 63-grain bullets will all properly fit the same throat in the barrel. I call to the attention of these same shooters what are without doubt the most accurate and carefully made factory bullets ever produced: the .25 Roberts as made by Remington. These bullets all have a rather full round nose, which enables the 87, 100 and 117-grain weights to fit the chamber throat equally well, and so make for fine accuracy.

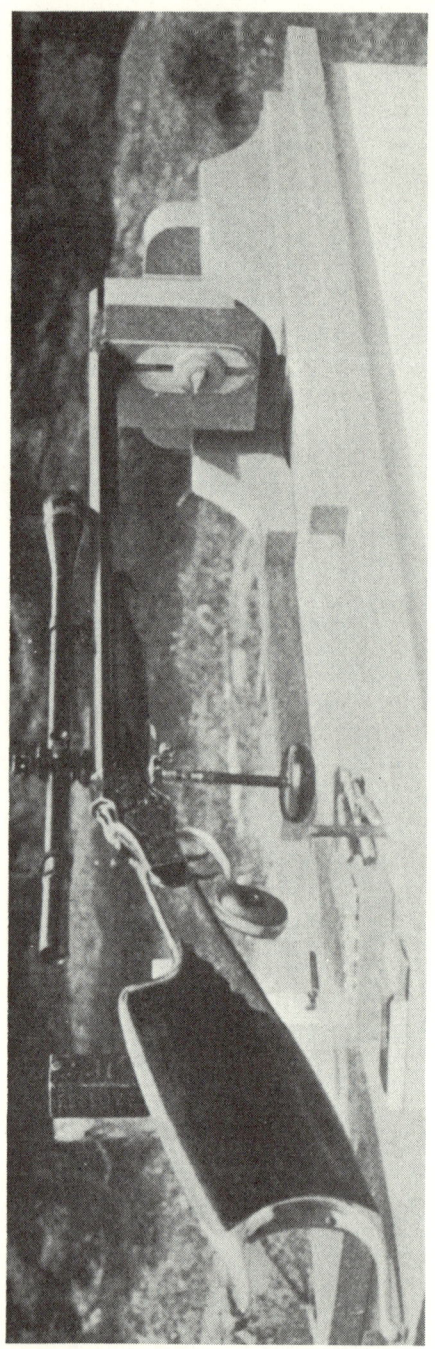

*An improved model bench rest that the author is now using. The V-rest is adjustable for elevation as well as for barrel length.*

# Rest Shooting and Schuetzen Loading

### By H.A. DONALDSON

**Reprinted from May, 1936**
*American Rifleman*

It is the purpose of the writer in this and other articles to show how to remove many of the errors in rifle, ammunition, and the human element, the results of which become evident in careful bench-rest shooting.

My own idea of an accurate rifle is one that will group within one minute of angle at all ranges up to the maximum. The Schuetzen rifles as made by Pope, Schoyen, Zischang, and Walker would do this, but only when the ammunition was properly prepared and the weather conditions ideal. For no rifle yet made is more temperamental than a Schuetzen, as so many of my readers have apparently discovered. However, under favorable conditions, when rifle, ammunition, and shooter are in tune, the Schuetzen is a hard proposition to beat, for it will send shot after shot through the same ragged hole, even up to two hundred yards. My friend Mr. C.W. Rowland has done this on many occasions. Yet the slightest change in components or method of loading will cause the groups to open up; in fact this will at times occur without apparent cause, and will call for a complete check-up on everything involved. For a slight change in bullet temper, lubricant, or even the moisture content of the powder, is enough to nearly double the size of groups.

No one enjoys using a Schuetzen rifle more than I do, but if I were called upon to produce a small group on each and every day in the year, taking the weather as it came, I should not select a Schuetzen rifle, but rather a sixteen-pound Springfield bull gun, in either .30-'06 or .300 Magnum caliber. For if there is any rifle made that can produce small groups on short notice in any kind of weather, even with fixed ammunition, it is the heavy Springfield.

There are shown herewith two of my five-shot hundred-yard groups shot from rest with a Schuetzen rifle. Only a short time after the first group was fired I made several more just about as good; and with the rifle and ammunition working the way they were, the bullets continued to group just as long as I did my part. Luck had nothing to do with it, unless it was that I was lucky in having no wind to contend with. I shall try to explain in detail just how that ammunition was prepared; but first a little history.

One dark, cold day in February 1931 I was visited by two riflemen — friends of long standing — and after quite a talk they asked if I would show them how the Schuetzen rifle was used in rifle shooting. I explained that good rest groups were hard to make on such short notice, and that this was especially so in winter, with two feet of snow on the range and shooting bench. But they insisted, and I selected for the test one of my .32-40 Schoyen-Ballards. This rifle had a globe aperture front sight and vernier rear, and was designed to have the bullet seated in the barrel in front of the case

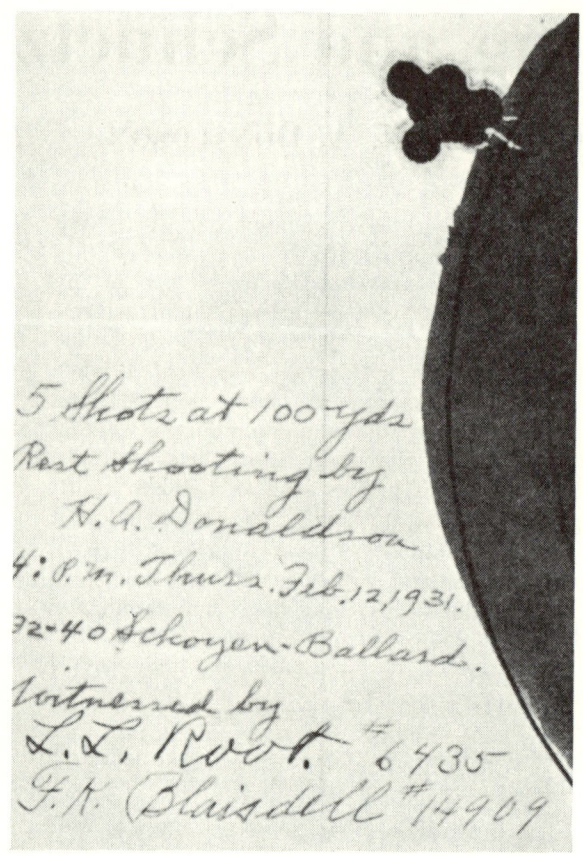

The five-shot hundred-yard group made with iron sights.

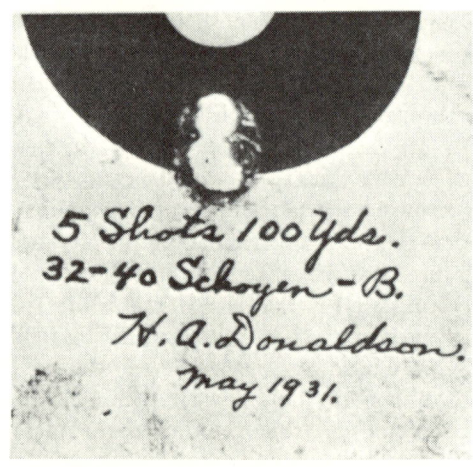

The five-shot hundred-yard group made with telescope sight.

with a ball starter. This is known as breech-seating, and gives good results with the proper bullet.

My reason for selecting this particular rifle was that, for some reason, it will shoot as well in cold weather as my Pope rifles will in warm weather. Also I had a psychological reason for choosing aperture sights instead of a telescope: when aperture sights are used it is impossible to see how the group is forming on the target, and this tends to keep the shooter in a calm state of mind, relaxed, and in good control of his nervous system. On the other hand, when a telescope is used the shooter is under more or less tension in his effort to do his best, for every shot fired can be seen at once.

For cold-weather shooting, bullets seated in the barrel just in front of the chamber appear to perform better than when muzzle-loaded. As different powders are used with the two systems this may have some bearing on the matter.

The target selected had a three-inch black bull, which I increased to six inches to fit the front-sight aperture and my eyes. The target was fastened to my one hundred-yard butts, the front of which is painted white, this white background permitting a smaller target to be used. Before beginning to shoot I moved the front sight over to bring the group into the white; for then by the prints the bullets make in the target, it is easy to see if any of them are tipping.

This may be a good time to mention that in working up a load for best results in a Schuetzen rifle, a powder charge should be selected which will carry the long, heavy bullets up to the target with the lowest velocity possible and still have the bullets fly point-on. If the shooter will watch the prints of his bullets on the white of the target he can tell when any are tipping; for with a tipping bullet the dark rim around the hole in the paper will be wider on one side than on the other.

This low velocity necessary for best grouping is one of the reasons why some loads that give fine results at one hundred yards will not do so at two hundred yards:

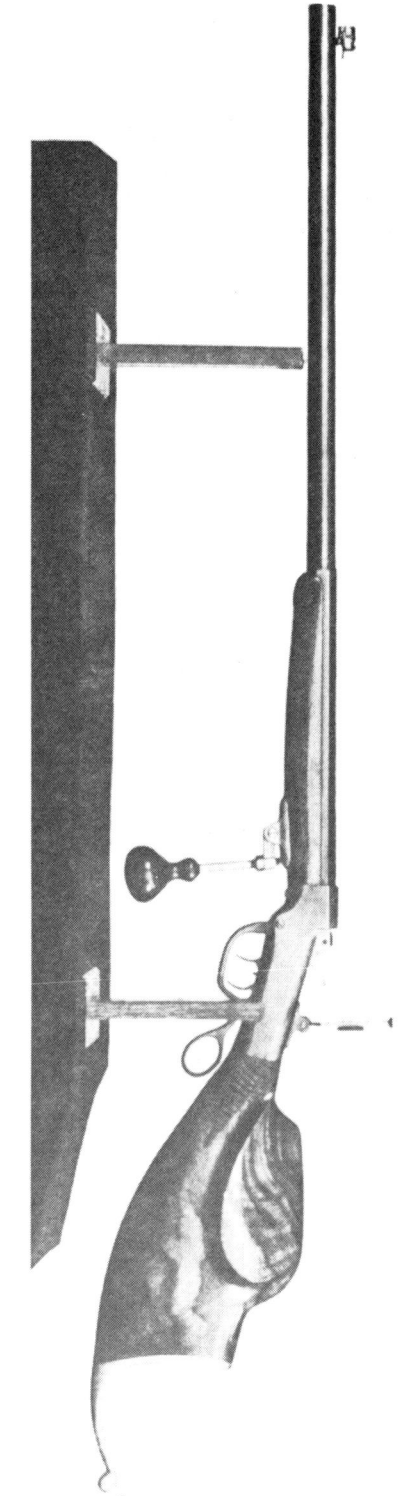

The .32-40 Schoyen-Ballard rifle used in making the two groups.

the bullets do not remain point-on at the longer range. Do not expect the one load to shoot equally well at two different ranges.

The aperture in the globe front sight measured .116 inch, or the size of a No. 32 drill. It was enclosed in a wide black rim. The aperture in rear eye cup was .025 inch, or the size of a No. 72 drill. The distance between sights measured 32-1/4 inches. Both front and rear apertures were made by the late Thomas Martin of Dorchester, Massachusetts, the sizes of apertures having been very carefully worked out from tests made by Mr. C.W. Rowland nearly fifty years ago. I find that these sights are as accurate as any scope when the proper size of bull is used; and they also are fine for offhand shooting on a twelve-inch bull at two hundred yards. This rifle I use for most of my offhand shooting.

And now we come to the components used in making the groups shown. Primers were No. 9½ Remington, to ignite nine grains of Du Pont bulk shotgun powder back of a 200-grain Pope bullet cast 1 to 25. Bullets were lubricated with Leopold's lubricant in a Pope grease pump. One greased wad was seated in the mouth of the case, leaving the powder loose. The bullet was seated in the barrel 1/16 inch ahead of the case. Powder charges were thrown with an old No. 5 Ideal measure.

The above load would appear to be a simple one to prepare and to use; however, when we go a little more into detail it may not look so simple. First, the primers are selected by weight, to insure uniformity. They will vary in weight, and I sort them into three different lots, to weigh 5½, 6, and 6½ grains; and I use each lot separately. The metal of which primers are made is very uniform in thickness, and the dies that make the primers are accurate; hence any variation in weight must be in the chemical mixture in the primer. This may seem like splitting hairs, but I have found that it makes for uniform ignition.

Each .32-40 cartridge case used has a small notch cut into the rim, and the case is placed in the chamber of the rifle with this notch up each time. I seat the primer in the pocket with the anvil in line with the notch in the rim of the case, so that the anvil will be in a vertical position when the case is placed in the rifle. This is especially important with a Stevens action, the firing pin of which may strike a little off center.

The white Du Pont shotgun powder is not used as it comes from the canister, it being first screened and graded into three different lots according to the size of grains. I use two small tea strainers for this purpose, one having eighteen mesh to the inch, and the other thirty. The powder is first passed through the eighteen-mesh screen, and what will not pass through is placed in a container and marked "Fg." The remaining powder is put into the thirty-mesh screen, that which is held on the screen being marked "FFg." The powder that has passed through is marked "FFFg."

If the powder were used as it comes from the can there would be no way of knowing the percentage of fine grains to coarse, but by screening, uniformity is assured. I have found that the size Fg works well in the .38-55 case, while I use FFg in my .32-40 rifles, and FFFg in the .25-20 S.S.

When any bulk powder such as Du Pont shotgun, or Schuetzen, leaves the factory it has a moisture content of about two percent, and it is very important to maintain this moisture content. With powders used for Schuetzen loads I do this by keeping the powder in a tobacco humidor. When powder has been stored in a dry attic in hot, dry weather it will burn at a far different rate than if stored properly. That is why it is often impossible for anyone to give the correct charge of a bulk powder to use in Schuetzen loads.

For some shooting I weigh the powder charges very carefully, but in preparing the loads used in making the groups shown, the charges were thrown with a No. 5 Ideal measure. This is a light load but one I have found to be very accurate for one hundred-yard shooting. Because of this being a low-velocity load it requires careful holding in offhand practice.

The powder is left loose in the cartridge case, the greased blotter wad being placed only 1/8 inch below the mouth of the case, a specially-made wad-seater being used for the purpose. My lubricant for this wad consists of one part rosin, two parts beeswax, and three parts tallow. I dip clean white blotting paper into the hot lubricant, let it soak for a moment, and then hang it up by one corner to dry. Wads are then cut from the sheets with a wad-cutter.

We now come to the 200-grain Pope bullets, which of course are selected carefully and weighed; but I wonder how many riflemen today shoot their cast bullets in exactly the same order in which they come from the mould? I do. It is an old method and one that makes for greater uniformity as to bullet temper. The block for holding the bullets is made from a piece of pine about an inch thick by six inches square. One hundred holes are bored in rows of ten each, about 3/4 inch deep. The holes are numbered with a pencil, and when the mould is working properly the first good bullet is placed, base up, in hole number one, and so on until the block is filled. The bullets are then lubricated with a Pope grease pump, and returned to the same holes in the block.

It will be seen at once that when bullets are fired in the same order in which they were cast there will be less difference in the temper of the metal, from bullet to bullet, than if a large number of bullets were jumbled up together; for the temper of the metal tends gradually to change during the process of casting the bullets.

If no grease pump is at hand one can use a small cake tin about seven inches square and one and a half inches deep. Mix up in another container, from the formula given, enough lubricant to fill the cake tin to a depth of one inch, and place the bullets in the latter in rows about one half inch apart, exactly the same as they were in the block. The hot lubricant is then poured in one corner of the tin until it reaches a level above the top grooves of the bullets. The lubricant is allowed to cool thoroughly; and then, with one hand placed over the points of the bullets, the tin is turned bottom-side up. A stream of cold water is run over the bottom of the pan to cause the lubricant to shrink away from the sides. Then the cake of lubricant, with the bullets, can be removed as a unit. The cake is turned over and each bullet pushed out with the thumb, and returned to its proper hole in

*Fred H. Harris, of Brattleboro, Vermont, demonstrating the proper position in rest shooting.*

the block. When properly done this is a clean and simple method of lubricating bullets. No grease sticks to the bullets except the small amount left in the grooves, and no lubricant is wasted. I can see no reason for using a Kake-Kutter when the cake of lubricant can be used for the same purpose.

Schuetzen methods are based upon maintaining the greatest uniformity possible. The finest accuracy is obtained by seeking out all causes of error, and then removing them so far as is possible. The actual load one uses is not so important, and in the old days nearly every shooter had his own pet load. It is uniformity in preparing and shooting the loads that is the big factor.

In rest shooting I usually fire several shots through the barrel to foul it. With the aid of a bullet seater the bullet is placed in position in the barrel 1/16 inch ahead of the case; this being done with one push of the seater. If several blows are used on the handle the soft bullet may be upset and the accuracy spoiled. The loaded case is then placed in the chamber, with the notch up, as before mentioned. The rifle is pointed upward to bring the powder back in the base of the case, and then carefully lowered to firing position, the muzzle resting on a soft rubber pad in the notch of the muzzle rest. The barrel should rest at the same point for each shot, in my own case about six inches back from the muzzle.

At the shooting bench the rifleman should take an easy relaxed position. He should have both feet flat on the ground, and try to hold the rifle in such a way that there will be no undue strain or tension at any one point. I take a position with body at an angle of about 45 degrees with the line of sight, hold the buttplate of the rifle on the upper arm, and not at the shoulder. The left hand is brought around and held under the toe of stock, with both forearms lying flat on the top of the bench. A rubber mat on the bench top is an aid to steady holding. When the buttplate is held on the upper arm the recoil effect appears to be more uniform, the rifle coming straight back. With a light load in a heavy barrel, recoil is usually light. Where the rifle is held at the shoulder with the face pressed tight against the stock, the recoil has a tendency to throw the comb of the stock away from the face, causing the rifle to twist as it comes back; and this twist is not constant from shot to shot.

The secret of fine rest shooting is to hold the rifle so that it will be free to recoil *in the same way* for each shot. I like to have my rifle come straight back, and when I see the crosshairs rise toward twelve o'clock in a straight line above the bull, I know that all is well and that I can expect a good group. If the shooter will carefully perfect his holding so as to get this effect, the matter of making small groups will come much easier.

Do not be in too great a hurry to shoot when once in position, especially when using a telescope sight. Wait until the pupil of the eye is adjusted to the scope. And try to get the same picture each time through the telescope or sight aperture, remembering that uniformity in *holding* is just as essential as in everything else.

On the February day mentioned, we found it necessary to sweep off the shooting bench, and shovel the snow away. It was four o'clock when I sat down to shoot, and the light was none too good, as it had been a dark day. However, there was no wind. My cases and bullets were in a block on the bench, and it was my intention to try to make several ten-shot groups.

I moved the front sight over to throw the group into the white of the target, fired several shots off to one side to foul the barrel, and then settled down to business. After the fifth shot the man who was spotting for me ran out and called to me to stop shooting saying all of my shots were going into the same hole. I wished to finish the string, but he removed the target and brought it to the bench. Both men were surprised when they examined the target, and one of them said he had no idea that any rifle could shoot like that. The spotter said the reason he had brought in the target was that, as I had already made what he felt sure was a record group, he was afraid I would spoil it if I continued to shoot.

I made several more close groups, until it was too dark to shoot. The first group shown is hardly what I would call a selected one, but it indicates very nearly the average performance of this fine Shoyen barrel, when conditions are right. It was witnessed by the two men referred to, whose names appear on the target. I would say that this group, as compared with some of Mr. Rowland's, is only fair. I have one five-shot one hundred-yard rest group made by Mr. Rowland a few years ago that looks as if only one bullet had passed through the target. I doubt very much if any other shooter can equal this performance in rest-shooting.

There is also shown herewith another of my five-shot rest groups. It was with the same rifle and ammunition, but an eight-power Fecker scope was used. I spoiled what started out to be a group made as Mr. Rowland makes them, by pulling the last shot to the top edge of the hole. The first four shots went into one hole. I noted this through the scope, and my attention was thereby distracted just enough to send the last shot one quarter inch high.

Of late riflemen who are trying to learn some of our older Schuetzen methods have written that they are unable to obtain very good results, complaining that they cannot purchase the same components that were in use thirty years ago. My own experience has been that we have better primers today than ever before, and I should say that most of the trouble with the modern shooter is that he is not using the methods in Schuetzen work that were in use thirty years ago. I would again call the attention of these riflemen to the groups shown. They were made with modern primers and powder. In my opinion our primers today will in every instance give as uniform ignition as did any of the old ones. Also, our modern Du Pont bulk shotgun powder will, when properly conditioned, make as good groups as any we used to get with Schuetzen or black powder, when bullets are seated in the breech. Mr. Rowland uses the No. 12 Peters primers, while I use the No. 9½ Remington. The F.A. No. 70 primers will also give uniform ignition. When any of these new primers are used, with a few grains of Du Pont bulk shotgun powders as a priming charge, Semi-Smokeless powder may be used in the muzzle-loaded rifles.

I have mentioned only a few of the thousand and one things necessary to obtain best results in rest shooting. There is still much to be written about ignition, conditioning of powders, casting of bullets, bullet fit and selection, and dies, swages, cases, targets, telescope sights, and the rifles themselves. All this, including the building of bench rests and shooting tables, will be dealt with in another article.

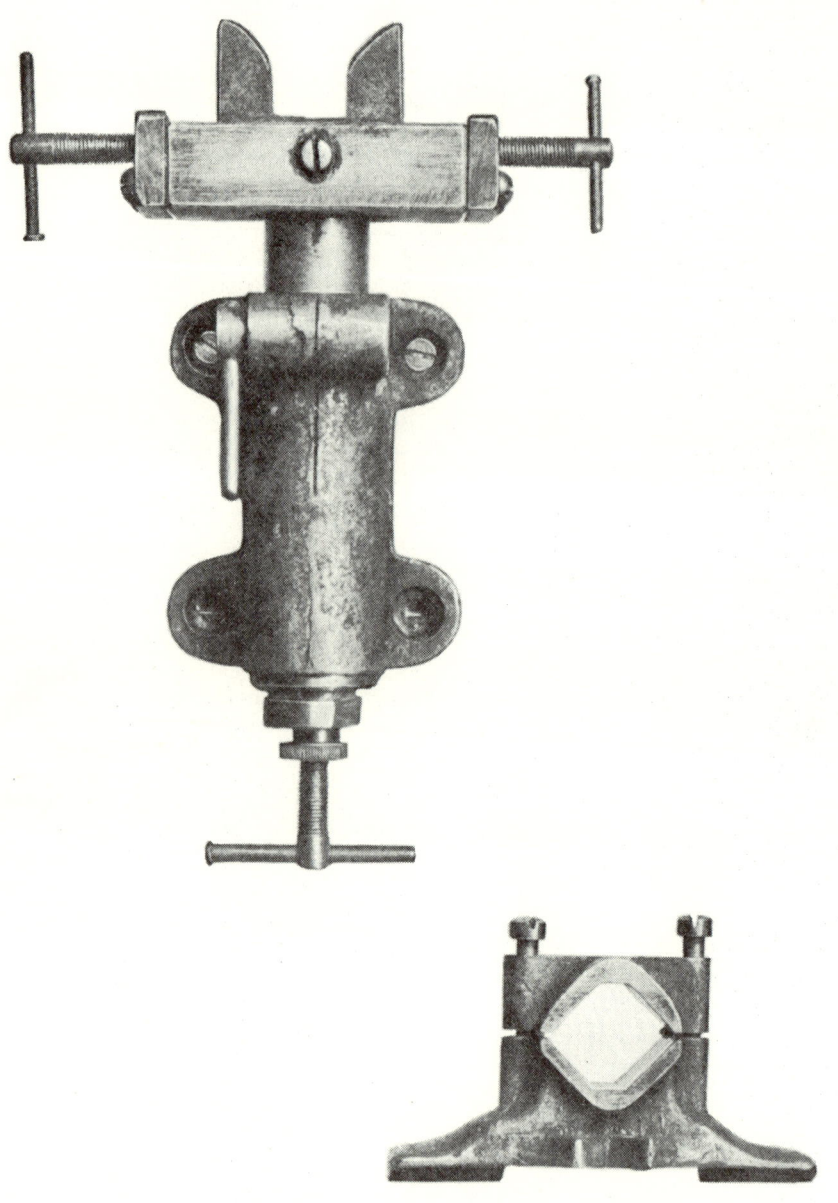

Machine rest made by Harry Pope, and used by fastening to top of shooting table, rifle being free to recoil.

# Rest Shooting and Schuetzen Loading

### By H.A. DONALDSON

**Reprinted from September, 1936**
*American Rifleman*

Uniform and complete ignition of the powder charge in Schuetzen loads has more influence upon the accuracy obtained than has any other one factor. The burning rate of any powder charge may be altered by a change in the ignition. With the proper selection of primers or the use of certain powders in priming charges, this matter of ignition may be kept under control. When the shooter understands all this, and is able to secure uniform ignition, he is well on the road to small groups.

With modern primers it is easy to obtain satisfactory ignition, but it is well to experiment with different components, and the shooter will be repaid for more than passing study of this subject. Most of the powders usually employed in Schuetzen loads are very easy to ignite, and with such powders as Schuetzen, Semi-Smokeless, No. 80, or Du Pont bulk Shotgun Smokeless, no trouble will be had with ignition. However, it should be fully understood that these powders burn at a far different rate with the modern primers than with the older ones. Some of our double-base smokeless powders that contain nitroglycerin will be found to ignite nearly as well even as black powder. These powders burn at so nearly a uniform rate that they give great uniformity of pressure, and ignite easily no matter what the shape or size of the grains.

In some Schuetzen loads employing a light charge of powder in a large case, ignition trouble may be had if the old low-power primers are used. The large air space dissipates the heat from the primer, and this condition is aggravated when the bullet is seated in the throat ahead of the case. In such cases conditions may be improved by the use of the more powerful modern primers.

All bulk powder should be carefully screened in order to remove the fine grains and dust particles that will be found in each canister. Du Pont bulk Shotgun Smokeless should be screened also for the purpose of having the grains uniform, for only in this way can the burning rate be closely controlled.

A good rule to bear in mind is that the most powerful primer will give the most consistent accuracy. Inaccuracy can in most cases be traced to faulty ignition, as from weak primers.

Proper lubrication is another important factor in Schuetzen loads. When some of the older powders are used, weather conditions will have a bearing upon the lubricant to be selected. With some powders, greased wads are used in addition to the regular lubricant on the bullet.

When certain smokeless powders are used with soft lead bullets, they will be found to fuse the flat bases of the bullets. Greased wads may be used to overcome this trouble, as well as to provide additional lubrication for the bore.

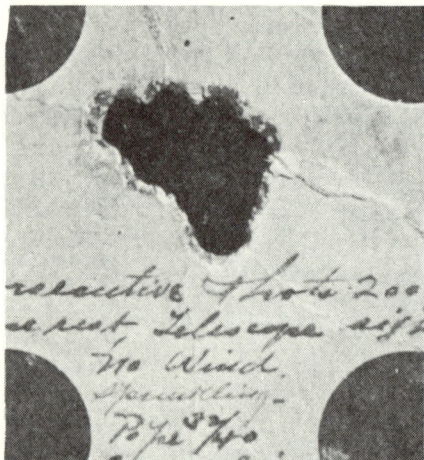

Ten-shot two hundred-yard rest group made by C.W. Rowland thirty-five years ago. No one has been able to equal this shooting with any modern rifle.

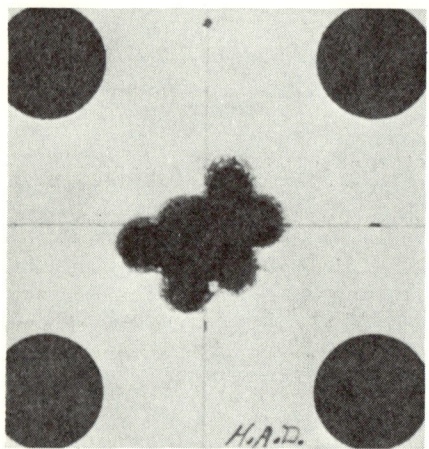

Ten-shot hundred-yard rest group made by author with .32-40 B-L Zischang rifle and six-power Peterson scope, bullets breech-seated.

A weak mainspring or a faulty firing pin will cause uneven ignition; or the fly in the hammer may be responsible, when double set-triggers are used. With my own double set-trigger Schuezten rifles I remove this fly from the hammer and grind out the safety notch. This often improves the shooting of a rifle that has a tendency to string the shots up and down on the target — just another instance of removing an error to improve the groups.

One should go over the action carefully before testing out a strange rifle, noting particularly the strength of the mainspring. The flat mainspring as used in the Winchester Single Shot action may often be improved upon and given increased strength by changing its position. This spring is fastened to a flat piece of metal dovetailed into the barrel. The face of this metal block can be filed off at a slight angle, to cause the end of the mainspring, where it comes into contact with the toe of the hammer, to bear at a different angle and increase the strength of the spring.

Any Winchester Single Shot action can be easily changed over to the Schuetzen double set-trigger, by obtaining the necessary parts from the Winchester Company. Be sure that the action and barrel are tight, and keep all dirt from under the extractor.

It is hardly possible in an article of this kind to cover properly the subject of bullet making. The Schuetzen shooter of today is again fortunate in being able to purchase his bullets lubricated and ready for use. I know of nothing in the preparation of suitable Schuetzen loads that calls for more experience than the casting of bullets. The very best commercial bullets I have ever used are those furnished by H. Guy Loverin, of Lancaster, Massachusetts. He uses my own method of casting bullets, and I can recommend his product for the finest accuracy.

The shooter interested in making his own bullets should obtain the handbooks furnished by the loading-tool companies. And I would advise anyone interested in Schuetzen rifles to collect all the good bullet moulds he can, such as were made some years ago by Pope, Schoyen, Zischang, etc. My own collection has often enabled me to obtain good results with rifles that were without moulds.

I use one very accurate muzzle-loading rifle that will make better groups with a bullet cast in a Zischang mould than it will with a bullet cast in the mould that was made for the rifle. Quite often a rifle will be found that has a barrel with oversize groove diameter. Where one has several moulds of different sizes it may be possible to select one that will cast a bullet of the proper size for such a barrel.

Nearly all of my Schuetzen moulds cast long bullets that are tapered from the base to the forward band. Such bullets are necessary when loading from the muzzle with a false muzzle and bullet starter. This same long tapered bullet will give good results when breech-seated in the barrel with a bullet seater. Quite often such a bullet with a base band diameter of .323 may be sized down in a Belding & Mull or Lyman bullet-sizing chamber to .320 or .321, which size may shoot more accurately when the bullet is breech-seated. When bullets are sized in this manner, care should be taken to size them base first; and the plunger used should fit the point of the bullet. My own Lyman sizing chambers are made in sizes from .318 to .325 inch, by half-thousandths, and with their use I am able to fit a bullet to any size of barrel in .32-40 caliber.

When the proper bullet is selected, the front part is tapered and only the last band or two is sized cylindrical. These bullets seat easily in the barrel, and when used in this manner they will be found to give remarkable accuracy. A little care in the proper fit and selection of such a bullet will give improved results in even the ordinary factory barrel.

The cases used in Schuetzen loads should be marked on the rim so that they may be placed in the chamber in the same position each time. My own .32-40 cases for use with black or Semi-Smokeless powder are chromium plated, which allows their being easily cleaned. Such cases wear well and are easy to extract after long use. Each particular rifle should have its own

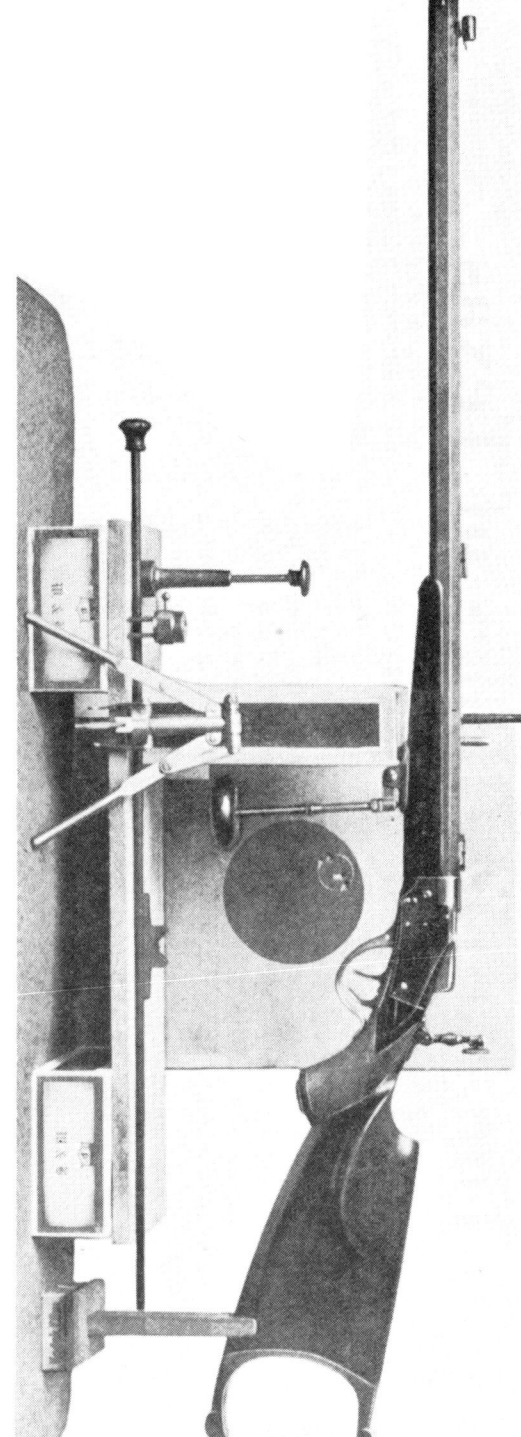

One of author's favorite Schuetzen rifles: .33-40 Pope M-L on Sharps-Borchardt action. Stock made by Zischang. Pope mechanical bullet-seater.

cases, kept separate in a box made for this one purpose.

A shooter should experiment in order to find the load that will give the best accuracy in one particular rifle. When this load is found it is well to stick to it, and use no other. But just because a certain load gives small groups in some particular barrel is no reason to believe that it will perform as well in another rifle of exactly the same groove diameter. Do not be too easily satisfied with one or two groups. Try every possible combination, and note well the effect of small changes in the components. Only a slight change in the lubricant or bullet temper, or the use of a different primer, may mean the difference between an inch group and one of twice that size. That is one of the reasons why it is well to keep on each target, as the groups are fired, an accurate record of the load, with all of the conditions noted. This information is of no value unless it is put on the target at once, and it should give every detail possible.

My first article on rest shooting, about a year ago, illustrates my particular form of rest target. This target provides sufficient space for an exact record of each group. The targets are then filed in a looseleaf holder which keeps them in good condition.

Any good telescope of from six to twelve power, with medium to fine cross-hairs, may be used in rest shooting. When a high-power scope is used it is well to practice regular oxygenation of the blood just before settling down for the trigger release. My method is to fill the lungs fully, then to expel all the air, again fill the lungs, expel about half, and hold steady in the final act of trigger release. This provides the system with the necessary air while the breath is being held, and it raises the ribs slightly over the heart and reduces body vibration. This method was used for years by offhand shooters in Schuetzen work and is still practiced by Mr. C.W. Rowland and the writer in rest shooting.

The size of the white sighting disc or center in the target should be chosen according to the range and the power of the scope, as well as the thickness of the cross-hairs. When a low-power scope with coarse cross-hairs is used, the white sighting disc should be large. The rifle should be so sighted that the bullets do NOT group on this white center, for just a few shots will destroy the aiming point. This recalls an occasion when a certain friend was watching me shoot some rest groups. He seemed to think it strange that, while I was putting them all in practically one hole, I could not seem to hit the center of the target!

If several different sizes of centers are tried, one will be found that gives better results with less eye strain than any other. Another method, for one hundred-yard shooting, is to use four black pasters set on about two and a half-inch centers, to form a square. A little experimenting will determine the size of paster to use, as well as the size of the square. It is surprising how the eye will center these four black spots at two hundred yards; and very small groups can be made with this form of aiming point. But no matter what form of target is selected, the important thing is to see it the same for each shot. Rest shooting with a heavy rifle offers an endless field for experiment, and different targets may be used until one is found that seems to give the best results with your own particular iron sights or telescope.

The secret of successful rest shooting lies in being able to discover the errors in your rifle, in the ammunition, and in yourself when doing the actual shooting. Only when these errors are discovered, and are eliminated as far as is possible, can there be any improvement in the size of the groups. The requisites of a successful rest shooter are endless patience and an eye to small details.

It is hardly possible to give dimensions for a shooting table or bench rest that will be suitable for all shooters. A rest that may be just right for one person may be too high or too low for another. The bench should be the right height to allow the forearms to lie flat on the bench top when the shooter is seated in an ordinary chair, with his feet flat on the ground. The legs of the table may be made from 4 x 4 fir or oak, but 6 x 6 material will make a heavier bench. The rails may be 2 x 6 fir, mortised into the legs or bolted on the outside. The top of the bench should be made from two-inch planks glued together with waterproof glue, and fastened with screws to the rails. One corner of the top should be sawed out to allow the shooter's body to be at an angle of about 45 degrees to the line of fire. If this opening is made so that the chest touches the edge of the bench top while the forearms rest easily on the top, it will allow steady holding.

Almost any sort of wooden V-block may be fastened to the front of the bench. My rest has a piece of half-inch sponge rubber glued into the notch in the block. The height of the V-block from the table top is more or less governed by the drop of the stock of the rifle being used. In my shooting I want the rifle as low as possible on the rest, and having the V-block adjustable for height allows its being used with any type of stock. My article in the May issue of *The Rifleman* shows a well-made bench rest with adjustable V-block. It is also adjustable for differences in barrel length as well as for height. The lower part of the legs of this bench are covered with sheet lead. This adds to the weight, and also protects the wood from the weather.

The bench rest should be well painted unless it can be protected by a shooting house. Some riflemen use a canvas cover over the shooting table, and this should be fastened securely in place or it may blow away.

I have one bench rest in my workshop which allows shooting in any weather, and is made ready for use by simply raising a window sash. This is a most convenient arrangement, and when used with a spotting scope it saves a great deal of walking back and forth.

No one should expect to do as good shooting from a strange bench rest as from one he is accustomed to. Constant practice will allow fair shooting from most any sort of bench rest, but when the shooter tries to adjust his position to a rest with which he is not familiar, quite often a strain is imposed at some point that causes the group to open up. That is the reason why a visiting rifleman will seldom be able to make as small a group from any rest as the man who made the rest and is accustomed to it. So do not try to beat a rest shooter on his home range: it simply is not done. Doctor Mann mentioned this in his book when he told of his experiences in testing one of his best rifles while on a visit to his old friend Dr. S.A. Skinner, at Hoosick Falls, New York. He said that for some reason his rifle had lost its gilt-edge accuracy and would not perform as well as it had done on his own home range.

## Whose Bullets?

**May 21, 1965**

Mr. David R. Wolfe
Peoria, Illinois

Dear Dave:

Enclosed is a copy of a letter I recently received from Harvey Donaldson. I thought you might be interested in it because of the twenty-shot nickel-size group mentioned in this letter. I just wanted you to know whose bullets were involved.

We are presently working on some .22 caliber match bullets that look quite encouraging. I will send you a box and you can either shoot them yourself or give them to Captain Nonte for evaluation.

Sincerely yours,
Joyce W. Hornady

# Twenty-Shot Nickel-Size Group

**Sunday - April 25, 1965**

Mr. Joyce Hornady
Grand Island, Nebraska

Dear Sir:

Yesterday I went over to Schaghticoke, N.Y., to visit our local jobber, John B. Beecroft. He gave me about a dozen of your new 53-grain boat-tail bench rest bullets that you gave him at the recent N.R.A. convention in Washington, D.C.

They look OK and I will try them out in my bench rest gun, and report later. I could use a box or two more of these new bullets, as John does not as yet carry them in stock. While I was at his gun shop I picked up a box of your new .25 caliber 75-grain open point bullets, made with your new type of jacket.

This morning I loaded up twenty of these new bullets in some new Norma brass, in .250-3000 caliber. I used the No. 250 CCI primers with 34 grains of 4064, to an overall of 2-7/16 inches length.

Then I went out and tried them at one hundred yards on my own range, and I sure was surprised at the results. The whole twenty shots could be covered with a nickel.

This shooting was done in a Model 54 Winchester Sporter, twenty-four-inch barrel, with a ten-power Weaver scope. This rifle happens to be the most accurate factory rifle I ever owned. A number of years ago, when I heard that Winchester would not chamber the Model 70 rifle for this .250-3000 case, I sent them a Model 54 action to have re-barreled in that caliber. When it arrived I was most surprised to find they had given me a good close chamber. It might be that it was chambered with a reamer that had been used considerably. Anyway, my rifle has a nice tight chamber, like a good custom job.

Even though I'm past 82, I can see and hold about as good as I ever could. Also, I keep in practice; I am shooting about every Sunday, as weather permits. Have been shooting all winter, and some days it was down close to zero. As long as the wind don't bother, I do not mind the cold.

But to get back to today's shooting: After I had fired the twenty rounds, I went back to my shop and loaded them up again, so I might try them on a few woodchucks. It was no trouble to find and kill three chucks. Here is where I got another surprise.

My experience in long-range chuck hunting is that one should use (to be sure of an instant kill), bullets which are semi-pointed, with some lead exposed on the point. Especially in bullets of .224 caliber. These .25 caliber 75-grain bullets were made with open point, so I wondered what they would do on animals.

I noted this morning that your bullets cut nice clean holes in the target, which indicates plenty of velocity, but I was hardly prepared for the damage one of these new jacketed bullets did on the one chuck I hit at around two hundred fifty yards. Mister, he never even moved.

It must have opened up perfectly as it passed through the chuck, for it tore quite a hole on the opposite side. This is my very first experience with your new type of bullet. If they all open up like that, you have a wonderful bullet for hunting.

Thought you might be interested in this experience of mine. I use your bullets in all of my own hunting rifles, and I have had fine results in one of my rifles in 7x57 caliber. This one rifle has a barrel with the twelve-inch twist, so I can duplicate results I get with another rifle in .270 caliber.

Would like to have you send me a few samples of your bullets cut on a slant, as Beecroft showed to me. I work part-time in a gun shop in Johnstown, so will show them where they will do the most good.

Sincerely yours,
H.A. Donaldson

## First Encounter

My first correspondence from Donaldson was a letter "out of the blue" in the spring of 1966. It could be that Joyce Hornady told Harvey that a copy of his April 25 letter about his "nickel-size group" had been forwarded to me. In any event, old Harve made it abundantly clear that there were still a few shooters around who remembered how things were done fifty or more years ago, and he had the answers.

If memory serves correctly, this letter prompted my inquiry the following February — would he impart some of his vast knowledge to readers of *Handloader?* The rest is history.

Dave Wolfe

# It's A Tricky Business

**May 1, 1965**

Mr. Dave Wolfe
Peoria, Illinois

Dear Sir:

I have just finished reading an article on the slug rifle and I cannot remember of ever reading an article on shooting that contained more errors.

For your information, I was brought up with a slug rifle, back of the kitchen door. My first woodchuck was killed with a .40 caliber slug gun. My uncle, who taught me all I know about shooting, was one of Berdan's Riflemen, and his shooting started back around 1840. I have been shooting for seventy-five years, so you might say his experience and mine goes back to 1840.

At one time I owned eighteen fine Schuetzen rifles, as well as about a dozen slug guns. I still have the fine slug gun my uncle used after the Civil War. Also I can lay my hands on guns made by Morgan James, George Ferris, George Schalck, and others. If you will look up the back copies of the *American Rifleman* for 1935 and 1936 you will find pictures of some of my rifles shown in articles by Ned Roberts.

I might add, a powerful lot of shooting was going on before 1900. I got in on the tag end of the slug gun era, but here in the Mohawk Valley we continued to use them 'til right after 1918, when most of the old-timers had passed away. There are still a lot of the old guns around, but try and buy one! None are for sale.

Writing for the shooting magazines is rather a tricky business. I pass up chances to write all the time. I am busy with other matters. When a man starts writing he should know what he is writing about. Soon as he starts to guess, he is done. Some old cuss like yours truly may still be around who KNOWS the answers. Harry Pope would kick the lid off his coffin if he read where a man closed the breech on a powder-charged metallic cartridge, then muzzle-loaded the greased bullet with false muzzle and starter. That sort of data might blow some man's head off.

Pope taught me to place a dummy cartridge, with a plug in the mouth of the case (that stuck out a sixteenth of an inch) into the chamber of the rifle. Then the bullet was inserted into the false muzzle and pushed down *carefully*, until it touched the plug in the dummy case. If the starter rod is a little snug, one should withdraw the rod *slowly*, or it will suck the seated bullet part way up the barrel, and thus ruin that particular load. (Read this over carefully, for you will not find such data in a Montgomery Ward catalog.)

You then take out the dummy case and replace it with a loaded one with a greased wad on top. Also, to keep from shooting off the false muzzle, most shooters had it tied to the shooting bench with a short piece of heavy cord.

If you ever travel our New York State Thruway, stop off and see me. This small town of Fultonville is right on the Thruway, at Exit 28. Better yet, why not visit us at the Pine Tree Rifle Club, in Johnstown, N.Y. We will be holding a shoot at the Club on June 12th, and again over Labor Day.

Cordially yours,
H.A. Donaldson

# Needed: Real Experts

**February 10, 1966**

Mr. Harvey A. Donaldson
Fultonville, New York

Dear Mr. Donaldson:

While you and I have never met, I somehow feel that I know you. I remember your correspondence to Joyce Hornady and me last year, and, of course, I'm quite familiar with your Donaldson cartridges. I wanted to write to you when I was editor of *Shooting Times*, but somehow never got around to it.

Would you consider writing a few articles for my new magazine, *The Handloader?* I realize you've had many opportunities to submit stories to all of the gun publications, but I think my magazine is quite a bit different. I'm in real need of articles written by genuine experts — people who have been in the gun game long enough to separate fact from fiction.

There's a wealth of topics that would be right up your alley. For instance, your experiences with bench rest rifles, cartridges, loads and bullets. I would also be interested in your early experiences in the shooting game, your acquaintance with all of the great names — like Dr. Mann, Harry Pope, Ned Roberts, etc. We might also do a story on the .25 caliber on varmints, the cartridges and bullets available. Just a few ideas . . .

If you consent to do some writing for me, what do you think of running your material as a series of letters? We might even put a heading on the series such as "Yours truly, Harvey A. Donaldson." In this way you could ramble on a variety of subjects, but all *meat and potatoes* material for the hard-core gun enthusiast.

Hope to hear from you soon on this proposal.

Very sincerely,
David R. Wolfe

**Yours truly No. 1**

# A Few 'Cutting' Remarks

*(The following letter is a kick-off to a series of articles by one of America's best known shooters. Harvey A. Donaldson was one of our pioneers in handloading; the data in his files, and letters from Harry Pope, Dr. Mann, Niedner, Lowe, Dr. Hudson, Farrow, Whelen, and others, would fill volumes. We will bring you this material in a regular feature called "Yours truly, Harvey Donaldson." If this doesn't become one of the most popular departments in this magazine, I'll eat my typewriter. — Editor.)*

**February 27, 1966**

Dear Mr. Wolfe:

Received your letter of the 10th announcing your new publication. I have wondered for a long time why someone did not start such a magazine; we have more handloaders in the country right now than ever before.

If my old buddy were still around, he could tell you that I have had seventy-five years' experience in reloading. I'm talking about Col. Townsend Whelen. You see, it was my own writing for shooting magazines back before 1900 that got Whelen deeply interested in handloading. I knew him before he joined the Army. For years our Uncle Sam supplied his ammunition, so he had no reason to load his own. But the results some of us were getting by reloading for the .30 Krag got Whelen interested.

My own rifle shooting started with the use of an old Stevens "Expert Model" .22 rifle. From that I went to an old muzzleloading squirrel rifle. You can bet we did plenty of handloading with black powder in those days. From 1900 to around 1915 I used mostly "Schuetzen" rifles, shooting off-hand at two hundred yards. All my life I have made a special study of rifle shooting. I was associated with Dr. Mann and Niedner from 1906 until the doctor's death. I have data in my files from Dr. Mann, via correspondence, that has never been published. Also, letters from a lot of the real old-timers — Wm. V. Lowe, Harry Pope, Dr. Hudson, W. Milton Farrow, and a host of others. I knew these men personally, and shot in matches with some of them.

Some of Dr. Mann's experimenting was carried on through suggestions that I sent him from time to time. My bullet making with hand-swaged metal case bullets started in 1906, with swages made by Niedner. I still have them. I doubt if there is another man living today that has had sixty years of experience in swaging metal case bullets. What pleases me the most is that I am still shooting. Later I'll send you a target that I fired on February 13 this year; it has five shots in a 3/16-inch group at a hundred yards.

As years go, I'm several past the eighty mark, but that doesn't mean a thing. I happen to be as active as a man only half my age. I work ten hours a day in a local machine shop as a tool maker, and I'm about the only man in the shop who can read a pair of mikes without the aid of a reading glass. And I read the papers without glasses. I have been driving a car since 1900, and driving sports cars these past twenty years. General Motors made a survey and they claim I am the oldest sports car driver in the country.

Yes, I would be pleased to send you data for your magazine as you suggested. And I have enough to fill several books. How would it be to include some of my letters received years ago from Harry Pope, that show the troubles he had in shooting and how he corrected these matters? You will soon find that I am about the only source that has such material that would interest the modern shooter.

For many years I wrote for the *Rifleman*. What soured me on writing for them was that someone was re-writing my stuff, cutting out the important parts 'til it made little sense. This got my goat, so I stopped writing for them. Trouble was, the fellow reading my material did not even know what it was all about.

Phil Sharpe visited me one time. He stayed about two weeks, looking over my files and taking notes. I gave him enough data that he went home and wrote a book on reloading.

It's strange about some of the old-timers. Neither Dr. Mann nor even Ned Roberts was what you might call a rifleman. Dr. Mann was more of an experimenter and scientist than a shooter. He required plenty of help in loading his ammunition. Niedner helped him a lot. Ned Roberts was a school teacher, and had to confine what little shooting he did to vacation time. He called on me to help out with the book he wrote.

I knew Roberts for about sixty years; he taught at one time only a short way from my home. He knew nothing about handloading. If you could see the way he mixed up his components, you would understand just what I mean. I don't believe he ever shot a one-inch hundred-yard group in his life. He was one of those fellows that was going to do so and so, if and when he got the right combination, but that day never came. He did considerable writing about shooting, but as my old "shooting uncle" used to say, "Those that can shoot, SHOOT, and those that can't, write about it."

Yours truly,<br>H.A. Donaldson

Harvey Donaldson (left) and his good friend Phil Teachout. Photo was taken in the early 60s when Phil was editor of Precision Shooting magazine.

Harvey's love for sports cars goes back to 1900 when he bought a Stanley Steamer. In 1961 he was featured in Corvette Magazine as the oldest known sports car driver.

Yours truly No. 2

# Finding the Cause of 'Flyers'

March 12, 1966

Friend Wolfe,

This letter has to do with the two targets I sent to you recently. They are my latest efforts to show the cause of what we shall call the *off shots* in the normal five or ten-shot hundred-yard group.

First off we go back to around 1900 up to 1910. At this time Dr. F.W. Mann was trying to determine the cause of what he called the X-error in rifle shooting. Today I call these the "off shots." You probably call them "flyers." I have in my files plenty of correspondence with Dr. Mann, so I'm well acquainted with his early experiments. I also have data that was to appear in his second book on the *Ballistics of Small Arms*. This data was never shown in print, for the good doctor died before it was published, and his manuscript was destroyed.

Dr. Mann discovered in his early experimenting the simple fact that the ball did not always fly straight from the muzzle of his rifle — that is, in the direction which the bore of his rifle was pointed. His theory was that the blast from the muzzle acted to deflect the bullet, and also that imperfections in the bullet caused these "off shots." Dr. Mann was more of a scientist than a rifleman or a bench rest shooter. And he was not an experienced handloader. That was one reason he had to invent his Mann V rest, to do his best shooting.

Today, the modern bench rest shooter can beat the best groups that Dr. Mann ever made with his V rest. He had to resort to data he received from A.O. Niedner, to help out with his handloading. Niedner was also a great help in his experiments.

We have far better components today than were available when the doctor was conducting his tests. Our metal case bullets are close to perfection, especially the process that produces the very accurate Remington Power-Lokt bullets.

My reason for writing the above information is to show that there is no evidence shown in the doctor's book that would lead one to suspect that he ever gave a thought to the fact that the uneven thickness of the case necks of the handloads we use today had any effect whatever on the cause of these off shots we get now and then.

For many years I have had the idea that our off shots were caused by the uneven thickness of the case necks. For a number of years I coached my friend Samuel Clark, Jr., in the ways and means of handloading for bench rest shooting. One of the first things he had to learn was how to segregate the cases that gave the tight groups, and to discard those that produced these flyers, or "off shots." Understand, this data is obtained ONLY by shooting.

I might as well mention that friend Clark did right well in his shooting, having held several World Records at the same time. It might do no harm to also mention these records were made with rifles chambered to cases of my own design.

There are several gages available today that will allow a shooter to determine the thickness, or shall we say the difference in the thickness, of the case necks in our handloaded ammunition. Having no such gages myself, I have to resort to other methods. I am more interested in just where the bullets are going out at one hundred or two hundred yards than I am in the amount of thickness one side of the case neck might have over the other side.

During the past several months my shooting has been confined to testing out a very accurate varmint rifle. As you know, I work in a machine shop during the week, so my time for shooting has to be confined to Saturdays and Sundays, regardless of weather conditions.

The data on the rifle used in these tests is as follows. The action is the Remington 722, with a light trigger. The stock is an old one made several years ago, well seasoned and action and barrel bedded carefully. The barrel was made by Douglas in .224 caliber from stainless steel, with fifteen-inch twist, sporter weight, twenty-six inches long, chambered for the .225 Winchester case.

Douglas fitted the barrel to my action, and then chambered it as well. He gave me a perfect job. Tolerance at case neck is as it should be made, the body of the chamber a perfect fit for the factory case. In fact the fired cases show no swell near the head of the case, as so often happens with the factory product.

My loading data for handloads used in my tests consists of No. 250 CCI Magnum primers, thirty grains of 4895 powder, and the new Remington 55-grain open point Power-Lokt bullets. Overall length of loaded case is 2 13/32 inches.

For some reason this rifle seems to do well with any of the bullets I have tried, but all in the 55-grain weight — Sierra, Hornady, Remington, as well as my own hand-swaged product. In bench rest shooting I use one of Gene Beecher's rests, together with Basil Tuller's fine sandbags. The trick in shooting a light sporter from the bench is to have the fore-end well bedded down in the front bag. Keeping the sides of the bag well up on the sides of the fore-end will prevent canting, as well as insuring a solid rest.

The sides of my rear sandbag come well up on the sides of the stock. My eye sight just happens to be keen enough that I can see clearly the figures of the ten ring at a hundred yards, through my ten-power Weaver scope. In trying for a tight group one has to hold on as small an aiming point as is possible. It might be that my years of bench rest shooting have made it possible for me to see them the same for each shot, as well as holding the rifle properly for each shot. As I have mentioned before, an experienced bench rest shooter can beat the best efforts out at one hundred or two hundred yards over any of the targets Dr. Mann ever fired from his famous V rest.

I had several reasons for testing this particular .225 Winchester rifle. First I wanted to learn just how well it might perform, since the crow and chuck season was fast approaching. I wanted to be prepared. Another reason was to test the new Remington Power-Lokt bullets I had heard so much about. It may seem strange to many that I am just as keen for chuck hunting now as I was some seventy-five years ago, when I first started hunting them.

The last few years when shooting a varmint rifle in testing for five-shot hundred-yard groups, I have noted that one shot out of five or two out of five would go some half inch out of the normal group. These shots were going either high or to one side. With the good bullets we use today I could hardly lay this to the bullets. Nor to my holding, as I was seeing the same each time. During the past few months in testing an especially accurate rifle, I came to the conclusion that the cause of these "off shots" was the same as friend Clark and I found out years ago. That is, the case necks of my new Winchester .225 cases were of uneven thickness.

So . . . I decided to do something about it by segregating my cases, not with any gage, but by shooting, and seeing each shot as fired through a spotting scope, and noting its position in relation to the normal group. The cases that went into the normal group were placed in a box marked MATCH LOADS. Those cases that delivered an off shot went into another box marked CHUCK loads. Before long I was able to collect quite a few cases that would shoot as well as I could hold.

Now we are ready to examine the targets sent you recently. The weekend of February 5th snowed and blowed so hard I was unable to do any shooting, but on Sunday, the 13th, the weather turned quite warm for February, about 35 above, but it was raining. Some of the best groups I ever shot were fired in the rain. Also, the best group my old friend Charles Rowland ever shot (but from a *machine rest*, not a bench) were made in the rain. That was on May 16th, 1901.

The 13th was a dark day, but no wind, and it was about the best day for shooting I have had this year. My shooting started around 1:00 p.m. A steady rain was coming down at this time but as my shooting bench was well covered, it made little difference.

My first group of five shots is shown on target marked No. 1. The first two shots were from cases that had shown "off shots" in previous tests. And the last three shots, that went into one hole, were from my MATCH CASE loads. This rifle was doing so well I then fired shots on the target marked No. 2. It was so hard to spot the shots through the scope that I then walked up to examine the target. This tight group was even better than I had expected, and it should give some idea of the accuracy of this particular Douglas barrel, as well as the Remington P-L bullets.

I am sorry now that I did not fire a ten-shot group, but on the other hand if I had been able to see how well they were doing I might not have made such a tight group. This is about as tight a group I have ever fired from a varmint rifle, but I have done better with heavy bench rest guns.

Yours truly,<br>
Harvey A. Donaldson

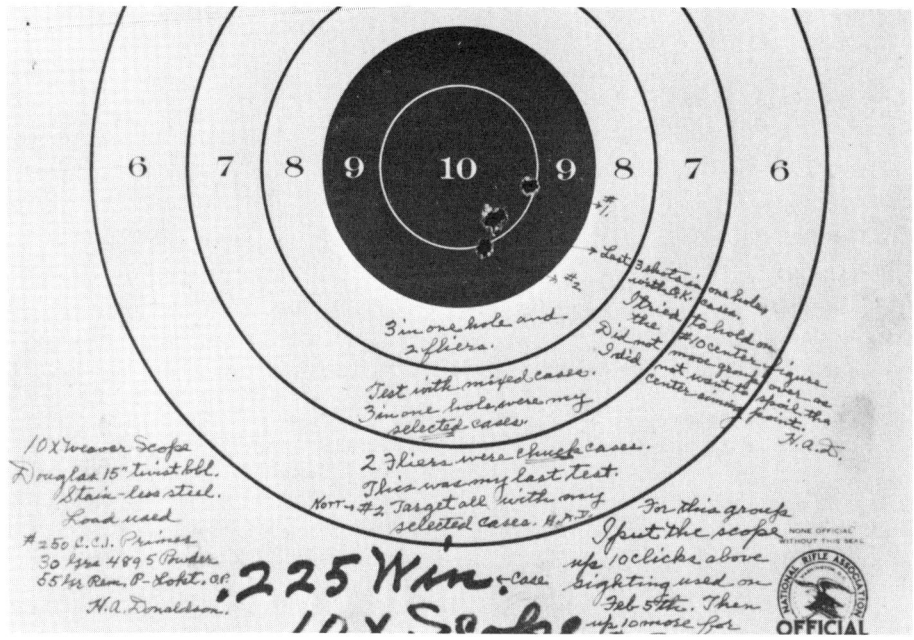

Top — Donaldson's test target with mixed cases. Upper and lower holes were made with "chuck load" brass, while bullets from three selected "match" shells went into one hole.

Bottom — Five shots in one hold at one hundred yards, all from selected cases. As Harvey says, it pays to separate "off shot" brass from your match cases.

Yours truly No. 3

# Origin of the .25-20 Single Shot

**May 10, 1966**

Dear Dave,

Perhaps our readers would like to learn the origin of the first cartridge and rifle designed in .25 caliber. Checking over some old copies of the *American Field*, dated in 1884, I found several letters from the pen of F.J. Rabbeth, the shooter who originated the .25-20 Single Shot cartridge, which throws some light on his early experiments.

I was surprised to learn that "J. Francis," as Rabbeth was called by the Walnut Hill riflemen, first worked on a .28 caliber case, the present .25-20 case being the outcome of experiments made after his .28 caliber rifle was in use. Mr. Rabbeth was interested in the development of a varmint cartridge — one that would give improved accuracy and as high velocity as possible with the components at hand.

To understand fully the situation as it existed over eighty years ago, it should be borne in mind that there were no rifles available for small game hunting, with the possible exception of the .32-20-115 that was used in the Model 1873 Winchester rifle. This particular cartridge, while accurate, had a low velocity with high trajectory, and was not entirely suited to squirrel and woodchuck hunting. Note that back in the old days, the chuck hunters were looking for high velocity, as is the case today.

This brings to mind the fact that most improvements in our modern rifles and ammunition during the last eighty years were brought about by the woodchuck hunters of this country. To the untiring efforts of such fine riflemen as F.J. Rabbeth, Dr. Henry Baker, Major Hinman, W. Milton Farrow, Dr. Skinner, Dr. Mann, A.O. Niedner, Horace Warner, Reuben Harwood, E.A. Leopold, H.M. Pope, Charles Newton, N.H. Roberts, Capt. G.L. Wotkyns, Capt. G.H. Woody, Col. Townsend Whelen, and a host of others I could mention, is due the excellence of our modern varmint rifles.

In working out the design for his .28 caliber case, Rabbeth proceeded as follows: First, in order to avoid the expense of an entirely new case, he selected the longest .32 caliber shell then on the market, this being the Frank Wesson .32 caliber centerfire case, which was 1 5/8 inches long. He then had his barrel bored for a bullet the size of the *inside* of this case, so that he could use a bullet of a uniform diameter, and to seat it to any depth in the shell. This, of course, made the bore approximately .28 caliber.

For the benefit of those readers who have never used nor seen a .32 C.F. Extra Long case, as used in the Frank Wesson rifle, I will explain that the bullets for this cartridge were really .29 caliber and had at the base only a heel of the diameter of the inside of the case, the rest of the bullet being larger. This bullet was held in the case by this heel, the same as in .22 Long Rifle ammunition in use today; the outside was the caliber size of the bore.

With a charge of 25 grains of fine black powder back of a bullet of eighty-five grains weight, Mr. Rabbeth did some good shooting up to one hundred and fifty yards. The April 1884 issue of the *American Field* shows ten-shot hundred-yard groups made by him that measured one and a quarter inches. This was remarkable accuracy for black powder and cast bullets in those days, and would be nearly on a par with some of our modern vermin rifles today, if they were loaded with black powder and cast bullets.

There is small wonder that Mr. Rabbeth's experiments aroused considerable interest among the small game shooters of that day.

This .28 caliber rifle he tried out on small game, but because of the way the bullet tore up ducks and gray squirrels, he decided that this .28 caliber was still too large for his purpose. Mr. Rabbeth then ordered from E. Remington & Sons, Ilion, N.Y., a barrel in .25 caliber, this being the very *first* barrel in .25 caliber ever produced. This was in 1884. Harry Pope did not come out with a .25 caliber barrel until around 1887 or 1888.

Rabbeth used the same 1 5/8-inch F. Wesson .32 caliber case, but reduced it slightly at the mouth to .25 caliber, thus making a slight bottleneck in design. And this is exactly the same .25-20 Single Shot case as we know it today. From the very first it has given fine results as a small game cartridge.

Loaded with twenty-two grains of Hazzard's No. 3 powder, and a 67-grain bullet, this cartridge made an "86" on the Massachusetts decimal target, or "48" by Creedmoor count, with ten shots, off hand, Mr. Rabbeth doing the shooting on the Walnut Hill range.

In rest shooting he frequently put ten consecutive shots into less than a 1½-inch group at a hundred yards. The hundred-yard mid-range trajectory height of this particular rifle, with twenty-six-inch barrel and shooting the above load, was 1½ inches, and 9½ inches at two hundred yards. The corresponding trajectory heights for the .32-20-115 Winchester case were 3½ and about 15 inches for the same ranges. The above trajectories were obtained on the same day at the Walnut Hill range by Mr. Rabbeth and Major Hinman, by shooting through tissue paper screens placed at intervals of twenty-five yards over the two hundred-yard range. These figures were checked and found to be correct.

The firm of E. Remington & Sons not only made this first .25 caliber barrel, but also made the bottleneck cases that were used in this rifle. However, Remington was in no way eager to put the .25-20 S.S. rifle and cartridge on the market; from Mr. Rabbeth's letters it would appear that the company was waiting to see how great a demand would arise for the new rifle before tooling up.

In the year 1884, the Massachusetts Arms Company of Chicopee Falls made the Model 1882 Maynard rifle, and it was quick to see the advantages of the new cartridge. The company at once adapted the Maynard rifle to take this new case. I might add that when this first commercial .25 caliber rifle appeared, it was received with the same enthusiasm as was the .22 Hornet which came out some fifty years later. The .25-20 Maynard barrel had a fifteen-inch twist.

The writer owns and shoots two very accurate .25-20 S.S. Maynard rifles in hunting gray squirrels. One of these has been fitted with a small firing pin, and with five grains of Unique and the Lyman gas check bullet No. 257420, it is possible to shoot fifty-yard groups of ten shots that will cut into one ragged hole.

There is shown on Page 2 of the March 1936 issue of the *American Rifleman* an advertisement by the Hercules Powder Company showing one of my targets made with this fine old Maynard rifle. Shooting was with iron sights, but today for some reason or other I have to use scope sights.

The Maynard rifles were all furnished with straight line bullet seaters for their .25-20 S.S. rifles. About the only way a person can obtain a .25-20 S.S. rifle today is to pick one up second hand. If the barrel is not in perfect condition this should be no cause for discarding the rifle. It is surprising how some of these guns with barrels in too poor condition to handle cast bullets will give remarkable accuracy with the use of metal case bullets.

Yours truly,<br>Harvey A. Donaldson

*Harvey operates his screw press, on which he made bullets in Niedner dies for fifty years.*

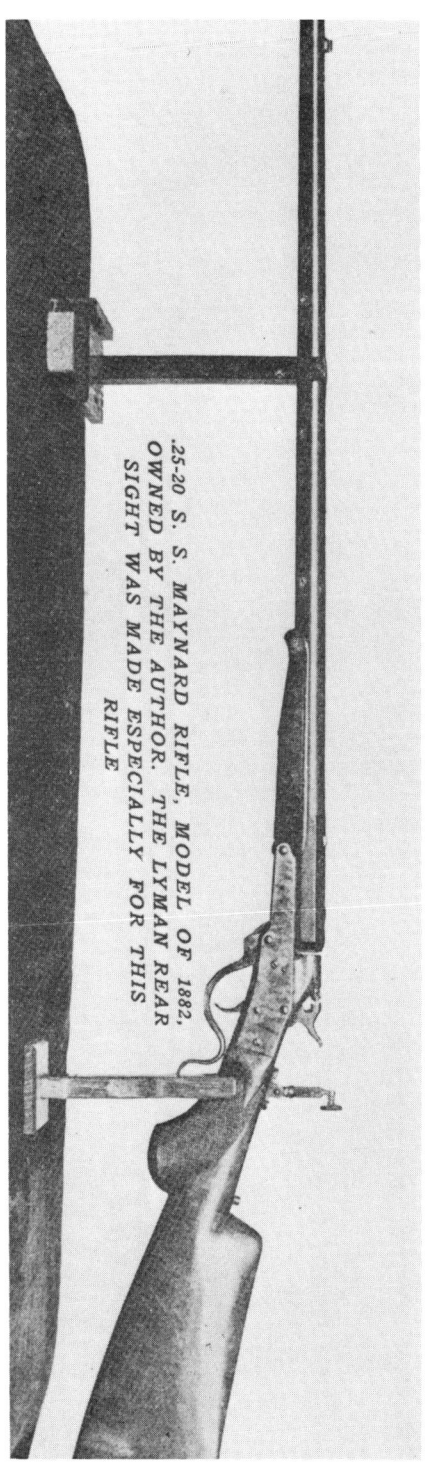

.25-20 S. S. MAYNARD RIFLE, MODEL OF 1882, OWNED BY THE AUTHOR. THE LYMAN REAR SIGHT WAS MADE ESPECIALLY FOR THIS RIFLE

## The .25-20 Maynard

**May 11, 1966**

Dear Dave:

I have just completed another letter for the *Handloader*, which I will send along in a day or so together with some more prints you can use.

A friend took some pictures of me in my shop, showing me at my loading bench. Will send these along under separate cover. Will send prints of my .25-20 Maynard rifle together with print of a target the Hercules Company used. Is this O.K.?

Later I will do an article on some old loading tools. I want to show prints of some of my old Niedner hand swages that still make fine metal case bullets. Also I have the patent papers of W. Milton Farrow's rifles as well as the re- and de-capper he invented. Could you use them later?

I have in my files the score cards that Mr. Farrow used when shooting in France over 80 years ago. He was about the best off-hand 200-yard shooter who ever lived. A World Record holder. I knew him well and have enough data on him to fill a book.

Best regards and lets hear from you.

Harve

# FINE TARGET PROVES ACCURACY OF UNIQUE

## H. A. Donaldson Makes Perfect Demonstration to Friend

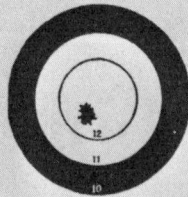

The accompanying target was made by Mr. H. A. Donaldson, of Little Falls, N. Y. It speaks for Mr. Donaldson's holding ability, for his loading skill, and for the quality of the materials he used. The following remarks are from the letter which accompanied the target:

"I read with interest your fine ads, "Reloader News," in the American Rifleman. I do a lot of testing and experimenting; you may have seen my articles and also the data I am sending F. C. Ness for the Dope Bag of the American Rifleman.

"What I want to say is that if more shooters would try your Unique Powder, they would be pleased with the results.

"I have used Unique for some 30 years. It is the powder that gives the best results in reduced loads for the .30/'06, .270 Winchester, .250/3000, and a number of other cases. With Unique there is no comparison.

"I find this so, especially with the gas check bullets. I am sending you enclosed a target I made a few days ago, at 50 yards, to prove to a friend what a fine load I am using in one of my squirrel rifles . . . . . I find Unique to be very reliable and it gives me wonderful accuracy, burning well when loaded loose in the case

"Another thing you should mention in 'Reloader News': I have found in my own testing that your new HiVel No. 3 is the *only powder made* that gives extreme accuracy with the 60-gr. open point, .25 cal. vermin bullet, in such rifles as the .25/35, .25 Remington, .250/3000, .25 Neidner Special, .25 Roberts, and the .25 Krag. Never before have I seen such fine accuracy with high speed with this short 60-gr. bullet."

# A Visit To Risley

**June 20, 1966**

Dear Dave:

I have received the second copy of our magazine, and note that the prints made of my targets show up clear and sharp. Nice work.

Am also getting more letters so send along more writing material with *Handloader* heading.

Enclosed find a letter I just received from my old-time gunsmith friend, M.S. Risley of Earlville, New York. I visited Risley some time ago and at the time he said some of my early experimenting should be shown in the magazines. Since my visit his wife died, and his health is failing. He is past eighty, and way over weight.

He had his daughter type out his letter, and sent it along to me Friday so I might have a photostat copy made for my own files, and he asked that I mail it on to you.

I know you are busy but how about taking time out for a letter.

Best regards,<br>Harve

## Where Credit Is Due

Mr. David Wolfe
*Handloader* Magazine
Peoria, Ill.

Dear Sir:

I have noted that several riflemen have been quoted as having been responsible for the design of the cartridge known as the .22-250 or the .22 Varminter, the same case design of which rifles are now produced by both Browning and Remington.

To give credit where credit is due, and to set the record straight, the credit for this design should go to Harvey A. Donaldson, Fultonville, New York.

I first met Donaldson in 1906, when he was living in Rome, New York. Even then he had been shooting for over ten years. Ever since that time I have been in close touch with Donaldson, and have known of his experiments in case designing, and in handloading for super accuracy.

When the Savage Company brought out the rifle chambered for the .250-3000 case in 1915, Donaldson was working for the Remington Arms Co. in Ilion, New York, as an inspector. Within a year from the time this cartridge was available, Donaldson took this case and necked it down to .228 caliber. He then obtained a .228 caliber barrel from the Savage Arms Co., (the cost at that time being only $4.00), and had Niedner chamber and fit the barrel to a Savage rifle. This was the very first .22-250 rifle ever made. The barrel had the .228 bore, same as the .22 Hi-Power Savage rifle, using the 70-grain Savage bullet.

The design was a success, right from the start. But when Donaldson tried to interest the Savage Arms Company in producing a rifle chambered for the new case, they told him it was a good case, but if they brought it out at that time, it might spoil the sale of their .22 High Power that they already had in production. All this happened some fifty years ago, long before those who now claim its design were doing any shooting.

Donaldson used this rifle in chuck hunting for some time, then when the Hornet and the .22 Lovell came out, he changed the design of both cases to a bottleneck design, the latter called the 2-R. Lovell and I made up the first reamers in this design, and he also chambered and made up Donaldson's complete 2-R rifle.

Along in the early Thirties, when J. Bushnell Smith was visiting Donaldson, then living in Little Falls, New York, he was looking through a cigar box filled with some empty fired cases, and he dug up a few of the old .22-250 (.228") cases. He asked Donaldson what they were, and when told, he decided he wanted a rifle made up to take such a case. Donaldson told him to go ahead. Later he was surprised when he learned that Smith had sent the fired cases on to Gebby, saying they were his own design.

This data above gives to the best of my knowledge the true history of the design of the case now known as the .22-250 or the .22 Varminter.

Very truly yours,
M.S. Risley, Gunsmith
June 16, 1966

Yours truly No. 4

# On .30 Caliber Cast Bullets

**July 14, 1966**

Dear Dave,

I have read the very comprehensive article by Ken Waters on handloading for the .30-30 case. Ken has done a fine job in preparing his material. I believe my old friend Townsend Whelen would have enjoyed reading this article.

I feel certain that there are many of the old-timers in this shooting game who will agree with what Ken has written. I fully believe if he had tried the Lyman gas-check bullet No. 31141 cast one to fifteen, and sized down to .311 inch, he might have made tighter groups. My own experience in shooting several rifles in .308 caliber recently has led me to believe that this particular 175-grain 31141 bullet will give far better accuracy than any other bullet in this caliber that I have tried. If shooters will go to the trouble to check over bullets No. 311291 in round point and No. 311375 in spitzer point, I believe they will agree that the bullet that I am using (No. 31141) is a lot better balanced. You might check with the No. 43 Edition of the *Lyman Handbook*.

You may note that this flat-nose bullet is much like the .32-40 bullet No. 319247 that we used in the old target rifles back around 1900. If anything, No. 31141 is even a *better* balanced bullet. With the advantage of the gas check, it can show a velocity of from 1,600 to 1,800 feet per second. In my experience, I always got far better results in regard to accuracy at 100 yards where the velocity was under 2,000 fps, by shooting a flat-nose bullet. If Harry Pope were around today, he would tell you the same thing. There was nothing to prevent Pope from having any bullet shape he wanted, but he found the flat-nose bullet gave the best results. So . . . who are we to argue with that old-timer.

Now it just happens that I have, within the hour, returned from my own rifle range, where I spent the afternoon shooting around thirty bullets No. 31141 through a very accurate .30-06 Springfield sporter. The load used in this rifle is as follows: No. 9½ Remington primer, sixteen grains of Du Pont's 4759 and this 175-

grain gas-check bullet cast one to fifteen and sized to .311. My loads were fired from once-fired MATCH F.A. brass, and I would have you understand the necks of cases were *not* resized. My bullets when lubricated and sized in the Lyman lubricator to .311 are just a nice smooth fit in the case necks.

They could easily be seated in the cases with the finger, but they were seated down into the case necks three-eighths of an inch with a Vickerman bullet seater. This same seater, by the way, has been lapped out to take a .311-inch diameter bullet. I mention this just in case some joker would like to know how to get a .311 cast bullet into a seater made for bullets of .308 diameter.

My shooting was five-shot groups only, and I am not even going to show you any of the groups. You might believe they were shot from a .308 caliber bench-rest outfit. But I can tell you that *every* group as fired was *under one inch*. You cannot do such shooting with any gas-check round-nose bullets. If you don't believe it, just try it.

Some shooters may complain that I have mentioned a powder no longer available.* It just happens I have an ample supply on hand, and the reason I used it was simply because it happens to give very accurate results. I'm still going to do more testing with the same rifle and bullets but with other powders. When these tests are completed, you will have a complete report.

Just in case some of our readers would like to know the secret of getting accuracy with *any* gas-check bullet, there are several things to keep in mind. First, one has to be able to cast *perfect* bullets, then apply the gas check as the bullet is sized down and lubricated. One should experiment until he finds the correct diameter of bullet for his own barrel.

If shooting in hot weather, the lubricant has to be just right. And again it takes some experimenting to find the correct temper of lead and tin.

While it is possible to drive gas-check bullets to over 2,000 fps, if you are looking for accuracy, keep them down to 1,800 or so.

The seating of the bullet into the case is also very important. Never *crimp* the case neck down into the crimping groove if it can be avoided. Sure thing, a lot of bullets have this crimping groove, but that does not necessarily mean one has to use it. For handgun loads, that is O.K., but when I take all the necessary pains required to cast a perfect bullet I don't want any case neck scraping the length of the cast bullet before it enters the barrel.

As one old-timer told me recently, he had found that some seventy years of experience in casting bullets was a damn handy gadget to have around. Maybe he had something there.

Yours truly,<br>Harvey A. Donaldson

* Du Pont had discontinued No. 4759 powder at the time *Harvey* wrote this letter, but was back in production in the early '70s.

**Yours truly No. 5**

# *Experiments in .25 Caliber*

**September 22, 1966**

Dear Dave:

This letter is written on the chance that our readers might be interested in some of my early experimenting with a rifle in .25 caliber. While I will agree that we have hardly reduced all aspects of rifle shooting to an exact science, if you will attend some of the recent bench rest matches you will see we are getting closer all the time to one-hole accuracy.

My own background in rifle shooting, from around 1900 to about the time of the First World War was devoted to off-hand two-hundred-yard Schuetzen shooting. You would be surprised at the many things we learned in those days, trying for accuracy with the old-time black powder rifles. Many of these things can still be applied to our modern rifles. For one, we tried to fit our loads to each particular gun, and this had to do with the proper twist, the correct weight of bullet and powder charge, that gave the best accuracy at the *range* where we were shooting. We used one load for a hundred yards and quite another for two-hundred-yard shooting.

From around 1905 up to around 1912 or later I was more or less associated with the experiments of both Niedner and Dr. Mann. We then used the very accurate Mann-Niedner .25 caliber Krag case design. My rifle was made up on the Winchester Single Shot action, with double set triggers, a Pope speed action, heat-treated receiver, and Mann-Niedner firing pin. I still own this fine rifle, but today it has a barrel chambered for my own .219 Donaldson-Wasp case. In fact, it happens to be the very *first* barrel ever chambered for this case. Niedner made the barrel in .25 caliber with a fifteen-inch twist (at my own suggestion), and he chambered the rifle originally for the .25 Krag case.

This particular rifle accounted for a great number of woodchucks and crows. I used a bullet of eighty-five grains made in a swage furnished by Niedner. This fine swage is still in use in my shop. I soon found that the twist of fifteen inches was *ideal* for this bullet. Even today I use rifles in .25 caliber having this same twist when I use eighty-five-grain bullets.

This .25 Krag case, as you can imagine, was a lot more powerful than necessary for strictly a chuck rifle, even if the fellows today shoot them with magnum rifles.

One might ask just why I selected this fifteen-inch twist. The simple fact that I owned a very accurate Maynard rifle chambered for the .25-20 S.S. case in fifteen-inch twist might have had something to do with it. Long ago I found it was a good plan to stay with something that gave RESULTS.

Looking for something not quite so powerful and noisy, I decided to do something about it, on my own. I simply took the Winchester rimmed .25-35 case, and came up with a bottleneck design with a thirty degree shoulder, about like the .225 Winchester case of today, but with a longer neck. Cases were fire-formed in my rifle. Niedner made my reamer and chambered my rifle, as well as making the barrel. He also made the straight line bullet seater. I still have these tools and dies.

This man Niedner was a super gunsmith if there ever was one. When he turned out a job it was a JOB and no fooling. He certainly gave me perfect work in every particular. We could use men of his caliber today, but don't rush out and try to find one. Those days are gone forever.

To make a long story short, I really had something in this particular rifle. You will note that I used only one weight of bullet, eighty-five grains. Also, this case held more powder than the regular Winchester .25-35, which was what I had in mind when I designed the case.

We soon found that this gun gave better accuracy, even out at two hundred yards, than anything either Dr. Mann or Niedner had seen. And I might add, at this time Dr. Mann was gathering material for another book, and had it been published, he would have mentioned this rifle and its accuracy. Niedner told me all the data for this second book was destroyed after the doctor died.

At that time, around 1910 or so, Charles Newton was keeping a close check on both Niedner and Dr. Mann, and their experiments. Somewhere in my files I have a long letter from Niedner stating that both he and Dr. Mann had figured it was from the data we got from my rifle that started Newton working on a design of case in .25 caliber. This came out as the .250-3000 case.

You should understand it was Newton's idea to use the .30 Krag case necked down to .25 caliber, but when he took that design to the Savage company, they told him it was not possible to use a case with such a large rim in the Savage magazine.

It is a long story how this was finally managed, but that can wait for another letter. If our good friend Whelen were still around, he could also furnish the details.

Some tests that Niedner made with my .25 caliber rifle, with the use of the eighty-five-grain bullet, showed he was getting a velocity of over three thousand fps which, of course, was due to the slower twist I used. Dr. Mann wrote up all this data for the book that was never printed. Niedner did very little writing for publication — most of his data was turned over to Dr. Mann, who took care of the writing.

Friend Whelen told me one time that so far as he knew, from the data he had received on my rifle from Niedner, this velocity would give me the distinction of designing the very first case, in .25 caliber, that gave a velocity of three thousand feet per second.

But all this is water over the dam, and is a small matter to me at this time. As you can imagine, what DOES interest me is the simple fact that I am STILL around, and able to shoot and to hold a rifle as well as I ever could. Whelen, Niedner, Dr. Mann, and a host of the old-timers I could mention, have left the range forever, but what we learned from them lingers on. May they Rest in Peace.

Sincerely yours,
H.A. Donaldson

*Harve charges some cases for future 'chuck and fox hunting. Photo taken in late 1960's.*

Yours truly No. 6

## *Those Flat Nose Bullets*

**November 10, 1966**

Dear Dave,

In reading over my letter for *Handloader* No. 4, I note that I made several statements regarding my choice of flat nosed bullets for better accuracy. This may be questioned by some of our readers.

With this in mind I want to qualify those statements. There is one round nose bullet in .308 caliber that I have found will give very fine accuracy. This happens to be the Lyman No. 308206 Kephart bullet.

This one has been around for a great many years; it was designed by Horace Kephart of St. Louis, Mo., some time before 1900. I will quote from a copy of the No. 16 *Ideal Handbook* dated 1903 that gives Mr. Kephart's own description of this bullet:

"The bands should be broad and strong to withstand pressure of gas from the rear, and the wrench of the ten-inch twist. There should be some provision for lubricating the bullet ahead of the first band, so that dry lead may not touch the barrel. Some means should be devised for pushing the fouling straight ahead and out of the barrel at each discharge. With these points in mind, I designed the bullet No. 308206 which has the three wide square-shouldered bands with a dirt catcher groove in front. This dirt catcher groove occupies the place of the usual crimp shoulder, and contains lubricant. Its function is twofold: to grease the rifle barrel before any lead touches it, and to push out fouling at each discharge. When the bullet of ordinary shape is fired through a dirty barrel, its point and crimp shoulder will wedge the fouling, usually forming a cake just ahead of the chamber. My bullet having the square shouldered band behind the dirt catcher scrapes up the fouling and pushes it out of the barrel."

Around 1900 and for some years later our military forces were armed with the .30-40 Krag rifle. Strange as it may seem to the shooters of today, it was common practice for the military forces to shoot cast lead bullets in target practice at the shorter ranges of two hundred and up to five hundred yards. This one hundred seventy-grain Kephart bullet, when shot in the Krag rifle, gave remarkable accuracy.

A later edition of the *Ideal Handbook* of 1905 states that the Kephart bullet was the *very first* bullet to give satisfactory results in any of the .30 caliber rifles. Moulds for this bullet in weights of one hundred twenty-five and one hundred seventy grains are still available from Lyman, and with our modern powders this bullet, if cast one to twenty, will still give very accurate results.

Down through the years I have tried any number of moulds to cast .30 caliber bullets, and with the single exception later of the Squibb-Miller bullet and this round nose Kephart bullet, I have never found any that would give the accuracy I get from the flat nosed gas check .30 caliber bullets. One should understand my experience covers both one hundred and two hundred-yard shooting, and not the five hundred-yard military shooting. I hope I have explained the situation to those shooters who use spitzer or round pointed cast bullets in their .30 caliber rifles.

In these letters I am only trying to give my own experiences and the facts I have found in my own shooting. It is one thing to put down in print any particular fact you have found through experience, but quite another matter to try to *prove* most any statements that have to do with shooting matters. I believe I can state as a fact, and get away with it, that "No one can fall out of bed if he sleeps on the floor." I only wish that shooting matters were that simple.

Sometime around 1910 I owned and used quite extensively a Winchester single-shot rifle with double set triggers in .30-40 Krag caliber. This rifle had the thirty-inch No. 3 barrel. I used the one hundred seventy-grain Kephart bullet in this rifle, and it was a tack driver. I sure wish I had that old rifle today. When I think back on the choice of powders we had in those days, I wonder that this gun shot as well as it did.

From around 1900 and even up to 1920, it was quite common in the woods of our Adirondacks in New York State, while deer hunting in the fall, to find hunters carrying single-shot rifles. These were experienced hunters, not the road hunters we find today. They used mostly the Winchester single-shot, but once in a while one saw a Ballard or Stevens. These rifles were in such calibers as the .25-35 Winchester, .32-40 Winchester, .38-55 Winchester, .40-70 Winchester and sometimes the .45-70.

Evidently deer were easy to kill in those days, for I know a number that were killed with one shot, with .25-20 and .32-20 Winchesters. But the fellows who used them were *hunters*, who depended on the first shot to do the job.

But times have changed, and the deer are getting harder to kill (or should I say hit) with anything but a Magnum!

I have just run across an item in one of the old *Ideal Handbooks* of around 1896 that will stand repeating. After giving several pages of instructions on how to cast bullets, down at the bottom of the page we read:

"The least trouble and best results in bullet casting may be obtained by purchasing your bullets direct from the Ideal Mfg. Co." They then state that there is a "knack in making good bullets that can only be acquired by *long* experience." That data is just as true today as it was some seventy years ago.

Writing about bullet casting takes me back to an experience I had with Harry Pope a number of years ago. It may do no harm to tell you about it. If memory serves me right (as it usually does), it was on July the 17th, 1938, that I attended the two hundred-yard off-hand Schuetzen Matches, held at Woburn, Massachusetts, on the old Walnut Hill Range. I will never forget that day, as it was the hottest I can ever remember. Most of the top expert off-hand shooters in the East were in attendance — men like F.H. Souther, the scope maker, John Kaufman, Paul Landrock, L.L. Heath, P.E. Brooks, A.L. Elliott, Charles H. Herrick (who designed the .28-30 case), William V. Lowe, H.M. Pope, J.C. Lippincott, and a host of others I could mention.

Along in the afternoon between relays, I sat on a bench visiting with Harry Pope. We had quite a long visit, talking over the old days, when I happened to put my hand in my pocket and brought out a .32-40 caliber hundred and ninety-five-grain bullet. I handed it to old Harry, who looked at it in amazement. Then he asked where in hell I had got that bullet. When I told him I had cast it in one of his own moulds, he said that it was impossible. He checked the bullet diameter with a pair of mikes he had in his pocket, and kept shaking his head, as if puzzled. Then he told me this story:

It seems the cherry that made the mould was made when Harry had his shop in Hartford, Connecticut. He had made up only three moulds with that cherry — one for himself, one for John Kelley, and one for Charles W. Rowland. When Pope went West to open a shop in California, he took this cherry with him. The day Pope figured to open his shop will be long remembered in San Francisco.

At 5:00 a.m. on April 18th, 1906, occurred the big earthquake. Harry said if the city was glad to see him they had no business to put on such a demonstration. To make a long story short, Harry lost everything he had in the world in the ruins of his shop, including the cherry that made the mould. Knowing that he had made only the three moulds from that one cherry, he figured it was not possible for me to have made the bullet.

The matter was soon cleared up when he learned that I had bought the mould from the family of Mr. Kelley, (together with a Pope rifle) sometime after Kelley passed away.

After examining the bullet once more, Harry turned to me and said, "After all these years I figured there were less than a half dozen men in the whole country who could cast a bullet that was fit to shoot. If you cast this bullet you can join that group, as I never saw a better cast bullet than this one I am holding." He wanted the bullet to keep and *"look at,"* as he said, so I was glad to hand it over to him.

Back in the 1920s, I used to cast bullets for Charles Rowland, who said they were just as good as his own, but the compliment from old Harry I will remember as long as I live. This was the last visit I ever had with Pope. I have in my files a number of letters from him down through the years, and some of them may be of interest to our readers. I will dig out some we might use.

The enclosed target shows the accuracy I get with the flat nosed .30 caliber bullets.

Yours truly,<br>H.A. Donaldson

This target shot by Donaldson shows a one hundred-yard five-shot group of approximately 5/8 inch, using his .30-06 rifle with 10-power scope. Load was 16 grains of 4759 powder, Remington primer and Lyman gas check bullet No. 31141, cast 1 to 15 and sized to .311. Case necks were not resized.

Harvey chats with his Canadian friend, Bob Snowball, at a bench rest match in the 1960's.

## *Bullet Not Listed*

**January 9, 1967**

Dear Sir:

In the November-December issue of *Handloader*, Harvey Donaldson mentions a Lyman gas check bullet No. 31141. My Lyman book does not list a bullet mould by that number. Could it possibly be No. 311467? If it is not too much bother, please put me on the right track.

E.B., Pompton Lakes, New Jersey

**March 2, 1967**

Dear Sir:

If you have failed to find bullet No. 31141 in your Lyman book, it is because this is a relatively new mould. Get a copy of Handbook No. 43, that I believe came out in 1964. On Page 117 you'll find the bullet shown under moulds for the .30-30 and .30 Rem. It is also listed under .30-06, .300 H&H, 7.62 Russian and others.

H.A. Donaldson

Yours truly No. 7

# Secrets of Schuetzen Shooting

**February 1, 1967**

Dear Dave,

I recently mentioned the name John D. Kelley in my letter to *The Handloader*. Mr. Kelley was a wealthy contractor from Williamsport, Pa. His business was building bridges. In Harry Pope's estimation, he was the finest bench rest shooter in the United States. During his years of active shooting he owned more than ten of Pope's best muzzle-loading rifles. This man was well liked by everyone who knew him. And he was absolutely honest and truthful in giving an account of his shooting experiences, which appeared from time to time in *Hunting & Fishing* back in the 1890's.

Mr. Kelley had a hired girl named Minnie Schenck; he taught her the fine art of bench rest shooting, until the time came when she was as expert as her teacher. I have, in my files, a copy of a target that she fired, five shots at two hundred yards. Those five shots went into ONE HOLE. This group is somewhat smaller than the famous ten-shot group by Charles W. Rowland from a machine rest back in May, 1901. By the old-fashioned string measure, her group was way under one inch. Later, when I have had a print made, I would be pleased to have you show it in *The Handloader*.

I believe this group was fired from Kelley's favorite Pope muzzle-loading rifle, chambered for the .38-72 case. The bullets were seated with the Pope toggle-joint bullet starter. This particular rifle is now in the possession of Ray M. Smith, the man who wrote the "Story of Pope's Barrels."

Along with this letter I am showing a print of one of my own .33-40 Pope muzzle-loading rifles. This rifle was No. 71, made up on a Sharps-Borchardt double-set

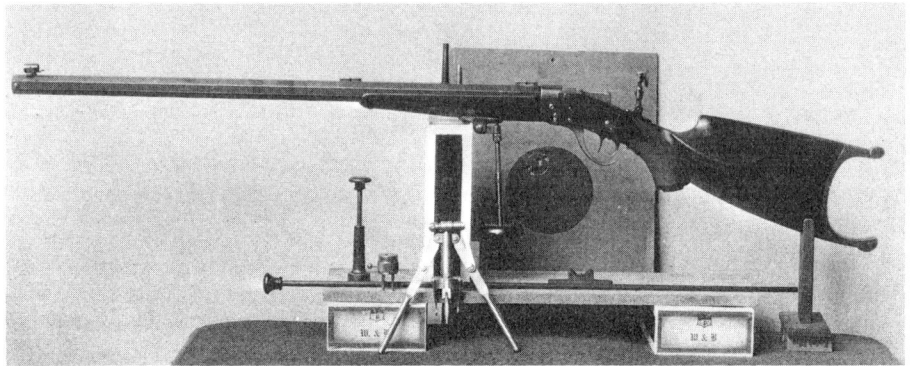

*The .33-40 Pope rifle No. 71 which Donaldson called his best Pope outfit.*

51

*Early photo of Donaldson showing his holding technique for Schuetzen shooting.*

trigger action by A.O. Zischang of Syracuse, N.Y. The target in the background was made at three hundred yards with the iron sights shown on the rifle. The loading or bullet-seating rod Pope made from rosewood. Long before Harry Pope passed away, those toggle-joint bullet seaters sold for over $150. Today they will bring most any price when offered for sale.

When casting bullets to use in these Pope barrels, the mixture of lead to tin had to be just right, and this was determined only by experimenting. The usual mixture was around one to thirty of tin and lead. Some used one to thirty-five. One reason, I believe, that the present-day shooter cannot seem to make the old rifles perform is because they cast their bullets too hard.

Back in the days before World War I, we shot our bullets in the same order as they came from the mould. In this way we figured we had better control of the mixture of lead and tin. More uniform, if you will. My own method was to use a board with a hundred holes bored in the top. When our mixture was the correct temperature and the mould was working right, we placed each bullet as cast into the board. The holes in the board were numbered from 1 to 100, and the first good bullet cast went into the hole marked "1" and the others in the proper order as cast.

Later, in shooting this lot of bullets, we used the bullet from hole Number One for the first shot, and so on down the line. This simple idea might be hard to prove but, as long as it worked out OK, we continued its use. So, as mentioned above, we figured we had a better control over the mixture, for there was a far better chance that the bullets from hole No. 1 to No. 10 would have a more *uniform* mixture or temper than say bullets picked at random.

One other technique in our system to keep components as uniform as possible was to run the powder through several screens, to separate the fine grains from the coarse. During this time I was experimenting with the use of white bulk shotgun powder, made by Du Pont. I remember at this time that Harry Pope learned from Lucian Cary that I was getting fine results in his own muzzle-loading barrels with a modern smokeless powder. The old master cussed me up-hill and down, telling Cary it couldn't be done. You must understand that Pope always used black powder in shooting his muzzle-loading rifles.

Somewhere in my files I have a long letter from Pope saying he wanted to take back, or apologize, for all he had said about me when he heard that I was getting good results from the white shotgun powder. Then he also wrote that, as far as he knew, I was the first one that had been able to get his rifles to perform properly with modern components.

An account of some of my early experimenting with shotgun powder in a Pope rifle was printed in the *American Rifleman*. We simply passed the powder through a couple of screens to separate the coarse from the fine grains. In some of the cans we found there was a greater proportion of fine grains over the coarse, so we figured the finer grains, or rather the greater amount of the fine grains, might have some effect on the course of the bullet. Here was a chance to control at least one matter that had to be considered, and I will show the method that I employed.

First off, we passed the powder just as it came from the can through a screen having eighteen holes to the inch, if memory serves me correctly. The powder that remained in the screen we called F.G. The finer powder was then passed through another screen having a finer mesh; the powder left on this screen was called F.F.G. The balance that passed through this second screen was called F.F.F.G., and it was the finer grains that gave us the most trouble. This simple method of separating the different size grains of powder soon began to show results. Our best accuracy was obtained from these efforts.

The amount of handling any one can of powder had received before it reached my loading bench had considerable to do with the amount of the finer grains of powder we found in the can. Back in the older days of rifle shooting we were careful to take advantage of every single feature that might be controlled, for there were plenty of others that were beyond control.

The average shooter today seems to think that the old muzzle-loading black powder rifles won't perform as well as they did years ago. Nothing could be further from the truth. The only thing is, most of the old-timers who did good shooting are long dead and gone. There are only a few left who can carry on, and only a few of those are still shooting.

Back in the old days one had to practically *live with a rifle* to learn how to shoot it properly. I can think of nothing being more temperamental than one of the old muzzle-loading Schuetzen rifles. Even a change in the weather from dry to wet would have some effect on those old guns. That may be one reason some of our modern-day shooters give up in disgust when they try to equal the results obtained by the original owner. All it takes is *know how*, and that is only obtained by shooting. For off-hand, two-hundred-yard shooting, very few ever used a telescope sight. Probably the reason was that there were few scopes available for this, with maybe the exception of the fine old scope made by Sidel, who had a shop on Race Street in Philadelphia.

We used iron sights or peep sights. The front sight had interchangeable apertures, to conform to the size of the target, or light conditions. Also, this had the wind gauge, as well as a spirit level attached, to allow the rifle to be held level. The rear sight was a vernier with apertures available to suit light conditions, or the specific ideas of the man doing the shooting.

Most of us used a front sight with a rather large aperture that would allow plenty of white to show around the large black bull of the off-hand, two-hundred-yard target. The size of the aperture in the rear sight had to be determined by the shooter as best for his own use.

When holding a rifle in the off-hand position, it was impossible to keep the rifle absolutely still. But to appearances, plenty of men could seemingly "hold like a rock."

Most of us used a palm rest, with the result that the rifle was more or less balanced and it was a little muzzle heavy to slow down the swing. The trick in off-hand shooting is to know exactly the right time to touch off the set trigger, as the front aperture is coming on the bull. The velocity of the bullets we used was seldom over 1,400 feet per second, which is slow by modern terms, so it took some doing to apply the pressure on the set trigger at EXACTLY the right moment to have the bullets go into the black. Harry Pope used to tell me, "Don't try every time for a ten. Just hold for the nines and the tens will take care of themselves." And the old-timer, as usual, was giving good advice.

The sight picture I liked best was to have the side of the bull just showing in the front aperture as I swung the rifle from right to left. By the time the finger touched the set trigger and the slow moving bullet had gone down the range (if your hold was correct), the bullet went into the black.

Not being able to hold dead still, and the balance of the rifle taking care of the high or low shots, most right-hand shooters came onto the bull from the right (my own method), but a number of other men would come on from the left.

The present-day bench rest shooter may think he does a lot of practice in getting ready for a match. I wonder what he would think if he knew it was a common practice for a rifleman of the old school to shoot say fifty shots off-hand almost every night during the summer months, as the light permitted, before he even ate his supper. This is what it takes, and such constant practice made holding and shooting in the off-hand position almost automatic.

One year I started along in April, getting ready for a match that would not be held until the following Election Day. Looking back, I cannot think of any summer when I enjoyed myself more. I did enough practice shooting that summer to take the edge off the modern varmint rifle, but with my Pope muzzle-loader it didn't mean a thing. No man could live long enough to wear out a Pope barrel.

I believe the one reason we do not see more good off-hand shooters today is the simple fact that such shooting takes a lot of practice, and the average rifleman does not have the necessary time to spend. During a long lifetime of active rifle shooting, I have known personally some of the finest riflemen this country has ever produced. From the early Nineties up until we started the bench rest movement, in Johnstown, N.Y., some twenty years ago, I practically lived with a rifle in my hands.

If I have learned anything about rifle shooting during that time, it was simply because I had available the help and assistance of the best shooters in this country. I have lived to see great changes in shooting. As I see matters today, there is still a lot of effort and work to be done if we wish to continue as a "Nation of Riflemen." The writer is still shooting and hopes to continue as long as he is able to prepare his loads and hold a rifle.

Yours truly,<br>H.A. Donaldson

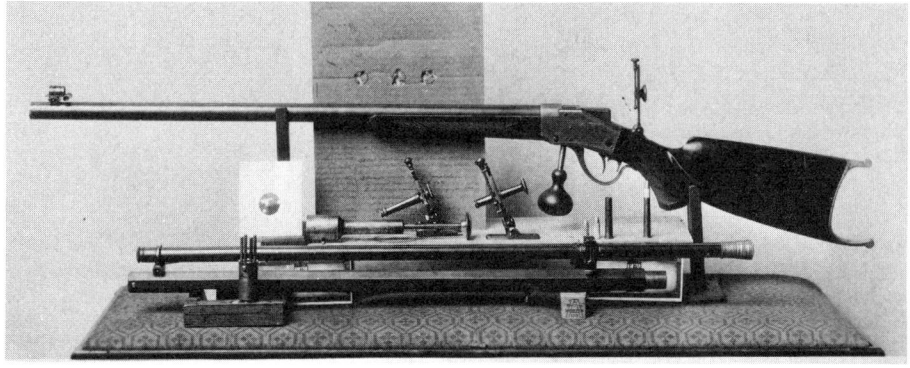

*Zischang barrelled .32-40 on Sharps-Borchardt action. Bottom barrel was made by Horace Warner, a .35 caliber M/L No. 4 octagon.*

# Bullet No. 31141

**March 11, 1967**

Dear Dave,

The latest issue of the *Handloader* has arrived and I am glad to have it. I am still getting a lot of letters from all over from shooters who claim they enjoy my letters. Why the devil don't they write to you? I'm also pleased to have your recent letter. I have had several letters from shooters who tell me they cannot find bullet 31141 listed in their handbooks. It might be a smart idea if you printed the letter from that guy from Pompton Lakes, New Jersey.

It seems a lot of .30-06 shooters are interested in the results we are getting with that Lyman bullet No. 31141, so someday I will send along a good target fired by my shooting buddy only recently. Sorry, but I will not be able to attend the N.R.A. convention. You see I will be taking off for a couple of months, June and July, up in Maine salmon fishing, so am busy at the machine shop in town.

I am very much interested in the article in this last copy of the *Handloader* on this matter of shallow groove cast bullets, by Paul Matthews. Would it meet with your approval if my next letter to the *Handloader* covered my own ideas as to this shallow groove business?

The Matthews idea, by the way, is nothing new. Back around 1900 some shooter from around New Haven, Connecticut, published some of his own experiments with shallow grooves in a cast bullet, and I believe it was published in the old magazine, *Shooting and Fishing*. If Paul had asked me about this matter, I might have saved him a lot of trouble and expense.

It simply boils down to the fact if you don't use *plenty* of the *proper* lubricant with any cast bullet, sooner or later you will run into trouble with leading. The idea Paul has might be O.K., but no one yet has been able to have it work out. If Paul wants to do away with lubricant, why doesn't he use a paper-patched bullet. They were used for years in the old days, but the shooters soon found those bullets wore out the soft steel barrels in short order.

History often repeats itself, and if someone at this late day wants to come up with something new, he had better *know* what has been going on in the shooting world for the last hundred years or so. Lubricant is put on a bullet for the sole purpose of lubricating the bore, so . . . no lubricant, no greased bore. I wonder if Paul would drive his car with no oil in the crank case? This matter is as simple as that.

What a letter my old friend Harry Pope would write you about this lubricating a bullet business, if he were alive today.

Thanks for your nice letter. Write again soon.

Harve

**Yours truly No. 8**

# *Favorite Hunting Calibers*

**April 3, 1967**

Dear Dave,

I have noted quite a bit of interest in recent years in Niedner's original .25-06 design of case. I had a rifle chambered for this by Niedner when it was first brought out, which was some time ago. This rifle was used for long-range chuck hunting, mostly with factory .25 caliber eighty-seven-grain bullets, as well as some ninety-grain that I made in a Niedner swage.

This standard Niedner design happens to be one of the oldest wildcats using .30-06 brass. With the faster burning powder of those days and the eighty-seven-grain bullet, I had it figured out that this case had more boiler room than was necessary. As friend Ackley has so often mentioned, "Like other overgrown cases, it is best with slow burning powders and relatively heavy bullets."

After several years' use of this rifle in chuck hunting, I discarded it in favor of my old Winchester single-shot rifle which had the fourteen-inch twist Niedner barrel chambered for his .25 Krag case. This was a far better all-around chuck rifle; accuracy was superb and with the fourteen-inch twist (with the eighty-seven-grain bullet) I got more velocity than was possible with the .250-3000 case.

Today we have better powders that are slow burning, and are thus far better to use in the large capacity rifle cases.

If any shooter is thinking of having a rifle made up for the .25-06, there happens to be a better case and caliber available. This is the .270 Winchester case necked down to 6.5 caliber. Today we have more good bullets available in this caliber than in .25, or shall we say we have more good *heavy* bullets in 6.5 caliber. This .270 case is *ideal* for our purpose, having a capacity to handle the heavy bullets. It is a simple matter to size down this case neck to 6.5 with the RCBS neck-sizing die correct for the 6.5x55 case. In seating bullets for this case, I use the Vickerman bullet seater for the 6.5x55 case.

If the reader is interested in shooting the long, heavy hundred and sixty-grain Hornady bullet, he should order his barrel with a ten-inch twist, in sporter weight. On the other hand, if he will use no bullets of over a hundred and forty grains, it might be better to have a barrel with the twelve-inch twist. This will handle any of the bullets available in this caliber of from a hundred up to and including the hundred and forty-grain.

This 6.5 caliber design (on the .270 Winchester case) will make an all-around hunting rifle. With hundred-grain bullets we have a long-range varmint rifle, giving wonderful accuracy. With the one hundred and twenty-nine or the hundred and forty-grain Hornady, one has a hunting rifle that will perform at the longer ranges for antelope hunting, and give better all-around results than any of the 6mm loads.

In my own shooting experience I have found that the lighter bullets gave as good performance out at the longer ranges as a heavier bullet. On the other hand, one cannot make a big game rifle out of a small bore job simply by the use of a heavy bullet.

In .22 caliber for chuck shooting, with a medium capacity case, I have had the best results with fifty-five-grain bullets. However, when I use my .220 Swift I favor sixty-grain bullets. In 6mm caliber I have no use for any bullets over eighty grains. If one wants a heavier bullet he might better go to the .25 caliber. In the .25, the limit is around a hundred and seventeen grains.

Now we go to the 6.5 caliber, and here we find we can use about anything from one hundred to one hundred sixty grains. So, I ask my readers, what advantage would a man have in buying a .270 Winchester or the .280 Remington rifle, over and above a rifle chambered as I have mentioned for this versatile 6.5x270 case? My own favorite caliber happens to be one in 7mmx57 caliber. Having used several rifles in this caliber from 1898 to the present time, I have never found an occasion to change. In the early days of this century we could only obtain 7mm bullets in a hundred and seventy-five grains. Today they are available in all shapes giving a selection of over a dozen or more weights. The 6.5 caliber was designed in Germany for a military firearm way back in 1884 or 1885, and the 7x57 caliber came out the next year, 1886. So I am shooting a caliber that has been around for eighty years. It seems obvious this caliber has *what it takes* to still be around after that length of time.

Down through the years I have used many good rifles, two of them being in .270 caliber — which I still have in my gun rack. These have shown wonderful accuracy, and for years I had the idea no rifle could beat a .270 for accuracy in the hunting field. But, when I started trying out the fine Hornady bullets in 7mm caliber, I soon found that my 7x57 rifles would give equal accuracy with any of my .270 Winchesters.

So, I still use my 7x57 rifle, and the .270's stand in the gun rack. Everyone to his choice, as the old lady said when she kissed the cow, but I still maintain that if any of the younger shooters are looking for an all-around hunting rifle, they might do worse than to select a rifle in 7x57 caliber.

For my own hunting I have no use for any of the magnum rifles, and this holds in any caliber. I will agree that there might be occasions when a magnum is necessary, but when I think of all the game that has been killed down through the years before the magnums arrived on the scene, I sometimes wonder. In hunting, it's where the bullet hits the game that is *still* the most important thing to be considered. And from the performance of some of these magnum shooters I have witnessed in the field, those fellows were *way* overgunned.

I am looking forward to the time that this new single-shot rifle, soon to be available from Ruger, will appear on the market. Bill Ruger is giving the shooters a rifle that should improve the hunting habits of the average shooter. It is *still* the first shot that counts the most in any sort of hunting. Thus, a man armed with this new rifle will learn the proper placement of his first shot, rather than the speed of fire obtained with an auto-loading outfit.

This new rifle must be seen as well as handled to be appreciated. Some time ago I visited the Sturm, Ruger factory in Newport, N.H. Len Brownell, one of the best men in the country or *any* country when it comes to stockmaking, showed us through the new factory. I was impressed with the balance and simplicity of the action, as well as the handling of this new rifle.

This action consists of only a few parts, and it is as smooth as silk. The trigger design is the best I have ever seen. The pull is sharp and crisp, and may be adjusted to any weight of pull. When a man buys this rifle he is getting a custom job in almost every sense of the word. The rifle is in a class by itself, for there have been few single shot rifles (and I have owned most of them at one time or another) that can be compared with it. Having such a short action, it can be fitted with the twenty-six-inch barrel, as it should be, and still be shorter over-all than the usual bolt action rifle.

The stock is attached with a long bolt through the stock, same as used years ago in the Winchester. No one ever found a better way to attach the butt stock. I was most impressed with the balance and handling of this gun. This will be appreciated by those shooters who are experienced in off-hand shooting.

With the many calibers that the new rifle may be chambered for, there should be little use for a second shot at most game.

The bench rest shooters, especially in the varmint class, will have a new rifle and action available that I feel certain will deliver as good accuracy as the rifles now in use. While at the Ruger plant, I saw groups that Brownell had shot on the factory hundred-yard range that would compare very favorably with any number of groups I have seen made with the heavy bench rest rifles.

When one considers these groups were fired from a run-of-the-mill factory product (and a light hunting rifle as well), it makes one wonder about some of the heavy varmint jobs we see on the line. I will have one of the new rifles as soon as they are available and, as you might guess, it will be in the .219 Donaldson-Wasp caliber.

I located a new chuck hunting territory this last fall on several farms over in Schoharie County that is posted to most hunters, but where I happen to have exclusive hunting rights. So something tells me, come next spring I may be found in these fields of clover and alfalfa. It sure will seem good hunting again with a good single-shot rifle.

Yours truly,<br>
Harvey A. Donaldson

# Many Schuetzen Fans Still Kicking Around

**April 18, 1967**

Mr. Dave Wolfe, Editor & Pub.
The *Handloader* Magazine
Peoria, Illinois

Dear Mr. Wolfe:

May-June 1967 issue of *Handloader* just came in and want you to know that this magazine is enjoyed by one of the old-timers very much; in fact, older than I sometimes like to think about.

It is with pleasure that I note you are giving consideration to the old-time single shot loading in appointing a very capable man for this job, Harvey Donaldson. This is being almost entirely neglected elsewhere in our publications and there are quite a number of this type handloaders still kicking around, and a lot of them new at the game, has been my observation. They need more detailed help, too! Not just generalities, and history, Dave.

Harvey and I both know that it was not *Hunting & Fishing* which started in the mid-Twenties but instead *Shooting & Fishing* (which I have copies back to 1889) that carried reports of John D. Kelley's fine rest groupings with the .38-72 Pope-Ballard rifle which, instead of owned by the late Ray M. Smith, is presently owned by the writer.

Think Harvey is right about the Schenck group being fired with the .38-72 rifle, but could look this up if deemed necessary for facts.

I question the serial (Pope's serial number) No. 71 on the original .32-40 Zischang rifle that Pope re-cut to .33-40 caliber with his toggle bullet starter. This is shown in current issue *Handloader* and was once shown in *Rifleman* years ago. Too, ask Harvey who has this fine rifle now, and if that serial number is correct.

Let's have more of this type data on old-time rifles using modern components; for the present black powder WON'T WORK as satisfactory as the old for these rifles!

Shootingly yours,
Claude E. Roderick

# And Harvey Agrees

**April 24, 1967**

Dear Mr. Roderick:

I have yours of the 18th, through the kindness of *Handloader* Magazine. A lot of water has gone over the dam since I last heard from you. That must have been thirty or more years ago. Since around 1930 I have given up the use of a Schuetzen rifle, and have devoted my time to the modern high speed varmint rifle, but I am STILL shooting.

The *Handloader* has asked me to devote some of my letters to the care and use of the old single-shot rifle, so I am doing the best I can in that direction. I certainly am surprised at the mail I have received since this last issue has come out. I had no idea so many shooters were still interested in the old-time target rifles.

Guess I made an error in my haste with this last letter, for of course I meant *Shooting & Fishing*, but I believe you are probably the only one in the whole country to note the mistake. I have several bound volumes of this old magazine in my files. Have noted that Mr. R.M. Smith has passed away. Did you get that rifle from his estate? I have never been able to figure out all the errors I found in his book on Pope's barrels.

Mister, there is *no mistake* about the Serial Number 71 on the rifle shown in the last *Handloader*. Old Harry stamped this number, with his name, on the under side of the barrel. You see this rifle was made years ago, although it had had very little actual use until I got it. The rifle was made for Dr. Guile, of Utica, New York. Pope made the toggle joint bullet seater quite a while after he bored the barrel. It originally, as you have mentioned, was a very fine .32-40 Zischang rifle. No one but this old-timer could make those fine set triggers. In fact, Zischang made the original rifle complete, some time before Dr. Guile had it made up into a muzzle loader by Pope.

From around 1900 up until 1930 or so I had something like 18 of the finest Schuetzen rifles ever made in this country. Strange as it may seem to you, some of my most highly prized rifles were made by George Schoyen of Denver, Colorado. Man, there was a barrel maker if there ever was one. I owned two good rifles by George Schalck, some by Pope, Schoyen, Zischang, George Ferris, Billinghurst, Brockway, and a few of German make. One by one I disposed of these fine rifles, and rifle #71 was sold to a man out in California.

Ned Roberts showed prints of some of my rifles in the *American Rifleman* back around 1935 or so. I have complete files of considerable data as to the old loads as well as some later ones, so if you are interested I could send some loading data along to you.

Dave Wolfe wants more letters about the old black powder rifles, so will have more letters before long that might interest you.

Have enjoyed writing to you once more, so when you have nothing better to do, write again. It sure is good to learn that at least some of the old-timers seem to appreciate my efforts with my letters to the *Handloader*. Tell me more about your fine old .38-72 J.D. Kelley rifle. That is without a doubt the best barrel Pope ever turned out.

Very truly yours,
H.A. Donaldson

**Yours truly No. 9**

# Letter from Harry Pope, 1903

**April 28, 1967**

Dear Dave,

Recently, in looking over some of my old correspondence, as received from Dr. Mann, Charles W. Rowland, Harry Pope, and others, I came across a letter received way back in 1903 from Harry Pope, when he was working for the J. Stevens Arms & Tool Co., of Chicopee Falls, Mass. I thought this might be of interest to those modern-day shooters who want to try old-style off-hand rifle shooting.

My files contain plenty of data on early rifle shooting, as it was performed by the most expert riflemen this country has ever produced, so it seems fitting that this data be shown in *The Handloader*, for what it is worth, for the attention of our younger riflemen. If left in my files, it will never be of much use to anyone. Mr. Pope's letter is shown exactly, as follows:

> P.O. Box 48
> Chicopee Falls, Mass.
> July 3, 1903

Dear Friend Donaldson:

It seems I have a half hour or so before it is closing time so I am going to give it to you. It seems I am a liar, but believe me, I am unable to help myself. Your rifle has been ready for over a week. But it happens the weather has been so rough all this time, that I have not been able to convince myself that your rifle is all I wish it to be. So, I want to keep it here until I am entirely satisfied. To date I have only shot your rifle three times, all in heavy wind. While the first hundred yards of our range is protected, the last hundred yards are a teaser. Having so far shot a few groups at two hundred yards, of from one and a half to two inches, I know your barrel is a good one, but I would like at least one good day to shoot, before I send it back to you. I have altered the twist slightly, in this barrel, from your old one, as my experience from recent experiments seems to indicate this would be for the better. Have also made you a new mould for my new style of bullet which is some 1/16-inch shorter, and I may make you yet another, so will let you keep whichever one you like the best, or both of them, just as you choose.

Your letter of the 15th I found on my return from the shoot at St. Louis, so can understand why you have not received my promised instructions. So, herewith, I will try and give you a little of my own style of off-hand two-hundred-yard shooting. I don't want you to think I have forgotten or neglected you, but you must remember that my life here for the past five months has been hell, and I would not go through it again (the experience, I mean), for any amount of money the Stevens Company could offer me. Right now, I am completely worn out, just working on my nerve. My weight is down to only 130 pounds, which is a lot less than it has been for years. My head bothers me more or less, so I am hardly my old self anymore. But enough of that, for here goes for my own method of shooting a *Schuetzen* rifle for off-hand two-hundred-yard shooting. I have not given you all the details of loading, as you already know about this matter. Sorry that I do not have any photos that would show you better than I may be able to explain it. First off, it might be well to say that you may often hear of my doing things that I tell my customers *not to do.* This results in my shooting, with no bullet in the barrel, and I have been known to even shoot off the false muzzle. This comes as a result of poor habits formed while shooting alone, from rest, when I do not look for my bullet in the target. This habit seems to stick, so I have trouble to overcome it, *BUT,* this is no reason why you should do the same thing in your own shooting. Most of my own trouble comes from those fellows who step up to ask questions, when I am at the bench either shooting or loading. It seems I am bothered to death, by people, everywhere I go, who want to take that time to talk to me when I am getting ready to shoot. This bothers me very much as it takes my attention from either loading or shooting.

There are shooters who can tell these inquisitive ones to go to hell, but I can hardly find myself doing just that.

But back to my own methods of off-hand shooting. About the first thing I do is to take my rifle to the firing point, putting it to my shoulder and directing it at the target. Next I close my eyes, and take a perfectly natural easy position, then I open my eyes, which will tell me if the palm rest is adjusted to such a height that the sights point just a trifle above the bulls-eye. If not, then I adjust the palm rest until it does, when you will find you are standing in a normal easy position, and thus do not have to strain your body or legs, to have the rifle in the proper position for shooting. Next thing I then insert a bullet into the breech of barrel, and shoot same into the ground or the back stop, to simply foul the barrel. It is never good to fire the first shot from any muzzle loading barrel, for record, from a *CLEAN* barrel.

I try to stand evenly on both feet, and have them about at right angles to each other, heels about five inches apart, line of aim about parallel with my toes. When shooting from a booth, as provided at some matches, the barrel of rifle is resting on window sill, right hand in place, then draw rifle to place on shoulder, with the right arm so elbow is nearly level with the shoulder, and at the same time drawing in all the air you comfortably can, as the lungs are distended by the opened arms, then breathe *ALL AIR OUT.* Next, draw in a very *FULL* breath at the same time raising the rifle with the left arm, then blow out nearly all this air while the rifle is getting somewhere near to position, settling onto the palm rest. Draw in slowly a not too full breath as the rifle is settling onto the bull, and stop breathing as soon as it is on. I then pull on the first satisfactory hold, if I can, but the rifle *MUST SWING SLOW,* if you want good results. My three fingers hold the lever back firmly, not loose, nor neither strained uncomfortably, so also does my left hand hold on the palm rest, my trigger finger is perfectly *FREE,* my thumb lying along the lower corner of the frame making a gage that holds my trigger finger off, so the point is just free of trigger. While aiming I keep continually touching the trigger with a very light pressure, but so I know at all times just where the trigger is, and when aim is complete a slightly harder touch lets it off, but *WITHOUT* the muscles of the other fingers *MOVING IN SYMPATHY* with the trigger finger, which is almost sure to be the case, if the trigger finger is held still till the aim is complete.

My last ace before aiming is to look at the wind flags, my first after firing the shot to see whether they have shifted, so as to call my shot according to the conditions.

I always move for wind before firing if possible, with iron sights, but with telescope however I set the windage according to the prevailing conditions, and hold for the variations. I use a pin head front sight for outdoor shooting, and an aperture front sight for gallery shooting, holding the pin head to just *TOUCH* the black, this pin head same size as the black bull, so a perfect shot looks like a solid figure 8.

My cheek piece is very high and full so my face rests firmly against the same while aiming, a very decided advantage. I do not aim long generally; if I begin to feel the need of more air I lower the rifle and breathe again. It is certainly a great advantage to get your blood thoroughly oxygenated as I have described, before aiming, as it takes away the violent heart beats, because the blood is satisfied.

Hope I have covered my own methods properly. I do not think many men will live long enough to wear out one of my barrels, if it has been properly cared for; time will tell. I could keep on writing you, for a week, if I had the time, but must close for now. If there is anything I have not thought to mention, about my shooting, would be pleased to have you question me. Just now, the way I feel, my head is pretty thick.

Yours sincerely,<br>
H.M. Pope

*Harry Pope (center) attended the National Matches at Camp Perry, Ohio, in 1923 with John Hessian (left) and Larry Nuesslein. Original photo could not be found; reproduction is from Handloader, 1969.*

## Pope Serial Numbers

**May 8, 1967**

Mr. Harvey A. Donaldson
% The *Handloader* Magazine

Dear Harvey:

You have no idea how delighted I was to receive your letter of April 24. I wrote you in 1965 as per the carbon copy attached, but evidently you never received it. I have since sold out to two of my top men, and retired. Still have complete machine shop with modern equipment in my back yard where I started in 1935.

You have no idea how many new shooters there are over the country now shooting and collecting these old single shot rifles. There are quite sizeable groups organized all over the U.S.A. They all need guidance such as the information given in Pope's letter.

I got the .38-72 Kelley-Pope outfit from Arthur Chafin of Huntington, West Virginia. T.J. Cooper got if from the Smith estate.

I thought possibly your toggler bullet seater Zischang-Pope could have been one of John D. Kelley's, and I presume No. 71 you mention is a Hartford series serial number, is it not? I have a Jersey City Zischang-Sharps-Pope (originally Zischang .32-40) that Pope recut and it is Serial No. 771. The Lucian Cary (last muzzle loader outfit Pope ever made) Highwall Pope .32-40 is Jersey City Serial No. 782, but of course he made other barrels after that. But I understand no more muzzle loader outfits.

I agree with you about Schoyen's barrels, and I consider them next to Pope's. I have one of his 25-pound muzzle loading .40-70 Ballard on Ballard that I'm going to limber up this year.

Shootingly yours,
Claude E. Roderick

*Editor's Note: Harvey's answer to this letter was never found in the thousands of letters in his loft.*

## Nonte Joins Staff

Maj. George C. Nonte, Jr. had been on the Technical Staff of *Handloader* since its inception, but in January of this year he moved his typewriter and library to our offices and assumed the title of Supervising Editor, a position he held for about one and a half years. During this time he assigned articles and edited manuscripts of most of our staff, but the Harvey Donaldson "Yours truly" column continued as one of my responsibilities. You could call it a "labor of love . . ."

And it continued so until Neal Knox joined the company in the Fall of 1968 as Editor of both *Rifle* and *Handloader* magazines. Shortly thereafter Harvey's "letters" began with the "Dear Neal" salutation.

The following three letters were found in the files in Harvey's shop — written when Nonte was Supervising Editor.

Dave Wolfe

## Darned Lead Smears

**June 28, 1967**

Friend Nonte,

I am sorry I missed Dave when he stopped off to see me recently. I was up in my gun shop loading some Swift cases, and if he had sat down on the porch for ten minutes, I would have found him. It is just one of those things.

I had a strange experience recently, and you might like to hear about it. Back in Issue No. 2 of the *Handloader* you will read about the fine results I was getting with the 55-grain Remington Power-Lokt bullet, with 30 grains of 4895 powder, in my custom-made .225 Winchester rifle. This bullet shot so well I thought I would try it in my fine pre-64 Winchester heavy barrel varmint rifle, in .220 Swift caliber. This happens to be the most accurate rifle I've ever seen in that caliber.

Well, first I started to use 36 grains of 4064 with this Remington open-point 55-grain Power-Lokt bullet. The group was only fair, but when I examined the target more closely I found indications of a smear of melted lead on the target. I then loaded up some more cases with 35 grains of 4064, and got better accuracy with no indication of any melted cores. What do you make of that? I have always figured that 4064 was the best powder in the .220 Swift, so I still use it. I had a Swift sent to me by Mr. Pugsley of Winchester some two years before they were available, for testing purposes, and it was at my own suggestion that they use the fourteen-inch twist and forget all about that light 48-grain bullet. My own heavy barrel Swift Varminter will beat the pants off a lot of varmint rifles I see on the line at our bench rest matches. I have made 200-yard groups of *under one inch* for ten shots. Few factory guns will do as well.

Recently I picked up several cans of H-375 powder. Somewhere, it may have been in *Shooting Times*, I remember reading that this was about the best powder one could use in my .219 Donaldson, or the .225 Winchester case. But, right now I'm unable to lay my hands on the article, which may have been by Ken Waters.

I would like to ask if you could furnish me with the proper loading data for the two above mentioned cases, with which I use only 55-grain bullets.

Best regards,
Harve

P.S. As I understand it, H-375 is some slower burning than 4064 or 4320. Is that correct?


## Sorry, Wrong Bullet

**June 29, 1967**

Friend Nonte,

After I mailed the letter to you yesterday I discovered that I had made an error. The bullets that made the smear of lead around the bullet hole were the regular Remington 55-grain Hollow Point, and not the Power-Lokt. I fired one group in my .220 Swift of five shots that were loaded with No. 250 CCI primers, 37 grains of 4064, and this Remington 55-grain HP bullet. I checked each shot through a spotting scope, and I noticed that the last shot in this group showed a discoloration, like the curved tail on a comet around the last shot fired.

Next I tried five more shots, but they were loaded with 36 grains of 4064 and the same bullets. Again on the last shot I saw this same dark spot around the bullet hole. I then tried five more shots loaded with 34 grains of 4064, and no more smears of lead were shown on any of the bullet holes. I wonder if the barrel heated up enough in five shots to cause the core to melt. I noted that each of the bullets that showed this color of lead around the bullet hole was out of the normal group about a half inch.

The hell of it is that I have used this load of 36 grains of 4064 with my regular Sierra semi-pointed soft nose bullets for several years, with no trouble at all, making long 300 to 400-yard kills on chucks. Several times this spring, when I used some cases loaded with these Remington open pointed bullets, I have had some misses out at fairly long range that I was unable to account for. I knew some of these chucks were hit, but they got in their holes. I naturally figured that these open point bullets did not open up properly out at long range, which might account for a chuck getting away.

This has bothered me for some time, so that is why I started to do some checking on a target at one hundred yards to see what in hell was going on. My .220 Swift is an accurate rifle, with a close chamber for a factory job. I'm still not sure that I know just what it is all about, but I have decided to cut my regular load of 36 grains of 4064 down to 35 grains. I never was much sold on that ultra high speed load that is possible with the Swift. I want accuracy most of all for the long shots, and I find that the Sierra or Hornady 55-grain soft nose bullets will do as they are supposed to do, if I do my part.

I went out with the Swift this afternoon and fired four five-shot groups at a hundred yards. Scope is 10X with a tiny dot and one that my old buddy John Unertl made up for me a number of years ago. All the shots could be covered with a nickel and the best group, made with Hornady's 53-grain open point Match bullet, is between a quarter and three-eighths of an inch. For some reason I cannot see so well when I try a long series of shots, as the target seems to fade. But for five shots, I do O.K. So I just fire five shots, then look away and sort of rest my eyes for a moment or so and the target clears right up. That does not bother me at all in chuck hunting, for usually I only have to fire one shot.

I'll be looking for word from you soon.

Sincerely yours,
Harve

## Melted Cores Not New

**July 5, 1967**

Mr. Harvey Donaldson
Fultonville, New York

Dear Harve:

Thanks very much for your letters of 28 and 29 June. I had been thinking about writing you, but felt you were probably still lashing the salmon streams to a froth, and wouldn't be back home yet. Am glad to hear that you are, and getting in some shooting.

I just talked to Dave Wolfe, and he is mortified that he missed you so narrowly on his trip East. You'll be hearing from him shortly, I'm sure.

On a couple of occasions over the years I have encountered the melted core phenomenon that has cropped up for you. Most recently it occurred (about a year ago) with a .17 caliber wildcat made up for me by P.O. Ackley. This particular one uses the .223 Remington case necked down to .17 caliber, but with the shoulder angle changed to about 30 degrees, producing a slightly longer neck, but leaving head to point of shoulder dimension same as .223. In driving Sisk 25-grain bullets at around 3,900 fps, I experienced quite a number of melted cores, and actually had a couple of bullets disintegrate in mid-air in a clearly visible puff of bluish smoke.

I have just checked the data I have from Bruce Hodgdon, and he does not list any H-375 loads for the .225 Winchester. However, in the April, 1965 *Shooting Times*, Ken Waters lists 33 grains with the 52-grain Speer open point, at 3,620 fps, 32.2 grains with the 53-grain Sierra hollow point and CCI magnum primer, at 3,597 fps and 46,400 psi chamber pressure. The only other H-375 load listed is 31.5 grains with the 63-grain Sierra semi-pointed bullet, at 3,416 fps and 51,600 psi.

While this data isn't precisely what you have asked for, I hope it will give you a starting point and thus allow you to use the H-375 you have on hand. If you want more data, why not write Hodgdon direct? Hodgdon did conduct the pressure and velocity tests for all of Ken's work with the .225 Winchester cartridge. Thus, he is certain to have all of the dope — a fair amount of which I am certain was not published in the *Shooting Times* article.

It would appear from interpolating and interpreting pressure and velocity data in my files that H-375 is somewhat slower burning than 4064. However, I would hesitate to make that as a *positive* statement. Again, Hodgdon will be able to furnish you with a positive answer. I am sorry I cannot do so.

All things considered, I would be hesitant to agree that the barrel could pick up enough heat in five rounds to cause the fifth and last round to spray molten lead, while the first four did not. Considering the fact that powder flame temperatures run as high as 6,000 degrees, and that the barrel can only pick up an infinitesimal percentage of this heat due to its mass and time of exposure, it doesn't seem that the barrel temperature at the end of five rounds (four rounds actually) would be elevated enough to cause the lead core to pass through the liquidus temperature.

Quite frankly, I would be more inclined to feel that it was simply coincidence that caused the comet trail of molten lead to show up on the fifth round. I could be wrong, but this is the way it seems to me. With the .17 wildcat referred to above, I might get a melted core on the first shot, or not until the tenth. Then, I might get a bullet that sprayed out plenty of lead, then the next three or four might behave normally. My thoughts at the time were that probably all of the cores were melting, but minor irregularities caused the spray to show up on some bullets, while it did not on others.

Incidentally, some writers have mentioned this phenomenon with high-velocity .22 calibers as far back as the early and mid-1930's. As a matter of fact, I believe Charles Newton mentions it as being the reason for his paper-insulated bullet.

Your Swift sounds like a mighty accurate rifle. Dave and I just returned from spending the weekend at the Speer bench rest matches over in Kansas — and I can assure you that there were a lot of $500.00 rifles there not shooting nearly as close as your Swift. You are to be congratulated on having lots of chucks to shoot out your way. Unfortunately, here in our neck of the woods varmint shooting is really quite scarce.

Best regards,
Major George C. Nonte, Jr.
Supervising Editor

**Yours truly No. 10**

# *An Insight into Primers*

**July 7, 1967**

Dear Dave,

Let me tell you about an experience I had recently. A young fellow came to me to find out why some of his loaded cases had misfired. This chap had an old .32-40 Winchester single-shot rifle. With the rifle he had an old No. 3 Ideal loading tool, a few old fired cases, and some old No. 2½ Winchester copper primers.

When I examined the case I knew at a glance just why it had misfired. I figured there had been no anvil in the primer. When he asked me how I could tell just by looking at the case, I told him it was easy — those old Winchester single-shot rifles had a rather large, as well as a loose, firing pin. On his case I noted that the firing pin had been driven far down in the primer, which would not have happened if an anvil had been in the primer.

I looked in his box of old primers and was not surprised to find several with no anvils. They were loose in the box.

Right off I can hear you say, such a thing would not happen today with modern components. But you will have to admit, it *could* happen any time!

Now let's go back to the good old days; I will try to tell you how we overcame such matters. If you are saying, "What was so good about the old days?" — well Buster, for one thing, I was a hell of a lot *younger*. From around 1890 up until nearly 1900, most of the shooting was done with black powder. A lot of my readers may doubt that the very *first* smokeless powder in the U.S.A. was made by Du Pont in the year 1893, and it was some time before it was perfected and made available to the average shooter. If anyone doubts what I have written, a note to the Du Pont Company will give the facts, or one can look it up in the old copies of *Shooting & Fishing* for 1893.

In one of my old Winchester catalogs of 1898 I find that they listed their Nitro primers for only $2.00 per thousand, but before that, around 1895, we could buy a thousand primers for anywhere from $1.50 to $1.80. Right from the start of my own reloading operations — nearly seventy-five years ago — we had trouble with these loose anvils in nearly every box of a hundred. The only way you could tell was to examine each primer, one at a time.

My own method was to place all the primers in the box on a table top, anvil side up — which would soon show any missing anvils. Then I would take an empty case to be primed, and push it down carefully over the primer. It was then placed in a hand-tool made for the purpose by the Ideal Mfg. Co., and seated by *feel* alone.

Just in case you are interested, I might add there has *never* been a better way to seat a primer properly than by *feel* alone. That was the way I was taught, and I might tell you that I use the same methods to this very day. I will say that it has been a long time since I discovered any loose anvils, but when I do it will be discovered before the primer is seated in the case.

When you stop off to visit me some time I will show you an arbor-type press that I made up back around 1906. I still use this tool in most of my loading operations. If you care to see what it looks like, turn to Page 220 in Phil Sharpe's book on handloading. This happens to be the only loading tool that will seat or de-cap primers in any case from the old centerfire .22 caliber Maynard case (bet you never saw one of those) up to a 10-gauge shotgun shell — with *no change* whatever in the tool. You see, I made it to work from the center of the case, where the primer is located.

The Lyman company furnishes what they are pleased to call a priming chamber with their No. 310 loading tool. This is a handy device which will enable the handloader to seat the primers properly, and in a short time one can tell by the feel when the primer is properly seated.

Why in the name of common sense (which you may agree is a rare commodity these days) it becomes necessary to resort to a loading press that is powerful enough to swage bullets, simply to seat primers, is beyond yours truly.

You can weigh your powder to a fraction of a grain, select your bullets with the greatest care and precision, but all this in itself amounts to nothing if your primers are damaged or seated carelessly.

It might be time well spent for any young shooter interested in handloading to attend some of the bench rest matches, if they are held in his vicinity. There he will soon learn, if he pays attention to detail, just what is required to prepare accurate shooting ammunition.

The primer in itself is a little thing, but make no mistake about it, even a small pistol primer is a mighty potent little package if handled carelessly.

We find that most of the large rifle primers today have a flat top surface. One should use a priming punch that has a flat surface with such primers. You might think such advice hardly necessary, but quite often we find ammunition that has been reloaded by some careless individual, with marks on the primer where a wrong seating punch was used. If the contents of the primer are crushed or damaged in any way, you can only expect improper ignition. It is as simple as that.

The primer is the very heart of the loaded case. If it should fail to function, you might be helpless if you are hunting big game that is ready and willing to put up a fight.

We handloaders today are fortunate in having available the best primers that were ever made. If they are used properly it may be years before you have a misfire, which even then could well be your own fault. In my own handloading, it has been so long since I have noted a misfire, due to a faulty primer, that I cannot even remember it.

But on the slim chance that you do have a misfire, go slow to place the blame on the primer. It may well be that your firearm is at fault. Firing pins do break now and then, and an anvil *can* be missing, or the primer not seated properly.

Much more might be written about the proper selection and use of the primers we use in handloading, but today we have considerable information in the many manuals available. I would suggest that anyone interested in handloading keep well up to date on these various manuals, as new powders and other components used in our loading operations are constantly made available.

One thing I would like to bring to the attention of any young shooter who is new to handloading. His ammunition will only be as good as his attention to all the little details necessary to prepare accurate shooting ammunition. Also, do not be too concerned about the *highest* velocity shown for your particular rifle. When the time comes that you really know your rifle, you will then find that the best results are obtained with loads several grains less than the maximum loads shown in the manuals. My next letter may show the inspection, care and preparation of fired cases before you start your handloading operations.

Yours truly,
Harvey Donaldson

## Lay Off, Buster

### September 22, 1967

Dear Dave,

Your nice letter received today, and I'm glad to hear from you. I have a letter, together with prints, that will be in the mail tomorrow. Will then get busy and send more later, to keep well ahead of the deadline. My only brother passed away last month, so things have been more or less upset ever since. He was 82 years old.

Today, in the same mail with yours, I got a letter from a friend in Elmira, New York. He wrote that a hunting buddy of mine was in the Arnot Ogden Hospital in Elmira. This shooter had been unable to obtain the last issue of the *Handloader*. As he has all the copies to date, he did not wish to miss a single copy. So . . . when I went to work this noon I had my favorite gal in the office put a phone call through to you, so that you might send him this last issue. Thanks again for your help in this little matter. I might add the girl friend said you had a nice voice. (Lay off, buster; don't try to beat my time!)

Give my best regards to Nonte. I sure am sorry that I missed you on your trip East, but try again some time.

Best regards,
Harve

*Editor's Note: Harvey had a severe hearing handicap, undoubtedly caused by so many years of shooting, which explains why he had the office "gal" place the call to* Handloader *headquarters.*

Yours truly No. 11

# Mann-Niedner 'Hamburg' Rifle

**August 30, 1967**

Dear Dave,

I wonder how many of our readers ever heard of the Mann-Neidner .25 Krag caliber Hamburg rifle. Only a dozen of these hand-made rifles were ever made, so one can imagine that they are plenty scarce.

Some time ago I wrote in one of my letters for *The Handloader* about the wonderful work turned out by Mr. Niedner in his gunsmithing operations. If some of our readers will turn to the pages of the *American Rifleman* of some fifteen years ago, they will find an article by A.O. Niedner as told to Mr. John Barsotti showing the pictures of this early bolt action single-shot Schuetzen rifle.

I have a friend, Henry W. Grillo, of Utica, N.Y., who owns one of these fine Schuetzen rifles in perfect condition; it is only the second one that Niedner turned out. Rifle No. 1 was made up only as an experimental and it contained several ideas that both Niedner and Dr. Mann had been working on for some time. First off they were looking for a bolt action job that was stronger and would stand higher pressures than either the Mauser or Springfield. That made it necessary for Niedner to design an entirely new type of bolt action.

His new design resulted (after many tests in which they tried to blow up the new action) in a bolt action that was without a doubt the *strongest* bolt action rifle ever made. The fact that they split and blew up four different barrels in testing the action, with no harm to the action, should show its strength. The pressures obtained in these tests were in *excess* of 100,000 foot pounds.

Mr. Niedner made up this first rifle early in 1912, when he had his shop on Beacon Street, in Malden, Mass. I believe it was Dr. Henry A. Baker, a great bench-rest shooter then living in New York State, who named the Hamburg rifle during a woodchuck hunting trip at Shushan, N.Y., some time in May of 1912 — when the pilot rifle of the new design was being tried out.

Dr. Mann, naturally, was anxious to see how the new rifle in .25 Krag caliber would work out on 'chucks. At Mann's request, Niedner made up a new stock, in a hurry, but the barrel and receiver were correctly bedded. Then double set triggers were added, and a sixteen power scope attached to the barrel.

This rifle then weighed eleven and a half pounds, which was rather heavy for a hunting rifle, but this weight made it hold nicely for off-hand shooting. On this particular 'chuck hunt at Shushan, N.Y., the first 'chuck that Niedner saw was out at two hundred fifty yards, but he decided to take the shot. He noted that the 'chuck disappeared at the shot, and both Dr. Mann and Dr. Baker thought he had missed.

Niedner then walked out to where the animal lay, picked it up and carried it back to show his friends. The 101-grain .25 caliber bullet had smashed the animal up so

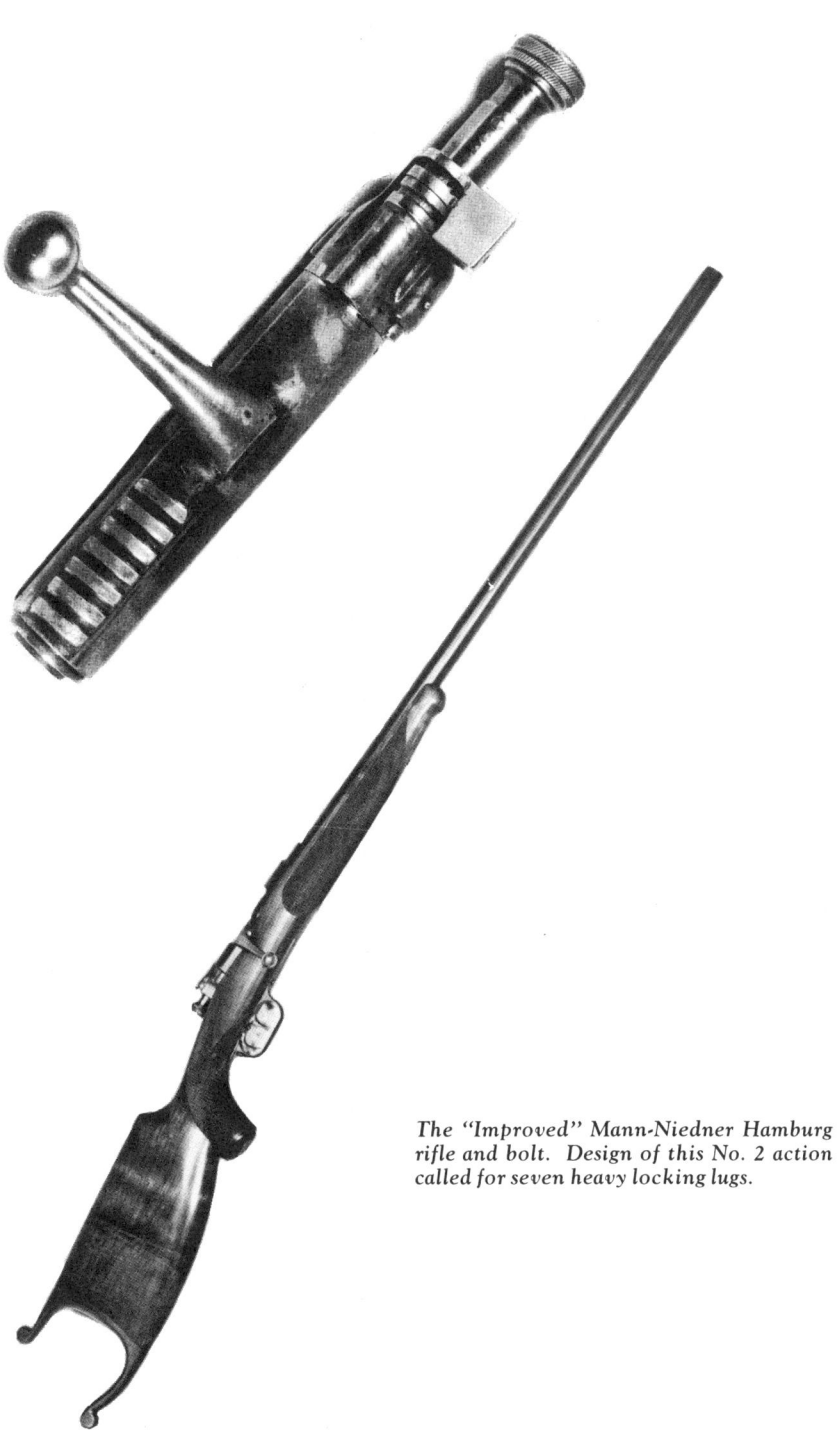

The "Improved" Mann-Niedner Hamburg rifle and bolt. Design of this No. 2 action called for seven heavy locking lugs.

badly that it was necessary for him to carry it in both hands. Dr. Baker took one look at the remains and remarked, "That appears to be a hamburg making rifle if I ever saw one." Thus the new rifle was named.

During that hunting trip the new rifle fired several very tight groups out at two hundred yards, and all were pleased at its performance. The load used at that time was forty-five grains of Lightning powder and Niedner's hand-swaged 101-grain bullet, in what was the first, or long design, of the .25 caliber Krag cartridges.

Both Niedner and Dr. Mann used that case up to August of 1913, when Niedner then improved on the first design. As mentioned, this Hamburg rifle was a single-shot bolt action, but the actual weight of the action alone was lighter than the Springfield, while a whole lot stronger.

Most of the weight of this action was in the front of the receiver, where it was required. The bolt of this first Niedner design was seven-eighths-inch in diameter, weighing some thirteen ounces, and it had two wide locking lugs on opposite sides of the bolt head.

The bolt head fits snugly into the *chamber*, behind and around the rear of the cartridge case. This, by the way, was the very first design of bolt that would not leave the cartridge unsupported on both sides. Today, both Winchester and Remington rifles are made with the same idea, but our friend Niedner worked out the design quite some time ago.

This Hamburg rifle action was made with a one-piece, strong extractor, separate from the bolt itself, but still it was operated by the bolt. Sliding in a groove in the bottom of the receiver, it would extract a fired case as positively as a rod pushed down the barrel. The firing pin was separate, and was screwed into the cocking piece of the bolt in such a way that it could not be blown back, or out. The original barrel for this first rifle was thirty-four inches long, had six lands, and a twist of one turn in twelve inches.

This rifle was chambered for a special longer Krag case, necked down to .25 caliber. For the record, when Ned Roberts saw the new case he started on his own design of .25 caliber cartridge, made from the 7x57 case, and later known as the .257 Roberts.

It seems that Dr. Mann had secured some five hundred unnecked and untrimmed .30 caliber Krag cases from a U.S. arsenal, and Niedner made up some of these in various body and neck designs, with different shoulder angles. After considerable experimenting Niedner later chambered his second Hamburg rifle with the improved bolt design (this being the rifle now in the possession of Grillo) for his final design of the .25 Krag, that called for a case of two and a quarter inches over-all. It is still known as the Niedner .25 Krag. Then later both he and Dr. Mann decided it was better to use the regular .30 Krag case simply necked down to .25 caliber, as the results with such a case were just as good.

I believe it was in August of 1913 that the first Hamburg rifle, No. 1, was rechambered for the shorter case, the same as is in use today, and the barrel was shortened to 27½ inches. It was at this time that I sent a Winchester high wall single-shot action to Niedner, to have him fit it with a new barrel that he rifled, and chambered for his latest design of the .25 Krag case. This same heat-treated action with Mann-Niedner firing pin, and strong flat main spring with Harry Pope's speed action, I still use to this day. I used that same action when my own No. 1 .219 Donaldson-Wasp rifle was made up soon after 1930. This first rifle ever chambered for the .219 Donaldson case is still in use today, and if I do my part it will still keep ten shots under a dime at a hundred yards.

During Niedner's experiments with his first .25 Krag rifle he used bullets in 86, 90, 101, and 103 grains, in the twelve-inch twist barrel. Later, having better results with the lighter bullets, in 86 to 90 grains, he made up his barrels with the fourteen-inch twist, which was what I ordered for my rifle. I used only the 85-grain bullet, and these were made in the swage Niedner made for me, which is still in use.

The first bullets used in the first model Hamburg rifle were made with a base band, to Dr. Mann's idea. *(Editor's Note: Band at rear of bullet of groove diameter, balance of bore diameter.)* This band was one-sixteenth-inch wide, and the bullet was seated into the case only about three-sixteenths-inch. Origin of the rifling for this base band bullet ahead of the case had a sixty degree throat. To prevent erosion with his high speed loads, Niedner used a mixture of vaseline and graphite, which was placed between two wads back of the bullet.

This first .25 Krag Hamburg Niedner rifle had seen some twenty thousand shots fired through the barrel when Niedner sold it to Mr. R.S. Hill. But even at that time it was still capable of making good groups.

The Niedner Improved Hamburg action was made with seven locking lugs and it is this first improved action, No. 2, that is now owned by Grillo. I believe that particular rifle was the one that Niedner made for Dr. Mann on their improved action design, in 1913, as this rifle is made with a beautiful stock, Schuetzen butt plate, and used for off-hand shooting. Somewhere in my files I have a letter from Dr. Mann written soon after this rifle was built, in which he told me all about it.

After the first action was made, neither Niedner nor Dr. Mann was entirely satisfied. Niedner had an idea he could improve the bolt design. This design called for seven heavy square threads instead of the two large locking lugs. They called this the screw bolt design, or improved Hamburg action. This rifle was chambered for the regular .30 Krag case necked down to .25 caliber.

I remember well, in one of the many letters that were received in those days from Niedner, that he mentioned he had only made up twelve rifles with this particular action. They were practically a hand-made product, which took much of his time. The prints shown with this letter will show the fine design of a 'chuck rifle, as well as one that could be used in off-hand shooting. After examining it carefully, I would say it is in mint condition.

Dr. Mann passed away soon after he received this rifle, so that could explain its fine condition. I believe I have forgotten to mention that Niedner was getting around 3,300 foot seconds velocity way back in 1912, with the first rifle having the larger case, in .25 caliber.

How Grillo came into possession of this really *rare* varmint or Schuetzen rifle is a long story, which will have to wait for some other time. It is hardly necessary for me to mention that this fine gun is simply not for sale, at any price. If my readers will understand this matter, it might save considerable correspondence.

Very truly yours,<br>
H.A. Donaldson

**Yours truly No. 12**

# Question of Proper Lubrication

**September 23, 1967**

Dear Mr. Donaldson:

Recently I bought a Stevens target rifle in .32-40 Winchester. It has the heavy, half-round barrel with a rear tang sight and adjustable front sight with hood. It is also equipped with double set triggers. To the eye the barrel appears very good, as does the rifle as a whole.

I was told this is a No. 46 action, but I am not familiar with this action.

My problem is mainly reloading. I load for several calibers but have little experience with casts, except .22 Hornet, and no experience with this type of rifle and caliber. I am planning to use Lyman cast bullet No. 319247 that you mentioned in *The Handloader*.

What I need most is a lubricant I can apply by hand; I don't have a lubricator but I can size bullets on my press with home-made sizing dies and punches. I have been using a mixture of water pump grease and graphite for my .22 Hornet and it seems to do the trick.

By the way, I paid $115 for the rifle and was told by a good gunsmith that it was a bargain.

Barry Dewick<br>St. Lambert, Que.

Dear Mr. Dewick:

From the description of your rifle I would say that you have indeed made a good bargain. I have seen good Stevens double set trigger actions sell for one hundred bucks — just the action alone.

Since your letter was mailed from Montreal, I suggest you contact my friend Bob Snowball. When it comes to any matter regarding shooting, Bob knows his way around. He might be of some help.

Your Stevens rifle, especially in the .32-40 caliber, is one to be desired — especially if you are looking for a super-accurate target outfit. They don't come any better. With fixed ammunition, with the bullets seated in the case, you can look for better than one-inch hundred-yard groups; and if you seat bullets in the barrel, you can obtain better than half-inch groups.

When seating bullets into the case, your choice of the Lyman bullet No. 319247, cast 1-25, is OK. For best accuracy, of which your rifle is capable, I would suggest that you use the old Ideal bullet No. 319289, cast 1-25, seated in the barrel ahead of the case.

It might be well to give you the history of this particular bullet, for you may not find it listed in the *Lyman Handbook*. Lyman has the cherry for this bullet, and they can send you a sample for your inspection.

Back around 1900 Dr. W.G. Hudson designed his famous .32 caliber two-diameter bullet No. 319273 for use in the Schuetzen rifles. They were seated into the barrel, ahead of the case, with a bullet seater, but you should know that the barrel had to be specially throated to take that bullet. A number of records were made at two hundred yards with this bullet. As I remember, the load used was fifteen grains of Laflin and Rand "Sharpshooter" powder on top of which is placed eight grains bulk of Cream of Wheat, and a blotting paper greased wad on top of all. Bullets were cast 1-15, but we later found 1-25 was better.

A number of shooters did not want to have the throat of their rifles chambered especially to take this Dr. Hudson bullet, so the Ideal company came out with bullet No. 319289, and this is the one I suggest you use. The three front bands fit the bore snugly, and the two base bands are as large as can be seated with the Ideal bullet seater. For years I used the following load with this bullet: first, three grains weight of Du Pont No. 1 smokeless, as a priming powder, then the shell filled with F.G. King's semi-smokeless powder, with a greased wad on top. Both of the bullets mentioned above should be used as cast, not resized, as they are two diameter; this is where my method of lubricating such a bullet pays off.

I have mentioned the use of a bullet seater, and if you are unable to locate one in .32-40 caliber, you just do as most of us did years ago: select a new .32-40 case and take out the primer. Fit a piece of wood, such as a dowel, snugly into the case, and have it stick out about a sixteenth of an inch from the mouth of the case. This end should be perfectly flat. To use this seater, simply drop the lubricated bullet into the chamber of the rifle, drop the dummy case on top and close the action. This seats the bullet properly in the barrel. Now remove the dummy and drop in the loaded case. The rifle is now properly loaded.

You could even use a caseful of FG black powder with bullet No. 319289, if you used a priming load of five or six grains of 4759 powder, or eight to ten grains of Du Pont white bulk shotgun powder.

Now we come to your questions about proper lubrication. This is a large order to try and cover in one letter. In fact, a book could well be written about it. I have noted that you will require a lubricant that can be applied by hand, not with a lubricator and sizer. That is the way all of us did it some seventy-five years ago, before lubricators were invented. With tapered or two-caliber bullets it is about the only way it can be accomplished, unless one has a lubricator made by Harry Pope. (I have a number of these.)

First, find a pan, such as a pie tin, and a small frying pan with a sort of spout attached, for easy pouring. There are many formulas available for making bullet lubricant, but I can do no better than to give you the one I have used for well over seventy years. It was used in black powder rifles years before it was given to me. It works properly in both hot and cold weather, as well as with modern high-speed loads with the use of gas check bullets.

My formula is simple to prepare, as well as to remember. It consists of one part rosin, two parts beeswax, and three parts tallow. I suggest you buy two ounces of powdered rosin and four ounces of clear beeswax. Then go to your grocer's and obtain a supply of beef tallow. Cook this tallow in your pan; when it is cold and in a solid mass, weigh out six ounces and place it back in your frying pan. Be sure you obtain suet that is free from salt.

Bring the tallow to a liquid state, then add the beeswax and powdered rosin. When I use graphite wads for handgun loads I add a small amount of the finest graphite, and stir in carefully. A long article by me in the March, 1936, issue of the *American Rifleman* went into more detail on this subject of graphite wads. Col. Townsend Whelen told me that this article was the first he had ever read on the use of graphite wads with modern, high-speed loads. He used my wads, and R.B. Sisk made them up for resale.

I still use these wads in all my high-speed .22 caliber varmint loads. It just happens that I have a .220 Swift rifle that was given to me for testing by Mr. Pugsley, of Winchester, over thirty years ago. All the loads ever shot in this rifle were with my graphite wads, and even today, after over thirty years of use and with 10,000 to 12,000 rounds fired through this barrel, it is still in fine condition, and will keep ten shots on a dime at a hundred yards.

Some shooters have complained that the rosin used in my formula is an abrasive, but the same thing might be said of tooth paste. Neither will harm the bore of your rifle.

This rosin is used as a binder and it seems to do the job properly; the lubricant will hold well in the grooves in either hot or cold weather.

But to get back to our use of the lubricant — the liquid in the frying pan should be poured into the pie tin, but only after you have placed the bullets, base down, in rows across the pan about a half inch apart. When pouring the liquid into the pan, be sure you have enough to cover the top groove of the bullet. Cover the pan with bullets in this manner leaving a space at one side to pour in the lubricant.

Let the liquid cool until it shows white or cream color on top. It should be firm enough to allow one to turn the pan upside down. In this position, hold the pan under a cold faucet, and let cold water run over the bottom. This makes the cake shrink so that the entire mass will come loose from the tin.

Hold the solid cake of the lubricant in your hands and push out the bullets from the top, one at a time, with your thumb. If you have done this properly you will find the grease, if you can call it that, only in the grooves of the bullet, with the bases clean.

If you have more bullets to lubricate, push new cast bullets into the holes of the lubricant, and place the whole thing back in the pie pan. Then heat slowly and repeat the process.

Lyman furnishes what it calls a cake cutter, to take the bullets out of the lubricant. This is OK, but a rather messy job; I think my method does the job a lot easier.

When lubricating bullets for Schuetzen shooting, we shot them in the same order they came from the mould. We had two boards bored with a hundred holes to hold the bullets. All the holes were numbered. When the lead was working right the first good bullet was placed base down into hole No. 1, and so on until the board was filled. This was to insure that the mixture of tin and lead was more uniform in say the first ten bullets than the last ten that were cast.

When the time came to lubricate these bullets they went into the other board, in exactly the same order. We thought we got better accuracy in doing it that way. Whether we did or not might be open to question, but just as long as the groups out at two hundred yards were satisfactory, our methods paid off.

If you have followed me thus far in this rather lengthy letter, I might mention that it is possible to use powders of recent manufacture that will work out OK in your .32-40 Stevens. *(Editor's Note: Hercules Reloder No. 7 powder may be substituted for discontinued Du Pont 4759 by reducing charge weight approximately five percent. It has not yet proved to do as well in the older calibers as 4759, but* is *probably the best substitute.)* I understand that some shooters in Quebec have trouble obtaining certain kinds of powder. Here is where my friend Bob Snowball might be of help.

I have used Schuetzen rifles for many years, so that is why I am interested in seeing that you have the proper information. It might interest you to know that a good Winchester or Stevens rifle in .32-40 will still beat the pants off the modern varmint rifle, accuracy-wise, if it is properly loaded. All you have to do is to look up the old records and then try to beat them with a .243.

Yours truly,<br>Harvey Donaldson

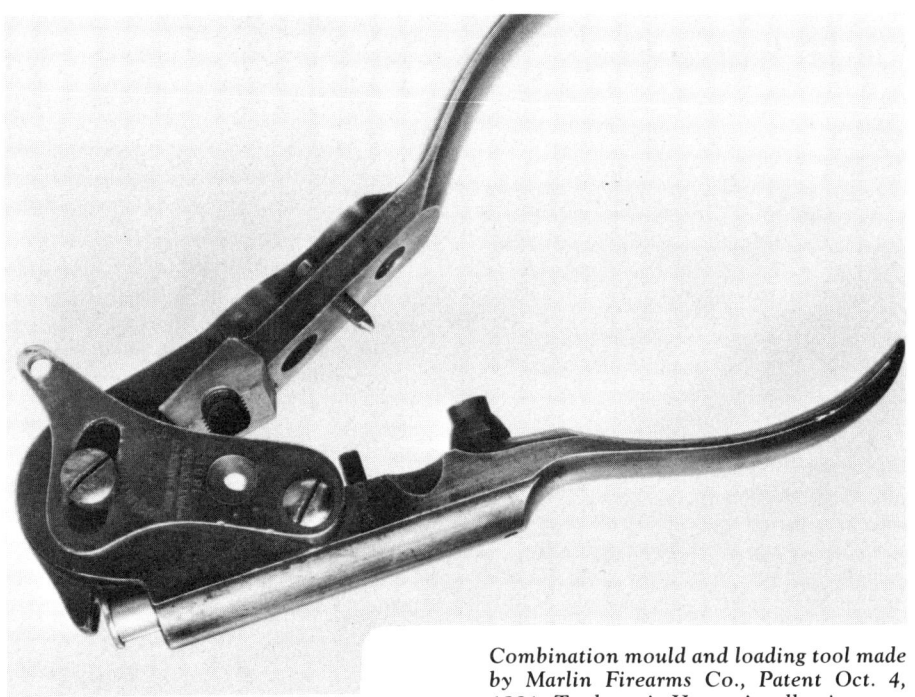

*Combination mould and loading tool made by Marlin Firearms Co., Patent Oct. 4, 1881. Tool was in Harvey's collection.*

## 85 Years 'Young'

**Jan. 12, 1968**

Dear Dave:

I mailed you a "letter" for the *Handloader* this morning. Drop me a card and let me know if this meets with your approval.

Around 25 below here this a.m. It seems as if our cold spell should break before long. If I can get a friend interested in the meeting (N.R.A.) in Boston, we may see you. Will you drive or fly to Boston? I understand it is on April 6-11. My birthday is April 6th (85 years) so I should celebrate. Will my buddy John Amber be on hand, I wonder? I'll have to write to John.

Best regards,
Harve

## .30-338 Wildcat

**January 12, 1968**

Dear Dave,

Enclosed find another letter. While it has little to do with handloading, still it may contain some tips that could be used by a young bird shooter.

I am experimenting with a new wildcat cartridge. I believe it is one that my friend Fred Huntington designed some six or eight years ago. A Model 70 Winchester in .30-06 caliber that takes a case made from the .338 Winchester Magnum, necked down to .30 caliber. Fred chambered the rifle and made the dies. Quite a cartridge, and Fred claims it is better than the .30 Winchester Magnum or the .308 Norma. Will have to wait some time till weather permits for testing.

Best regards,
Harve

## Forming .30-338 Cases

**January 17, 1968**

Dear Harve,

We'll be able to use your latest "Yours truly," even though it is a good bit different. The comments of experienced old-timers like yourself are always welcome, even though they might not be devoted entirely to our little narrow handloading field.

The .30-338 is an excellent cartridge. As you may know, the Army rifle teams have been using this cartridge — very carefully handloaded — for a number of years. If memory serves me correctly, the first batches of cases were formed by simply running .338 Winchester Magnum cases into standard .308 Norma Magnum dies.

Best regards,
Dave

## The Last One Left To Tell the Story

**January 23, 1968**

Friend Dave,

I have read over your letter of the 17th carefully, and note you want data on my early high velocity shooting experiences. Mister, it just happens I have enough of that data to fill our magazine for a year to come.

Just to give you a sample, of which it may take several more letters to cover, I am going to send in the first letter that covers the first really *"high speed"* varmint cartridges designed in this country. I want a reply from you soon to see if this meets with your approval. I have been in on all the early experimenting, and it also happens I am the last one left to tell the story.

Unless this appears in print now, it may be lost in my files when I pass on. Write again soon and tell me if this last letter is O.K.

Best regards,
Harve

**Yours truly No. 13**

## Tale from a Bird Hunter

**January 12, 1968**

Dear Dave,

I wonder if a little bird hunting I did this past fall might interest our readers. While it has little to do with handloading, I hope you will pardon this lapse from an "old-time bird hunter."

In the early part of October, while visiting a friend's gun shop, I noticed a 16 gauge L.C. Smith double barrel shotgun standing in the gun rack. While I own more shotguns than I will ever use, I was attracted to this piece. When I picked it up and put it to my shoulder, I found it was a perfect fit, just as if it had been made to order. The stock was the right length and quite straight, which I like. I like to see all the way up the barrel, or rib, as the gun comes to the shoulder.

This gun was in mint condition, as well as having a beautiful custom stock and wide beaver-tail fore-end, both made from well figured English walnut. Usually a 16 gauge is chambered for the 2 9/16-inch cases, but this one had had the chamber altered to take the modern 2 3/4-inch shells.

I looked it over carefully and found the left barrel was bored full choke, and the right either modified or improved cylinder — just right for a bird gun. To make a long story short, I found I just *had* to own it.

The gun was purchased on Tuesday, Oct. 10th. The following Friday was a beautiful fall day. It had rained all the night before, so the going would be quiet underfoot. Sun was out bright and warm. I got to thinking about a favorite woodcock cover of mine along Brandy Brook, up in Herkimer County, New York. I told my foreman that it was too nice a day to work, and took off with the new gun. After a drive of some forty miles or so I parked the car near the lane that led down into the alders.

As I entered the trees the thought came to me that I was sort of crowding my luck, to go bird hunting on Friday the 13th, but it would take more than that to change my plans. In hunting woodcock I usually have cases loaded with No. 8 shot in the left barrel and No. 9's in the open barrel. Also, with 8's in the left, if you jump a partridge in the same cover you have a better chance on him.

I had no sooner entered the alders when I found plenty of sign; there were still birds in the old cover. These would be the native birds, for it had not been cold enough for the flight to start moving. Until recent years I had always hunted this cover with a well trained bird dog. Now I have to be my own dog. There is always a certain fascination in coming back, year after year, to the same cover for both partridge and woodcock hunting. One learns just where to locate the birds, as well as which direction to take in covering the ground properly.

This particular cover is rather open, with cow paths leading down to the brook. The walking was easy and quiet. I had only gone a little way when I heard a bird get up and head down toward the brook — but I was not able to see it. My hearing aid is a great help in bird hunting. One can hear everything, and it is easy to hear a woodcock whistle as it takes off.

I was working along toward the west, along a cow path, taking it easy, when another bird got up, out of range. This led me to believe that the cover had been hunted recently, although I found no fired cases on the ground. When I hunt birds without a dog, I move carefully. I take one step, and stand still three, as my old hunting buddy used to say. But this method pays off, especially in hunting for partridge. If a partridge is near and should hear you, he cannot stand the suspense and takes off. You are standing still and in a position for a quick shot. I learned this trick from an old market hunter, and it sure pays off.

After putting up the second bird, I had only gone a few steps when a third got up and took off to my left. I heard him whistle as he rose, and then saw him. Waiting an instant till he leveled off, I dropped him with the open barrel. An easy shot. At this same instant another got up and took off straight away. Just as I was about to shoot I saw the bird pitch down sharply, and something told me to shoot very low on this one. When I fired I was holding at least three feet low. I heard this bird hit the ground, and knew I had made a double on woodcock — something I can't remember doing before in a lifetime of bird hunting.

I had the first bird marked down OK but sure had one hell of a time trying to find the second one. I tried to figure just where he had pitched down. The usual method used to find a bird that is downed is to walk to the spot where you last saw the bird, tie a handkerchief to a tree or bush, then circle around as a bird dog would do. I'll bet it took me all of twenty minutes to find that second bird.

About this time, with the two birds in my pocket, I figured it was about time I sat down to have a smoke and sort of figure things out. Here it was, on Friday the 13th, and I had two birds that I had killed with the *first two shots* I had ever fired from a gun I had never used before. Do you wonder I sat down to think things over? The thought came to me that a part of wisdom is to *know* the value of today, before it is gone forever. I believe you will agree to that.

After I had smoked a pipe and eaten a sandwich, I figured it was too nice a day to crowd my luck with woodcock any further, so I worked gradually up the hill, where I knew there were some crab apple trees. I might just jump a partridge.

At the edge of the alders there used to be a few old apple trees, and part way up the grade were some crab apple trees as well. Here it was more open and one could see up the grade above the alders. Some fifty yards up the grade was an old stone wall, and all along this wall some real old spruce trees — the kind with the lower limbs that come right down to the ground. In years long gone we used to jump partridge under the apple trees, and the trick was to get them before they reached the spruces or the stone wall.

With this in mind I started to work up through the alders. I had taken the No. 9's out of the right barrel and put in a shell loaded with No. 8 shot, with another of No. 7½ shot in the left barrel. This is my usual way when hunting partridge, but if the cover is very heavy I use No. 6's in the left and No. 7½ in the right barrel.

Just as I was about to leave the alders and bent almost double in getting under a limb, a partridge jumped from the ground and headed for the stone wall, a left quartering shot. Not being able to straighten up or even get the gun to my shoulder, all I could do was to swing the gun to the left and swing ahead, shooting the open-bord barrel. I believe I was more surprised than the bird when I saw it pitch to the ground. A clean kill at around 25 or 30 paces. Well, after I had this bird in my coat pocket, I was satisfied to call it a day. I believe I might have had more luck if I had followed up along the old stone wall, but I find it sure pays off if you leave some for another day.

While I had only spent a short time in actual hunting, I had enjoyed every moment. It was good to know that it was still possible to find a few birds in the same old cover I had hunted for so many years. Guess it goes without saying that I am most pleased with the performance of this fine Smith gun. I hope to do some white rabbit hunting next winter, with some fox hunting in mind in late January or February.

Yours truly,
Harvey Donaldson

Yours truly No. 14

# Early Varmint Cartridges

**January 23, 1968**

Dear Dave,

In reading some of the magazines devoted to shooting matters I have noted that some "experts" would have us believe that the modern, high speed varmint cartridges began with the appearance of the .22 Hornet, brought out by Winchester some thirty years or more ago. Nothing could be further from the truth.

(In regard to experts, by the way, I have it figured these guys may not know any more than their readers, but they have it better organized.)

One fault I find with the rising generation of riflemen is that they seem to think rifle shooting, in this country, started the day they bought their first rifle. The real rifle shooting in the U.S.A. started way back around 1720 or so, down in and around Lancaster, Pennsylvania, with such gunsmiths as Charles Leman, and many others.

The simple fact that this writer was in on the early work and experimenting with the forerunners of the present high-speed smallbore varmint cartridges, should give him some authority to now write about it.

To such men as Dr. Mann, A.O. Niedner, and later Charles Newton, should go the credit for our early high-speed varmint cartridges. Newton was one of our early experimenters, and a good one. He was no rifleman, when it came to testing or actual shooting. Niedner did his early gunsmithing, and it was through Niedner that I met Newton.

Evidently it was through Niedner that Newton sent me several of his experimental rifles for range testing. I had to work up the loads from data received from Dr. Mann, and then I did the actual shooting and testing. Newton lived in Buffalo, New York, and was a lawyer by profession.

It may be well to go back some sixty or more years and review the experiments which more or less paved the way for the modern high-speed cartridges that are in use today.

The original cartridge which, to the best of my knowledge, represented the first attempt to use metal cased bullets and smokeless powder for a high speed varmint cartridge was designed by Charles Newton with the help of both Niedner and Dr. Mann, in the winters of 1905 and '06. These dates check with correspondence I received from Newton and Niedner at that time.

The cartridge used was the long .25-25 straight Stevens case, tapered down to .22 caliber. I still have some of these cases in my collection. With this case Newton tried three different bullets — 50, 66, and 87 grains in weight. These metal case bullets were made in the dies furnished by Niedner. And it was at this time that the writer started making .22 caliber metal case bullets for Newton.

But when I tell modern shooters I have been making my own metal case bullets for over sixty years, they get that far off look and evidently think I am nuts. I believe Niedner got the hulls for these bullets from the Remington company. We got them from Niedner. Practically the whole problem in producing the ammunition lay in the making of these metal case bullets, one at a time and entirely by hand. This, in itself, required considerable study and experimenting, most of which was solved with Niedner's wonderful bullet dies.

The principal object in all this was to obtain a rifle cartridge that was better than any other available for long-range 'chuck hunting. We soon found that the sixty-six grain bullet was the most effective; thus it was used almost exclusively. If memory serves me correctly, Mr. Newton had an article in the December 1908 issue of *Arms & The Man* (the forerunner of *The Rifleman*) in which he wrote all about this cartridge, and rifle, which by the way gave an instrumental muzzle velocity of 2,075 foot seconds.

Looking for even more velocity, Newton, at the suggestion of Niedner and Dr. Mann, then tried yet another case, made from the .28-30 Stevens, with a straight taper down to .22 caliber. A rifle then chambered for this second case, when the case was loaded with nineteen grains of Lightning powder and the same sixty-six-grain bullet, gave a velocity of 2,550 foot seconds.

Still, Dr. Mann was not entirely satisfied. To see if they could make the powder burn better, they took this same case and made it into a bottleneck design. This *did* improve the burning rate of the powder.

This third cartridge design was practically a duplicate of the present .22 Savage Hi-Power case, as far as ballistics are concerned.

With all the above data at hand, Newton then went ahead and designed the regular .22 Hi-Power Savage case and submitted it to the Savage Arms Company. Savage then tested the cartridge and announced a rifle would be made for it. But from my correspondence with Newton, we learn Savage requested that Newton not mention the fact until the rifle was ready for market.

Right about here is where we learn that Newton was never entirely satisfied with what had gone before; in fact he was one to often change his plans, and this "indecision" later held up production of the Newton rifle.

Just when the Savage officials announced they were interested in this new cartridge, Newton again changed the design. He suggested that they use the .32-40 case necked down to .22 caliber, for use with an eighty-six-grain bullet. Newton got this latest idea from Dr. Mann.

To understand the situation, while Newton was doing all this experimenting, both Dr. Mann and Niedner were busy with a case design of their own. They had worked up this .32-40 case idea, necked down to .22, and Niedner had already made up a rifle and had prepared the ammunition. When Newton heard about it, he felt that this case, with the use of the eighty-six-grain bullet, would give improved ballistics.

Now, for the record, we find from correspondence that the Savage officials would not follow Newton's suggestions; they used the .25-35 Winchester case necked down to .22 caliber, with the seventy-grain bullet. So the .22 Savage Hi-Power was born. From the above facts one could arrive at the conclusion that the credit for the .22 Savage Hi-Power cartridge should go to both Dr. Mann and Niedner, as well as to Newton and the Savage Arms Company.

Very soon after his submission of a design to Savage, Newton again changed his plans. This time he decided to go the limit in producing a high-power .22 caliber cartridge. At first he used the 6mm Navy case necked down to .22. Soon after this he again changed plans and decided to use the 7x57 case. This latest case, when a rifle was later chambered to take it, worked into a very accurate long-range 'chuck cartridge. But the trouble all of us had at that time was the fact that there was no slow burning powder required for the larger capacity case.

Newton even went to bullets of ninety grains in .22 caliber to see if he could improve the burning rate of the powder. But after considerable experimenting he found, as Niedner had predicted, that a smaller capacity case, with a lighter weight bullet, was far more efficient, and it gave improved accuracy.

Several years before this, between 1910 and 1912, the writer, on the suggestion of Dr. Mann, took the .30 caliber Krag case and necked it down to .22. At first the full length case was used, but we soon found it held too much powder.

Next we tried a case of a smaller capacity, and this was found to be the most accurate and efficient yet tested. With Lightning powder and the sixty-grain bullet, I was able to get a velocity of 3,200 foot seconds (muzzle velocity) which was really *something* back around 1910.

Checking back on some of my older data I find that when Newton, Dr. Mann or Niedner, or the writer, first used the .22 caliber metal case bullets, in weights of 56, 60, or 63 grains, the bullets were made with the .22 (Short) hulls, so we made them with lead exposed at the point, a *soft nose* bullet — about the same as the .30-30 bullets used at that time. At the slower velocity that we got with the first experimenting, we thought we had to use such soft nose bullets. On long shots at 'chucks we drilled holes in the points to have the bullets expand properly. Then later, when the longer .22 Long Rifle hulls were available, we found we could make *open point* bullets simply by using a shorter lead core, and the bullets as made in the Niedner swage were about the same as are in use today.

In my later .22 caliber Krag design I used 32 to 34 grains Lightning powder or 34 to 36 grains of 1909 military powder with sixty-grain bullets. This rifle gave very good accuracy out to four hundred yards. I recall very well on one occasion, when hunting 'chucks with Byron Cottrell, the gunsmith from Galeton, Pennsylvania, that I killed a 'chuck that Cottrell claimed was fully four hundred yards. When Cottrell reads these lines he may remember the occasion.

In my next letter I will try to give more data covering the early testing and experimenting that was carried on for years in the efforts to obtain better rifles for long range 'chuck hunting. I have seen 'chuck rifles come a long way in the last sixty years. It may even be that this early experimenting *was* worthwhile.

Yours truly,<br>
H.A. Donaldson

*Harvey Donaldson at one of his loading presses in his shop. This second floor of an old barn he called Angler's Roost — out of love for fishing, no doubt. Photo was taken in 1966.*

## He's About Fed Up!

**April 25, 1968**

Dear Dave,

Sorry I have been so late in answering yours of April 6. I have been as busy as the devil. In fact I had so much work to do at the machine shop that I was unable to see you in Boston.

It seems that I am *way behind* in my letter writing. Our trout season opened on April first, and for the next couple of months fishing will take all my attention. Chances are that I will be in New Brunswick for the salmon fishing in June. Right now I have some thirty letters to answer, but no time to do this amount of writing. Not a single letter had a stamp in it for my reply. Guess the shooters around the country have the idea that all I have to do is to sit tight and then write and answer a lot of *damn fool* questions when they should be reading either the Lyman or Speer handbooks.

Mister, I'm about *fed up* on this writing business, as of *right now*. You should read some of my mail. Since writing for *Handloader* I get mail from all over this country. Some of the information requested would take several letters as well as more time than I can spare to answer. If you expect me to keep writing for the *Handloader,* you had better print a notice in your next issue that letters to me will be answered by someone else on the *Handloader* staff.

These shooters ask how to build everything from a Civil War musket, down to a super accurate varmint rifle.

While it always gives me great pleasure to answer all the questions I am able to, I must admit that to answer some of these letters as they *should be answered* would require an exhaustive article which, of course, is impossible. It sure would help a lot if more folks would confine themselves to only a few specific questions instead of writing a letter of a dozen pages asking how to build a Schuetzen rifle, for instance, or a bullet mould, or reamers, etc. You see a lot of fellows who have a lathe have the idea they can build most anything. Yeah, if someone will only tell them how to go about it. Hell, man, they might as well expect to buy a violin and start playing it as soon as they take it from the case. It simply isn't done that way.

If friend Nonte could read some of my mail, I am sure he would understand this problem of letter writing. For instance, just ask George which is the best hunting dog — a black one or a white one, and then have him write a book explaining the reasons for his particular choice. Then mail the book post paid to some character out in Walla Walla, Washington.

And another instance, in a letter received today. How would George go about answering a letter from a fellow who wants to know what kind of a bullet mould he should buy for a rifle he is *thinking* of building (yeah, a muzzleloader, no less) and this shooter is undecided just *what caliber* barrel he will order?

Then these Schuetzen shooting fans. They want data on loads for rifles that were in use 75 years ago. They fail to understand that most of the components used in these old rifles are no longer available. When I tell them to use black powder, they write back to learn just *where* they can buy a few cans of powder that was taken off the market about 1900. Then others want to locate bullet moulds made by Harry Pope.

I could write a book on the care and use of a Schuetzen rifle, but very few of the modern-day shooters would even know what it was all about. So . . . . as I have mentioned above, due to the fact that I will spend the summer months fishing, there will be very little time devoted to letter writing.

I'll make an extra effort to forward another "letter" for *The Handloader* in a short time, as I want to continue some of the data contained in the last letter. If I miss out on this, you can simply print on the last page of *The Handloader* that one H.A.D. has *Gone Fishing,* and will return late in the fall.

Best regards,
Harve

## *Let George Do It*

**May 1, 1968**

Dear Harvey,

I can well imagine how disturbed you get over this letter writing business. I suggest that you send me the ones you do not want to answer. Perhaps George Nonte will write these fellows and tell them that you are just too busy. We will try to help you in every way.

Also, please send me carbon copies of the letters that you write in answer to *Handloader* readers. We will reimburse you, which helps pay for your time. Also, I need the original letters so that both yours and the questions can be printed in the magazine.

I hope that you will find time to bang out a couple of letters for me prior to your fishing expedition. I would hate to run an issue without a "Yours truly" column. You are very well read in this magazine and your "letter" is a definite part of it.

Fond best regards,<br>Dave Wolfe

**Yours truly No. 15**

# More on Early Case Design

**May 4, 1968**

Dear Dave,

    This letter has to do with early case design, and is a sort of follow-up to my last letter. For a great many years, Charles Newton has been given the credit for design of the .250-3000 Savage cartridge. Actually Newton had little or nothing to do with the design of this case. If any of our readers doubt this statement, all they have to do is check with the Savage company.

    Mr. Newton was naturally interested in the results my friend Niedner was getting with his .25 Niedner Krag cartridge. This was back around 1912, or a little later. He thought that a shorter design of the Krag case would be more efficient. With this in mind he took the Krag case, cut it off to about the length of the .30-30, then reduced the taper of the case and necked it down to .250 caliber.

    The Savage company used Newton's idea of a .22 caliber Hi-Power, *after* making several changes in it. Newton naturally thought the company might also be interested in a new .25 caliber case, so he submitted the design. But he overlooked one major detail.

    As most riflemen know, the Savage 1899 rifle has a rotary magazine about like the Mannlicher. This means that the size of the head of the cartridge is more or less determined by the inside dimensions of the 99 action. When Savage officials examined the .25 caliber case, made from the .30 Krag, they found that it would be impossible to use such a large diameter of case rim in the standard Savage magazine and receiver.

    Newton asked Savage to change the rifle so that this new case might be used. But they told him it would cost too much to tool up for a larger width action. After the Savage company refused to have anything more to do with his new cartridge, Newton took the design to Winchester, which at this time was producing the 1895 Model Winchester in .30 Krag caliber. But Winchester was not interested in any new .25 caliber case, for it already had the .25-35 in the Model 1894 rifle.

    I believe I have neglected to mention that Newton's case (the one he submitted to the Savage company) called for a hundred-grain bullet. All of the above information is in my files, in correspondence from Newton.

    About this time I was living in Rome, New York, which was only a few miles west of the Savage Arms Company (at that time located in Utica, New York). I knew

John Pierce, the ballistic engineer for Savage. When I was working on a new case design I would run down to Utica to visit friend Pierce, and have him chronograph my test loads. I remember quite well that one time John complained about testing some of the loads I had worked up — when I was interested in my .22 Krag. He said, "Don't bring any more of that high speed stuff in here; it just about ruins our metal backing on the range. It has pock marks all over it!"

On one of my many trips to the Savage factory, I asked Pierce what they were going to do with Newton's .25 caliber case. He told me they could do nothing with it because the large diameter of case rim on the Krag case prevented its use in the Model 99 Savage. You should know that at this time the Savage company was making ammunition as well as firearms in the Utica factory.

This gave me an idea, so I asked John, "Why not use a case with a smaller rim?"

He looked at me in surprise. "Just what case would you suggest?" I then told him to take the .30-06 and cut it off to the proper length, with the bullet seated so it would work in the Model 99 action. I suggested a gradual taper to this case design with a 30 degree shoulder, and use of a bullet of around seventy-five grains. What I had in mind, of course, was a new 'chuck rifle cartridge.

About then John mentioned that Savage had never chambered a barrel to take a rimless case, and I came right back with the question, "Why not?" All that is required is a slight change in the extractor, and then headspace on the shoulder of the case.

John looked at me for a moment before he replied, "You know, Harve, maybe you have got something there, at that."

If my readers will compare a .30-06 case at the head together with a case in .250-3000 Savage, they will find that both will measure the same, so it could well be that Savage acted on my own simple suggestion.

At any rate, soon after this I got word to run down and test out a new Savage rifle. The company wanted a new rifle that would deliver a velocity of 3,000 feet per second, for sales talk. Newton wanted the hundred-grain bullet, but when that did not give enough velocity, the company used one of eighty-seven grains, but I figured the seventy-five grain would be even better. They also used a different shoulder angle than I had suggested.

When you have read over the above data you can well understand why, ever since that time, a rifle chambered for the .250-3000 Savage case has been one of my favorites. Right now there is one, but of Winchester manufacture, standing in my gun rack. I also had one of the very first rifles in this caliber that ever left the Savage factory.

An experimenter is really never satisfied with anything, for inside of a year from the time the new Savage .250-3000 came out, back around 1914 or '15, I had the same cartridge necked down to .22 caliber. I obtained one of the heavy Savage barrels in .228 caliber, (not .224) that they used for their .22 Hi-Power rifles. Then I necked this .250-3000 case down to .228 to take the seventy-grain Savage bullet. This, as you can easily understand, was many years before any other case designer had given any thought to the modern .22-250 case, as now put out by Remington.

At that time I tried to interest Savage in bringing out a rifle chambered to take my .22-250 case. I have in my files a letter from the company in which they said my new case was a good one, but that they were not interested in another .22 caliber design, as they already had a good .22 Hi-Power cartridge in production, and that a new case might reduce the sale of that rifle.

Well, time marches on, and what ever happened to the .22 Hi-Power Savage rifle? It has been out of production for years, and such concerns as Remington and Browning today chamber rifles for the case I used and designed long before some of our present-day riflemen were born. My correspondence with the Savage company, as well as correspondence with the old-time gunsmith M.S. Risley, (lately deceased), should show to anyone interested, just where the credit for the design of the now popular .22-250 case should go.

My later design in .22 caliber was the .219 Donaldson Wasp. I never saw any .22-250 that would equal a good rifle chambered for the Wasp case, and I believe even today that many shooters would be better off if they used a "Wasp" rifle. It seems fashions change in rifles, same as in ladies' hats, but how often is a simple change an improvement.

Any rifle that gave super-accuracy twenty years ago will *still shoot* with the modern .22 caliber bullets that we have today. My Wasp made its reputation for accuracy back in the days before we had such good bullets. Also, back twenty years ago, my .22 caliber case design had plenty of competition in all the matches.

Yours truly,
Harvey Donaldson

P.S. Several years ago, when visiting with my old friend Col. Whelen, I told him about my experiences with the Savage Arms Company, as contained in this letter. He said he had also heard that Savage, not Newton, had designed the .250-3000 case. I suggested that he contact Savage and learn what they had to say about it. On one of my last visits with Whelen he told me that they had designed the case in question, and for the very same reasons I have mentioned in this letter. I believe you now have in your files a photostat of a letter I received long ago from Risley, in regard to this .250-3000 case design.

H.A.D.

## Another P.S.

Dear Dave:

I believe I should add a P.S. to my letters each month, as a tip to the younger shooters. In something like seventy-five years of shooting, a fellow is bound to learn something about it, and maybe I can offer some things unknown to the modern-day shooter.

For instance, see Page 54 in Issue 14 of *Handloader* on the O'Connor .270 load — about filling a case with a capacity load. Some of us old-timers had the same trouble years ago when we tried to get a *full load* of black powder into the old-style straight cases like the .38-55, .40-70, or .45-90. In those days the old Ideal powder measures were furnished, on special order, with a long drop tube, (twelve or eighteen inches). They were made of brass, since we were afraid of static electricity under certain weather conditions.

If you own Phil Sharpe's *Complete Guide to Handloading,* turn to Page 203 and you will see how I showed Phil how to get more powder into the shell than it would normally hold. If you have a file of the *American Rifleman,* turn to Page 268 in the July 1935 issue, and see where I told Fred Ness about it. About half the data in Phil's book he got from my files. Also see Page 220 in Phil's book, and you will see a picture of my arbor press loading tool I made over sixty years ago, and it is still in use.

Now, if you want to get more powder into a case, make up a funnel with a long stem, that fits on the *outside* of the case, (have stem say two or three inches long). Then pour powder into this funnel. Next you take a short piece of brass rod, some three or four inches long, and drop it into the funnel neck on top of the powder. Make this rod a loose fit.

Tap the base of the case a few times on top of the bench. The weight of the rod causes the powder to settle more uniformly and it will thus occupy a minimum of space in the shell. I got this tip from Rube Harwood back around 1895 or so.

You will find that a lot of the methods we used in our handloading of years ago can still be of use. Only trouble is, there are not many of use old-time shooters around who can still tell you about it.

We had problems in the old days, same as now, but we usually figured out some method to overcome them. You should read some of my old note books on loading data. By the way, there was a lot of interesting reading in the last *Handloader.*

H.A. Donaldson

Yours truly No. 16

# Black Powder & Cast Bullets

**August 2, 1968**

Friend Dave,

In one of my recent letters to *The Handloader* I recounted some of the experiences of Charles Newton in his efforts to produce a modern high-power .22 caliber rifle. This experimenting, of course, was with smokeless powder and metal-case bullets. I have in my files information that might interest our readers, so we will go back long before the days of friend Newton, when only black powder and cast lead bullets were available.

Only recently I came across some letters received years ago from that fine old rifleman and target sight maker, Thomas Martin of Dorchester, Massachusetts. These letters are very interesting, but more than that, they contain data and information about the very first of the centerfire .22 caliber rifles. I always like to give credit where credit is due, and therefore will say that while Mr. Newton began his early experimenting back around 1910 or so, this was not the real beginning where the centerfire .22 caliber rifles were concerned.

Disregarding all .22 caliber rimfire cartridges, I would say that the very first attempt to produce a .22 caliber centerfire cartridge with more power than the rimfire cartridges in the same caliber, came about when the Massachusetts Arms Company, of Chicopee Falls, Massachusetts, then makers of the Maynard rifle, produced the .22-10-45 centerfire cartridge, and also the rifle chambered to take this fine little cartridge. Very few of the riflemen of today have ever seen one of these cartridges. I believe this was around 1880 or '82.

This particular cartridge was regularly manufactured by the Union Metallic Cartridge Company. The case was made from thin brass, having a folded head, and taking the No. 0 copper primer. The capacity of this small case was only ten grains of fine black powder. In use, it was soon found that the primer pocket was far too thin, and the cup of the small copper primer was so weak that the firing pin would puncture it and enter the primer pocket in many cases. This fault soon led to the adoption of the later .22 caliber Extra Long centerfire case.

This case had the solid head and used the No. 1 primer, made by Winchester. The extra amount of metal in this newer case reduced the powder capacity to only eight grains, and it was soon found that this particular cartridge did not perform as did the older and original .22-10-45 Maynard. The cartridge was reloadable, of course, but it was a real nuisance to clean and load. However, if this operation was performed carefully, it would produce excellent scores in the hands of an expert rifleman.

Probably the one man who made this cartridge famous was Bert Wentworth, of Dover, New Hampshire. He was the first shooter to make TEN consecutive bullseyes, at two hundred yards, shooting off-hand. Incidentally, Mr. Wentworth was also the originator of the then well known "Dover" barrel, which was made extra heavy for the Maynard rifles.

When I was a young man, I used one of the first of the No. 16 Maynard rifles made for the .22-10-45 cartridge; this rifle was owned by an uncle. This particular gun was very accurate, even out at two hundred yards. The weakness of the primer pocket, as well as the difficulty of cleaning and loading such a small case, made it rather unpopular, and quite a few of these rifles were later rebored to the .32-35 centerfire case by the makers of the Maynard rifle.

This one gun, owned by my uncle, had a twist of one turn in sixteen inches — the same as the more modern Hornet rifle used today. I well remember that I tried in every way possible to obtain a higher velocity, with the only smokeless powder available at the time, but with poor results; it only resulted in a loss of accuracy.

Mr. Martin wrote that when this cartridge first appeared he also tried out the early smokeless powders, such as "Dittmar," "Brackett," "Wood," and "Gelbite." He could improve the velocity but was unable to obtain the accuracy of black powder loads. Both paper patched and the grooved cast lead bullets were furnished or prepared by the riflemen for use in this .22-10-45 case — the former with a temper of one to fifteen, and the latter one to thirty. These paper patched bullets were usually seated in the barrel with a bullet seater, and placed about one-sixteenth-inch ahead of the case.

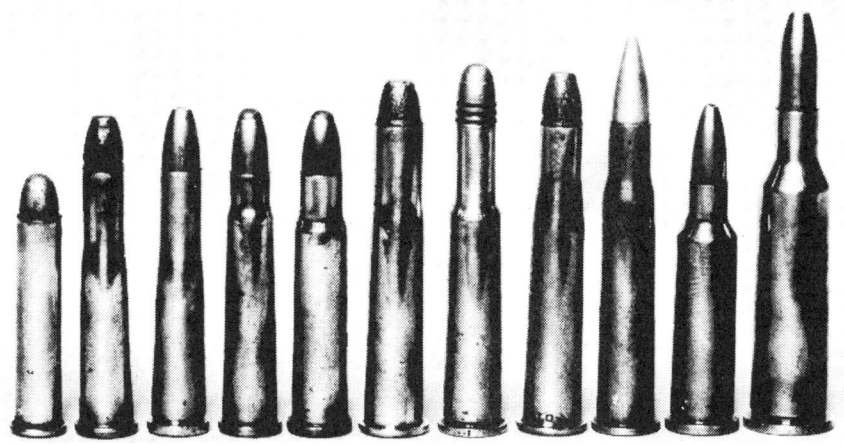

This photo, reproduced from HANDLOADER, shows eleven early varmint cartridges, but the original caption listed only ten, as follows: left to right, .22-10-45 Maynard, .22 WCF, .22 Hornet, .22 Donaldson Hornet, .22 K-Hornet, .25-20 Stevens SS, .22 Harwood Hornet, .22 Lowe Hornet, .22 Bee and .219 Donaldson Wasp. The editor and a half dozen of his usually reliable cronies could not identify the extra case. We therefore must trust that our readers are wiser, and just as forgiving.

For some time after the advent of the .22-10-45 cartridge, no further advance was made in the small caliber centerfire cartridges, except as some of the manufacturers improved their products.

Along around 1888, the year of the great blizzard that swept through the Eastern states, a well known Massachusetts rifleman, Reuben Harwood, far more widely known by his pen name "Iron Ramrod," opened a modest repair shop for gunsmithing, as well as a salesroom, on Avon Street in Somerville, Massachusetts. He was a rifleman himself, and in touch with most of the expert New England shooters, and made a specialty of furnishing fine selected and tested rifles. This testing he did himself, personally, before any rifle was delivered to any customer.

During his testing and experimenting, Mr. Harwood found that the majority of his customers were looking for a small caliber rifle, taking a case that was both accurate and easy to reload. They wanted slight noise and recoil, yet something capable of fine results in either small game shooting or target practice. As an outcome of this, some time around 1890 or so, Mr. Harwood designed and brought out what was practically the *very first* high-power .22 caliber centerfire cartridge, and this may come as a surprise to the modern rifleman — he called it the HORNET .22-20-55. Martin wrote that it was the late Mr. A.C. Gould, at that time the editor of *Shooting and Fishing*, who first called this cartridge the "Hornet," saying that the buzz of the bullet in flight reminded him of that insect. It was Harwood's idea to use grooved and lubricated bullets only, the fifty-five-grain for a hunting load, and the seventy-five-grain for target shooting. I believe I have neglected to mention that this new Harwood case was one of the *early* ones having the bottleneck design.

In this particular case we have our first glimpse of a real high power .22 caliber rifle. One giving high velocity, with flat trajectory, and yet with very fine accuracy out to two hundred yards. Mr. Harwood made and sold moulds, swages, shell resizers and bullets, as well as the loaded ammunition. He also sold Maynard and Stevens rifles adapted for his new Hornet case. He made up special barrels for this cartridge to fit other actions, and then later recut worn out or rusted out .22 caliber barrels up to .23 caliber for use with the unsized bullets.

One bright fall morning some sixty years ago, I was hunting gray squirrels on Florida Mountain, near Hoosac Tunnel in the western part of Massachusetts. I was using a very special .28-30 single-shot Stevens target rifle with a Pope breech loading barrel, and a Stevens scope in Pope mounts. This was an accurate rifle and I might add, it still is. I used a sharp pointed bullet for squirrel hunting, and at this time with such an outfit I figured I had the last word in a squirrel gun.

While hunting that morning I came across an old man who was also hunting squirrels. He had as fine a Maynard rifle as I had ever seen, with a barrel recut by Mr. Harwood to a .23 caliber, but using the .22-20-55 cartridge. The rifle had a fine Malcolm scope on it, and was a very accurate outfit, as I soon found out. I tried to buy this fine old rifle but soon found it was not for sale. The old-time squirrel hunter, who at that time lived up near Monroe Bridge, told me it was the most accurate and best shooting rifle in those parts, and that money could not buy it. I have often wondered just what finally became of that fine old Maynard.

I still own a nice Maynard rifle, but in .25-20 single-shot caliber. This rifle has also accounted for a countless number of gray squirrels.

Back around 1892 or '93, Mr. William V. Lowe, a prominent expert rifleman as well as gunsmith, who had formerly been in partnership with Horace Warner (also a famous rifleman), started business for himself at 27 Mechanic Street in Fitchburg, Massachusetts.

Martin wrote me that he had considerable correspondence and business dealings with both Mr. Lowe and Harwood about this time, and so was in a position to know what they were doing. In referring to his friend Lowe's booklets of that time, Martin stated that Lowe made a specialty of quick-twist small bore express and target rifles, as well as the supplies for same.

He wrote that Mr. Lowe was prepared to make up his .22 caliber rifle barrels with a twist of twelve inches, to handle the seventy-five-grain bullet for the Harwood Hornet case for target shooting. This case held twenty grains of powder. Lowe claimed that this cartridge case was an excellent one for loading for small game hunting and target work. Also, that it required no cleaning between shots (black powder in those days usually gave much trouble in this respect), and that it possessed accuracy equal to that of the .25-20 case, but with less recoil, smoke and noise and entailed less expense and labor in loading compared to the larger calibers. And last but not least, that worn out or rusted out .22 caliber barrels could be restored to .23 caliber and still use the same bullet cast from an over-sized mould.

From the above data it will be seen that Mr. Lowe had adopted in their entirety the ideas of his friend Harwood, and he also put the cartridge on the market under the name of Hornet. That this cartridge was the first really practical .22 caliber high power actually made and put on the open market seems to be without a doubt.

Here again we find two expert woodchuck hunters coming to the front with the best high speed 'chuck rifle of its day.

Yours truly,<br>
Harvey A. Donaldson

Harvey holds a Marlin loading tool. Patented in 1881 by John M. Browning, it was claimed in Marlin literature to be the only complete tool made — consisting of mould, wad cutter, decapper, recapper, and crimper.

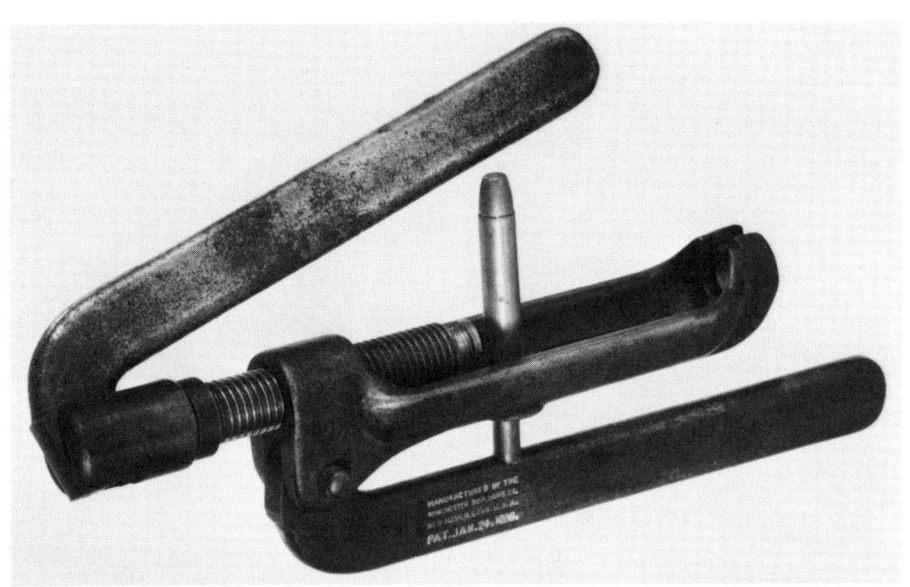

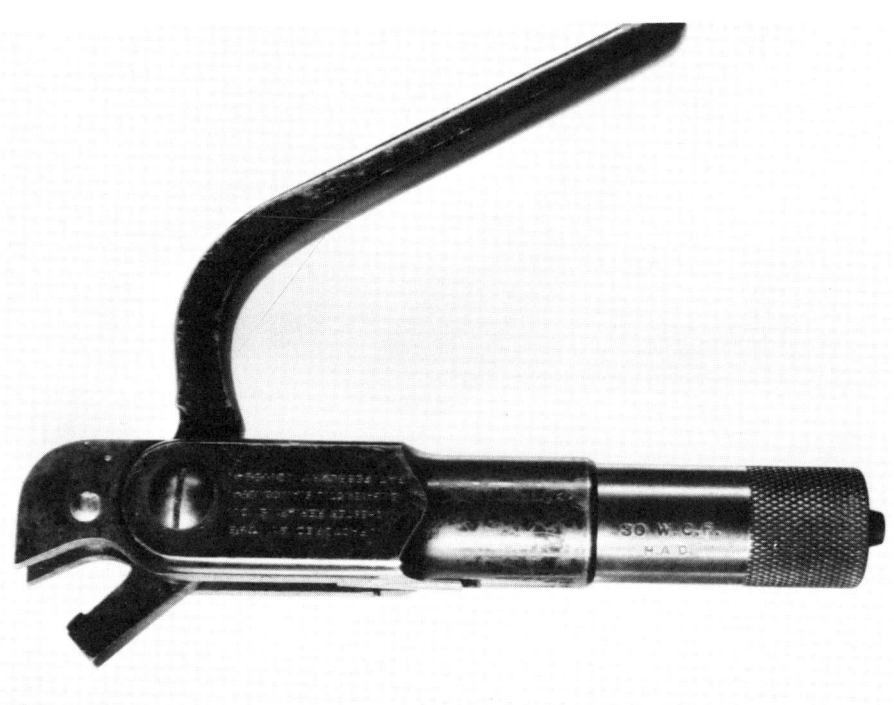

Two old Winchester loading tools in Harvey's collection. At top is the New Model which was capable of full-length resizing by turning the large lever and forcing a die over the cartridge case. Below is the Model 1894 tool, the last one produced by Winchester and offered until 1914.

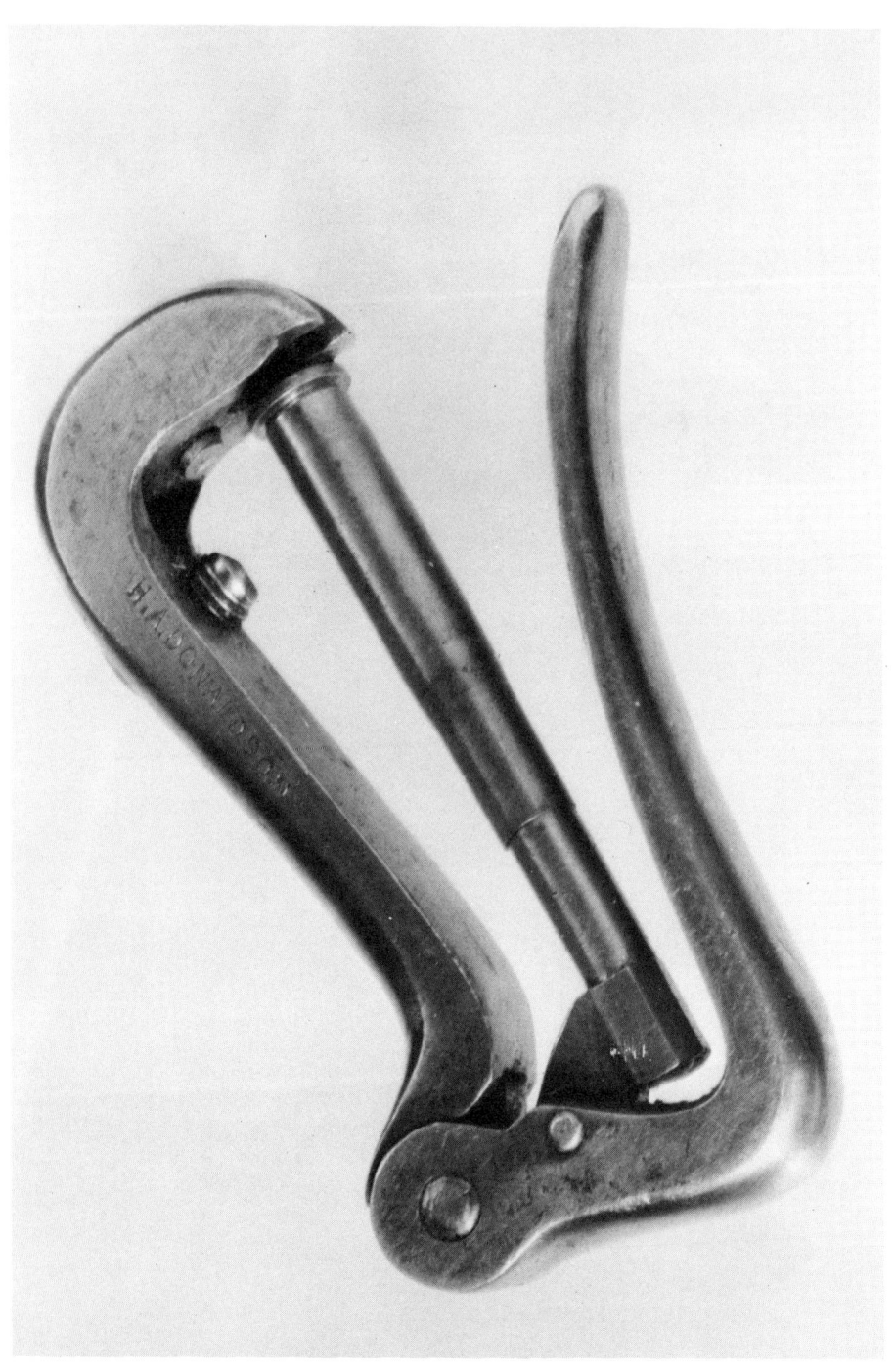

*Another tool owned by Donaldson was the W. Milton Farrow capping and decapping "implement." A copy of the patent drawing for this tool (right) was found in Harvey's personal effects.*

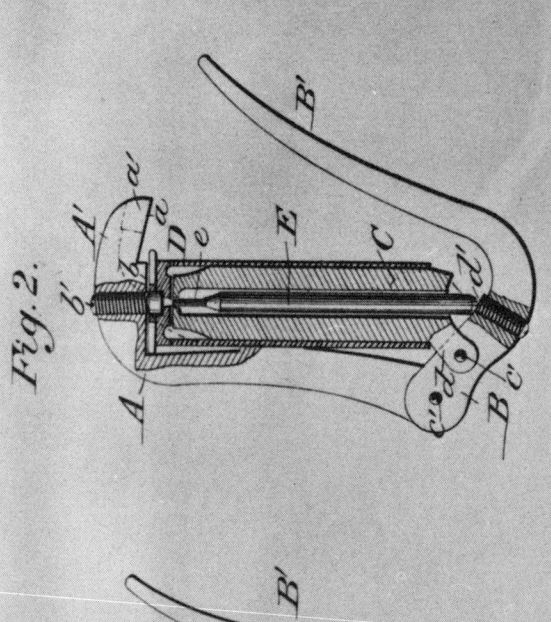

## A New Magazine

**August 23, 1968**

Dear Harvey,

Very confidentially, we are planning to start another magazine, entitled *"The Rifle."* This will cover all facets of the gun, including shooting, ballistics, the old-timers, competitive bench rest shooting, new guns, handloading, etc. It will be a technical book, one for the active shooters rather than armchair hobbyists. I would like to see a Donaldson feature in this magazine, but I don't want to work you to death. What do you think about an article or two a year on the early target rifles, and the developments that you were in on? Or would you rather do a regular feature? Let me know your thinking on this.

Fond best regards,
David R. Wolfe

## Good Service!

**August 26, 1968**

Dear Dave,

Yours of the 23rd came in the mail this morning. After reading it over I came right back to the house and sat down to do the first article for the new *Rifle* Magazine. So here it is in the afternoon of August 26, when this article will be placed in the mail and on the way to Peoria, Illinois.

How's that for service? But don't expect this every time. I will try and get busy on those other letters you have in mind for the *Handloader*.

Have been doing considerable shooting the last few days since I returned from my vacation in Maine. Had a new idea about a load for my Swift with the Sierra 53-grain bench rest bullets; guess it worked out OK as all of the forty shots fired can be covered with a penny.

Best regards,
Harve

## Knox New Editor

**August 29, 1968**

Dear Harve:

Your first article for *The Rifle* Magazine arrived and we have gone over it for initial editing. You did a good job and I believe this manuscript will be well received by the readers. I will need photographs, however.

I certainly appreciate your constant and continued cooperation. I wish I had a dozen staff writers just like you.

Beginning October 1, both *The Handloader* and *The Rifle* will have a new editor — Mr. Neal Knox who has been editing *Gun Week* newspaper. Neal will be contacting you soon about future articles. I will remain as publisher and hope to do some traveling selling advertising and doing general promotion. I hope to have a chance to see you on one of my trips East.

Very cordially,
Dave

## Harve, Meet Neal

**October 7, 1968**

Dear Mr. Donaldson:

I am sure that when you received Dave's letter telling you that Neal Knox was going to take over the editor's duties here at *Handloader* and *Rifle*, your first reaction was "Neal who?" — unless you happened to have been reading *Gun Week* newspaper. I'm a young fellow just getting started in this business. As such, I'm certainly going to need a lot of help from the men who know what the shooting business is all about. I'll certainly appreciate your keeping a close eye on my work here and letting me know if I go astray. After all, you had burned a lot of powder before even my Daddy was born.

I started shooting when I was seven and was given my first gun when I was nine, (for that matter my wife got her first gun when she was nine, too, so ours is a shooting family). It didn't take me long to learn that every time you went out with a gun you learned something. I am awed when I think of the knowledge gained and stored up during your three quarters of a century of shooting, particularly when I realize you learned your guns along side such men as Pope, Niedner, Mann and the other greats of years ago.

We young shooters need to know of your early experiments and how you went about them, for they are of great value to us. Guns have changed during the last sixty or seventy years but not nearly as much as the manufacturers would like to have us youngsters believe.

Take for instance Winchester's "new" .225; as soon as that case came out I recognized it as nothing but an unshortened form of your .219 Donaldson. Winchester left the case body length about the same as the .219 Improved Zipper, probably thinking that the little extra dose of today's slower burning powders would produce considerably more velocity than the Donaldson, but I don't think they got enough extra velocity to matter and I think the .225 is somewhat more temperamental than the Donaldson.

I noticed in one of your columns that R.B. Sisk of Iowa Park, Texas, had once marketed graphite wads for high velocity loads. If I knew it, I had forgotten it. Ralph's shop is only about three blocks from my Dad's auto parts house in Iowa Park and I know him well. In fact, we talked about my going in business with him about three years ago. His bullets have probably won more bench matches than any other commercial make, but many of the young shooters today never have heard of Sisk bullets, much less tried them.

You might be able to solve a puzzle that has bothered me for a long time. A friend of mine has a long-barreled Colt Single Action with factory serial number stampings on the barrel and the brass detachable stock. As I remember, the barrel is about 10½ inches and was one of the last long barrel single actions ever made. Its serial number was in the 110,000 range. The thing that puzzles me is that on the brass skeleton stock is stamped H. Pope. I have always wondered how that stamp got there and if it was *the* H. Pope.

Dave tells me that we do need one of your columns as soon as possible. One subject that would be particularly helpful to the new generation of shooters is exactly how to go about casting bullets for accuracy. I'm particularly thinking about the slug guns such as are used at the muzzle loading championships at Friendship.

I have often wondered how you cast bullets back in the old days, particularly how you determined correct hardness. You have mentioned that various barrels shot better with different alloys and I have wondered how you went about determining that alloy. Although it must have been largely trial and error and lots of shooting, I'm wondering if you also didn't have some techniques and hints from the gun which indicated whether the alloy should be somewhat harder or somewhat softer. In other words, were there any particular signs that you watched for to give you an indication as to how to change the alloy?

Remembering Pope's comments about your bullets cast from one of his moulds, I'm sure you could give some good advice to anyone who is casting bullets whether for black powder guns or the more modern types. Although most big bore shooters can produce a cast bullet that will shoot fairly well after a reasonable amount of experimenting, I know most of the boys run into problems when they try casting for .22 and 6mm bores.

I don't know when I'll again have a chance for such a long visit with you, but these are some of the things that I've been wondering about and I'm sure many of the readers would like to know. Keep an eye on how I'm doing here and if I goof up, kick me in the shins.

Best regards,
Neal Knox

**Yours truly No. 17**

# Bottleneck Case Controversy

**October 10, 1968**

Dear Neal Knox:

So you are taking over Dave's job on *Handloader* and *Rifle* magazines. From here it looks as if Dave is passing the buck — sort of shifting the load from his shoulders to yours. Well, I sure hope he gets away with it and I wish you all kinds of luck.

Your recent letter is so interesting that I hope you will pardon me if I refer to it before I start on other matters. I note well that you admit you are just a young fellow getting started in this gun editor business. Whether you realize it or not, right there you have a lot going for you. It's getting *started* that counts. Guess a few of us old-timers wish we were back to the days when we started handloading. You can rest assured that I will be only too glad to help out in any way possible.

You mention Paul Morton of Wichita Falls, Texas. I have seen some of his work and it was of high order. When he made a stock it *looked* like a stock, just the way it should. Maybe I am old-fashioned, but I'm not interested in the modern trend in gun stocks. When Tom Shellhamer, Niedner, Bob Owen, Risley, (and today, Len Brownell), made a stock, you had something to be proud of.

You mention the National Bench Rest Match held last August in Ohio. I had planned to attend, but at the last moment something came up. I have never missed a match held on the Pine Tree Range, in Johnstown, New York, where all this bench rest shooting got started over twenty years ago. For a number of years I attended all the big matches, but sorry to say so many of my old friends have passed away that I feel like a stranger at some of the shoots.

From your letter I learn that you once lived in Iowa Park, Texas. That address is quite familiar to me, for I have known R.B. Sisk for a great many years. Back in the early thirties I wrote for the *Rifleman* for several years, and experimented with several new cases that led up to my design of the .219 Donaldson case. While I was making my own .22 swaged bullets at this time, I was glad to test out the bullets made by Sisk. This was before the days of Sierra, etc.

Friend Sisk made good bullets — so good in fact that they made groups in my own experimental rifles that the shooters around the country found it hard to believe. I wrote about my results in the *Rifleman*, and Sisk claimed these articles helped make his bullet making business a success.

A number of years ago I attended a BR match out in San Angelo, Texas. Those Texans certainly showed me a wonderful time. That was the year that my old buddy Charley Hankins from Buffalo, Wyoming, cleaned up at the Nationals. I drove the whole width of Texas, from east to west, so know first hand it is a BIG country.

To again refer to your letter of October 7, the name stamp Harry Pope always used was simply "H.M. Pope," not H. Pope as you mentioned in your letter. And I note well your inquiries about casting bullets for accurate shooting. This is rather a large order that would require several letters to cover properly. My own idea of *accuracy* might differ considerably from another shooter. This matter will be covered in the future.

No. 16 issue of *The Handloader* has just arrived. It is full of interesting data, as usual, but what appeals to me most is the article by Ed Yard on Hornet versus K-Hornet. You may be surprised when I tell you that I have waited since the early 1930s for such an article to appear in print. I agree one hundred percent with all Yard has written. Here is a writer who knows where-of he speaks, with both feet on the ground and not up on Cloud Nine.

Some day I will show you a letter that I wrote to Fred Ness, the late Dope Bag Editor of the *Rifleman*, when I had finished my own experimenting with a bottleneck .22 Hornet case design. That letter was never mailed, but this letter will try to explain matters.

First off, let's go back to the time Winchester brought out the ammunition for a Hornet rifle, before any rifle was available to use such ammo. At this time I was living in Little Falls, New York. My gunsmith friend M.S. Risley was living in Utica and later near Hubbardsville, New York. The late Lysle Kilbourn lived in Utica. Both were good friends of mine and we often hunted chucks together, in the country around Hubbardsville.

My friend Col. Whelen sent me a box of the first Hornet ammunition I ever saw, and this was some time *before* you could buy it over the counter. Of course, I just had to own a rifle for the new case, so I took the ammunition and one of my good Winchester single-shot actions (with double set triggers and Pope speed lock) over to Risley. He made a half reamer for the new case in no time (sometime I'll explain this half reamer idea), and then he fitted and chambered a new .22 barrel to take the new Hornet case. This was before our friend Kilbourn even saw a .22 Hornet rifle.

The rifle was a success from the start, and it was very accurate up to two hundred yards, when conditions were right. Risley and I used this gun all one summer, but he often complained about the lack of power on the longer shots.

One day when Risley and I were visiting in his gun shop, he came up with the idea of making this Hornet into a bottleneck case, so it might hold more powder. I was not interested in the idea for I figured at best we might only gain a half grain to the load already in use, and all the extra work was hardly worthwhile. But Risley figured the only way to find out was to rechamber my rifle.

With this in mind he made a new reamer for the bottleneck design. I have every reason to believe that this same reamer was used later to rechamber the first K-Hornet barrel, as Risley did all the barrel work at that time for Kilbourn.

Well, to make a long story short, after we had used the bottleneck design for some time, we were unable to find that it was enough better than the original Hornet design to bother with.

About this time Risley told me that friend Kilbourn was going all out on the bottleneck in Hornet caliber. When his first rifle was made up, Risley told me that he (Kilbourn) had written to Fred Ness of the *Rifleman*, giving him a full account.

The Kilbourn account of the K-Hornet was printed and Ness himself praised the new caliber before he had even seen a rifle.

After I had read the accounts of the K-Hornet from data written by Fred Ness, I sat down to write to him about the results Risley and I had. When this letter was written, something told me to hold it to see what happened, so it was never mailed.

Kilbourn was a good friend of mine, so I figured that if he had a good thing going, who was I to throw cold water on this "K" business. Now I am glad that letter to Ness was never mailed.

What really burns me up is to have a young writer who covers the technical side of one of the West Coast magazines (this data incidentally being about as technical as a plate of corn beef hash) giving Kilbourn credit for *inventing* the idea of fire-forming a case. Every case that was ever fired in a rifle chamber is fire-formed to that chamber!

About now you will understand just why this article by Yard attracted my attention. He found out, just as did Risley and this writer, that if the K-Hornet has any advantage over the regular Hornet case, as brought out by Winchester, this made little difference out at a hundred yards. Not enough to bother with.

All a new case requires is a good press agent and man, have we got some among the new crop of writers on gun matters!

Just in case some joker writes in to find out what bullets we used in the early loading for the Hornet case, before Winchester was able to furnish the forty-five-grain bullets in .22 caliber, you might tell them that I was making my own metal case bullets in .22 caliber in a hand swage furnished by Niedner, long before the Hornet case was designed.

Also, when we could get them we used the full metal patch Velo-dog bullets in 5.5mm. But we put them upside down in a hand swage so we could make soft nose bullets. I believe Col. Whelen at that time used these 5.5 caliber bullets in his early experimenting with the Hornet case.

If you will look close at the photo shown with my letter on Page 66, in No. 16 issue of *The Handloader*, you will note that the second cartridge in line is the .22 WCF case. This happens to be the original case from which the Winchester Hornet was designed. The next case in line is the .22 Winchester Hornet.

All that was done was to simply take the old Winchester black powder case and load it with a smokeless powder and a metal case bullet. My old friend Col. Whelen had as much to do with this case as anyone.

Yours truly,
Harvey A. Donaldson

# J. Bushnell Smith

**October 29, 1968**

Friend Knox,

Would you and the readers of *Handloader* be interested in reading about some of the early experiences my old friend J. Bushnell Smith had in his early loading of custom ammunition? You see, I helped get Smith started in that business. He used to correspond with me when he was still in the Navy during World War I. When he left the Navy, I gave him several notebooks that contained some 30 years of my own handloading experiences.

This data contained loads for almost every cartridge, and it was kept up to date as the new powders came out. I was in close touch with Smitty from the start of his custom loading business. I could write a book about Smitty, and some day I may do just that. The fact of the matter was, I knew Smith's father, when J.B. was just a boy. He was a fine old man, and an expert with a handgun. We traded loading data for years. So it was from letters that the father had written to J.B. when he was in the Navy that J.B. started writing to me.

A lot of this data on J.B. I have in my files from the letters we exchanged for several years. I used to visit him in Vermont quite often, and J.B. would come down to visit me in the Mohawk Valley, where I could show him some *real* chuck hunting. These old letters will make interesting reading for any handloader. This data is as sound today as the day it was written, and unless it is shown in print, it may never see the light of day.

I could give you plenty of data on casting bullets for super accuracy, but Jim Carmichel is doing OK even if he has one hell of a lot to still learn about making bullets that Harry Pope would OK as fit to shoot. It takes *years* for that. Let's hear from you soon.

Best regards,
H.A. Donaldson

# Loading for the 7x57

**November 8, 1968**

Friend Knox,

I have had several letters from shooters since my method of handloading for the 7x57 Mauser cartridge was shown in *Handloader*. Thought perhaps I had better explain what I had in mind when I worked out that system.

When the 7x57 case was designed soon after the 8x57 came out, it was intended for a military rifle, and I believe it was used in the Model 92 Mauser rifle. My first rifle in 7x57 caliber had a twist of 8.86 inches. I used the 175-grain full metal case bullet. It was the only ammunition we could obtain. Later I was able to get some German ammunition that used a lighter bullet.

My second rifle in this caliber was a custom job, which had a ten-inch twist. With this rifle I tried to work up loads with both the heavy and the lighter bullets that would shoot into the same group out at 100 to 150 yards, without much success.

Then I began to wonder why anyone would choose a cartridge for our Adirondack deer hunting (where a long-range shot is under a hundred yards, as a rule), that used the long 175-grain bullet designed for long-range military shooting. Soon after the Second World War it was possible to obtain bullets in 7mm caliber of different weights; today they may be obtained in a dozen or more different sizes.

This started my experimenting all over again. The loads shown in the loading manuals for the different weights of bullets were tried out. I was able to get good accuracy with most of them. But having them group the same out at a hundred yards was something else again.

About this time the idea came to me, why not make up a new rifle in the same caliber, only with a *twelve-inch* twist. The more I thought about it, the better it seemed. At this time the Hornady round

Photos on these two pages were found tacked to the wall just left of Harvey's loading bench. Above photo has a notation, "J. Bushnell Smith's bench and tools used in making Smith's custom loads."

*Inscribed on the rear of this picture: "Print of J. Bushnell Smith's gun case. He sent this to me November 23, 1935. Photo shows my .32-40 Winchester Ballard." (Note the initials H.A.D. on the gunstock.)*

nose 154-grain bullet in 7mm was available, so I figured here was the bullet to use for deer hunting in the woods of New York.

So a new rifle was made up with the twelve-inch twist, and at long last, after a lot more experimenting, I found I really had something. Again the loads in the handbooks were tried, and while they gave as good accuracy as my custom-made .270 Winchester, I was not satisfied.

I found I had to work out a new system of handloading, which is the one I wrote about in *Handloader*. While the twelve-inch twist may not stabilize the 175-grain bullet out at a thousand yards, I do no thousand-yard shooting. With this slower twist I can get better accuracy, as well as a higher velocity with *less* pressure, and while my loads are greater than are shown as normal for the 7x57, the pressure in my rifle is normal.

At long last I have obtained what I was trying for. The load with the 120-grain Sierra bullet gives tight two-hundred-yard groups — O.K. for long-range varmint hunting. The 154-grain Hornady bullet is used for deer hunting, while the 175-grain bullet still gives enough hundred-yard accuracy that it can be used while hunting in heavy cover.

The best part of the whole system is that with the *same* sight setting I can put four different weights of bullets into the end of a beer can from the bench at a hundred yards.

Yours truly,
H.A. Donaldson

## A Common Friend

### November 15, 1968

Dear Friend Harve,

I enjoyed your reply to my letter. We'll have it in the January-February *Handloader*. As you will note in the enclosed memo to the Staff, the first issue of the *Rifle* will be out about November 26 so you should have your copy shortly after.

I think the readers might like to know of the experiences of J. Bushnell Smith, but I think it would be more readable if you would write them up in your own words, rather than simply printing the old letters. Also, although Jim Carmichel writes regularly on bullet casting, I think your experiences and techniques would be of great interest.

I received a note from my Dad down at Iowa Park, Texas, last week. He said Ralph Sisk had brought him over a copy of *The Handloader*, the one telling about my becoming the Editor. I had wondered if you and Ralph didn't know each other and I'm glad to know that we have another common friend.

Best regards,
Neal Knox

*The following feature appeared in the First Edition of* Rifle, *January-February, 1969. Readers will find some material is repeated from various "Yours truly" columns, but most is both fresh and refreshing — especially to present-day riflemen and hunters.*

# My First Chuck Rifle

This writer's first real interest in rifle shooting started back around the year 1892, when my shooting uncle loaned me an old Expert Model Stevens rimfire .22 caliber rifle. This was a very accurate shooting outfit, with target sights and a nice stock, designed for off-hand shooting.

Some time before that I used an old Flobert single-shot rifle, but it never gave very good accuracy, so I like to believe that I started rifle shooting with the old single-shot Stevens. This rifle was quite heavy for a kid to handle off-hand, so my uncle showed me how to shoot it prone, with rest stock, in 'chuck hunting.

My own rest shooting may properly date from this early experience. Guess I never did get over the habit of using the rest stock, for to this day I use it when taking long shots at 'chucks out at 300 yards and over.

Very soon after this I was instructed in the ways and means of loading and shooting a Schuetzen rifle. At first this only consisted of shooting off the bench with sand bags, but as I got older and stronger I was taught to shoot off-hand at 100 and 200 yards. This was truly the golden era of the Schuetzen rifle, from around 1895 to 1905. Every copy of *Shooting & Fishing* gave the scores of the most expert off-hand shooting riflemen in the country.

Also, plenty of data was available if one would keep his eyes and ears open when attending a match. In some of my old files are letters received from Dr. Hudson, Harry Pope, C.W. Rowland, L.P. Ittel, Rube Harwood, W. Milton Farrow, E.A. Leopold, Dr. Skinner, F.J. Rabbeth, John D. Kelley, Dr. Baker, and a host of others. The names of these old-time riflemen, with the possible exception of Harry Pope, may mean very little to the modern shooter, but back in the old days, having a writing acquaintance with any of the above-mentioned riflemen meant considerable to the young shooter just starting in Schuetzen shooting. From Leopold, as well as some of the others, we learned how to prepare and use the proper bullet lubricant, which was far more important back in the old days of black powder than it is today.

Rube Harwood showed us how to prepare the loads for my .25-20 Stevens single-shot rifle. Then later I got considerable advice from data received from F.J. Rabbeth, John D. Kelley, William Hayes and Charles W. Rowland on the finer points of bench-rest shooting. My correspondence with Mr. Rowland continued for over thirty years, up until his death. He was a wonderful man as well as an expert old-time rifleman. Looking over the old records shown in *Shooting & Fishing* will show any of my readers that the above-named riflemen were the most expert rest shooters this country ever produced.

If I have learned anything about bench-rest shooting down through the years to the present time, and I am still shooting, the credit should go to the fine old riflemen who got me started in the right direction.

It is surprising how many of the old methods still give the best results in shooting the modern high-speed, small-bore varmint rifles from the bench. Many young shooters today are using ideas that they believe are modern. Such is often not true. Take the use of sand bags, for instance. From some of the old records we learn that sand bags were in use for bench-rest shooting well over one hundred years ago, under both barrel and stock.

Spectators at some of our local bench-rest matches think the use of sand bags is a modern idea. The same thing applies to the targets we use. Our targets are not exactly a new idea when we find that about the same type of target was used some time before the Civil War. The telescope sight has been used in bench-rest shooting also for well over a century. Some of the early telescope makers later took up gunsmithing, as well. Old Morgan James made telescope sights even before he started making his fine match rifles. I have often examined many old targets that were found in the box that came with a fine old muzzle loading match rifle. If one is fortunate in locating one of these old rifles, he may find the outfit complete, with false muzzle, bullet mould, cast bullets, patches, etc.

These old targets were often fired at 110 yards instead of 100, as is done today, and many targets show the bullets cutting into the one ragged hole.

I have noted quite a change in some of the younger shooters of today. Some seventy years ago the youngster was ready, and we might say, very willing to take each and every bit of advice on shooting that was handed out by some wise old-timers. But today it seems this situation has changed, more or less.

Today, if one attends a bench-rest match and keeps his eyes and ears open, he may find a young shooter who hardly knows the difference from wind drift or bullet yaw, rushing up to the old-timer to try and explain just what is wrong with the performance of said rifle. The way I have it figured, no man can build much of a reputation on what he is *going* to do.

Very often the young shooter will have trouble with the horizontal dispersion of his group. This is quite often caused by only a slight movement (hard to detect) of the barrel or fore-end in the front sand bag at the instant of shooting. This is a common fault, easy to accomplish but hard to discover, since very little movement is necessary to throw the shot out. My own advice to any shooter having this trouble is to use a stock having a wider fore-end, and have it well bedded down into the sand bag. Having used both the old black powder rifles of seventy years ago and the most modern high-speed, small-bore varmint rifles of today, I would say it is a lot easier to make small groups now than it was years ago. This is due mostly to the use of modern components. I hardly believe the barrels themselves are any better than the ones used in the old days, as far as the bore is concerned. But today we have better barrel steel, as well as modern methods of manufacture, unknown in the old days.

Back in the black powder era, low velocity, in many cases barely over 1,200 foot seconds, was common. Mister, one had to hold, in the old days, even after the hammer fell. And with some rifles in larger caliber even the recoil had to be handled the same each time. Today, with the modern varmint rifle, the recoil is a minor matter.

Today, the modern shooter can become expert not only a whole lot easier, but in a much shorter length of time. The art of handloading has advanced very rapidly in the past few years. More shooters are better informed, and also have available far better components than were in use years ago.

One can place an order with any one of several custom gunsmiths, have the barrel of his choice fitted and chambered, and the addition of the proper scope sight, and with the research as regards the components readily at hand, one can have a tack driving outfit. Today this rifleman can expect fine accuracy almost from the first shot fired.

But back in the old days, it never happened that way. One had to do plenty of experimenting to get a new rifle to shoot properly. If we did get a load to shoot well on the first trial, we had a right to get suspicious. No new rifle was supposed to perform like that. Usually it took some time before one got all the components in tune. Then about the time this was accomplished, a slight change in bullet temper or a different lubricant was used and it would require a lot more experimenting. The old-time shooting called for precise methods, but it certainly weeded out those shooters who were even then trying to get by with slip-shod methods. You see, in the old days one never had to worry about the barrel wearing out. Some might worry — or rather wonder — if they would live long enough to get the dog-gone rifle to shooting properly. Understand, it wasn't easy.

Today, it is an entirely different story. One buys a new rifle and a box of ammunition, and it starts to shoot properly from the first shot fired. Naturally, all and sundry are highly pleased. Then we sit down and shoot, not so much for the practice as to show some of the other fellows what a humdinger we just got from, say, Bob Hart. Next we take it out 'chuck hunting, and are amazed at its long-range performance. Then back on the range several nights a week to satisfy ourselves we have the best rifle in four counties, yeah, and can prove it. Then we spend the summer hunting 'chucks. Along in the fall we start getting ready for the benchrest matches, and we note the fine accuracy of our new rifle is falling off. Our tack driver fails to drive any tacks. Next we check over the amount of primers used in shooting the rifle, and are amazed to find we have fired from 3,500 to 4,000 shots through our new rifle.

Now, there is little doubt that our rifleman has had a good time and has enjoyed every shot fired, but to one who has been through the mill, it seems the wise thing to do would be to reserve the *match* rifle for use in *match shooting* only. Have a spare rifle to practice with, or to use in 'chuck hunting. To my eyes, the saddest sight I can imagine is a shooter on the range, just before an important match, with a rifle barrel which has lost its tack hole accuracy. No chance to replace the barrel. That is when a fellow needs a friend.

Now to get back to some of my early shooting, which is what I really intended to write about when I started this article. I soon found in hunting woodchucks with the .22 caliber Stevens that they took considerable killing, unless shot in the head. My uncle had a .22-10-45 Maynard rifle, which took the small centerfire cartridge, and this fine, accurate little rifle was next used on 'chucks.

Right about here it might be well to mention that as a 'chuck rifle, it made a doggone fine little squirrel rifle. Usually, when I did hit a 'chuck anywhere but in the head, said 'chuck very promptly slid back into the hole. The barrel of this rifle fouled badly, due to the small bore as well as the black powder residue left in the barrel after every shot. Thus it required cleaning very often.

At just about this time I was looking for something that would really bust a 'chuck wide open but I did not have far to look.

My uncle owned a very fine old muzzle-loading percussion turkey match rifle, which he was pleased to call his eighty-rod gun. It took considerable coaxing on my part before I was allowed to shoot it from the bench-rest, in his own back yard. He said it was no rifle for a kid to use. (I must have been around eight years old at this time.) He might have had something to back up his argument, as this piece weighed over twenty pounds.

After I was allowed to shoot the rifle from a rest, in his own yard, I naturally had the desire to try it out on a woodchuck. Maybe this idea was fostered by the fact that I knew where a fat woodchuck lived in a cut bank over in my grandfather's cow pasture, not far from my uncle's bench-rest range. Never were better plans laid for a 'chuck hunt than this one.

At first both my uncle and I walked over to the edge of the pasture, to see if the 'chuck was at home. He was, and he promptly slid back into his hole. My uncle had figured the range was some 80 paces, but to me it looked much longer than that. The next thing in order was to rig up some sort of prone rest to hold the rifle. This took considerable time, so the day was almost gone before I was even ready to do any shooting. The very next morning bright and early I was on hand to carry on the hunt. I can remember, even to this day, how I had to wait till the sun had partly dried the dew off the grass, before my uncle even started to load the rifle at the house. First off, he handed me the percussion cap, and told me to hold it till after the rifle had been placed in the crude rest. Next, he wiped the bore carefully, finally blowing down the barrel, to moisten it he said, as well as to see that the nipple was clean. Next he placed the charge of black powder, which I now believe must have been around 80 grains in weight, carefully, in the barrel. The next operation was to place the .40 caliber bullet in the ball starter and seat it into the barrel. Then the bullet was pushed down very carefully on the powder with the rod, the end of which fit the bullet exactly.

With the percussion cap still in my hand we both started for the back meadow. When we arrived the 'chuck was nowhere in sight. The rifle was placed carefully in the rest with the muzzle pointed at the 'chuck hole in the bank.

At about this time the 'chuck came out, probably wondering at all the activity going on across the meadow by one old man and another very excited youngster. Before the hammer was cocked to place the cap on the nipple, the 'chuck went back in the hole. There was nothing to be done then but lie there and wait. Rheumatism had prevented my uncle from taking the prone position I was in, so he soon left and walked back to the house. The rifle had a nice pair of set triggers, which I was careful to set properly, as well as a small aperture rear sight with a fine pin head front sight, that had a shade over it.

I lay there in the hot sun, hardly daring to move, till my neck ached. I was holding that pin head on the entrance to the burrow for what seemed to me like hours. After quite a spell I saw the nose and top of the head of the 'chuck appear, but that was all. I waited and waited till my neck seemed as if it would break. Then another spell of waiting, and finally the entire head was in sight. I still wanted more of a mark, but was afraid I could hold my position no longer. Carefully centering the head, as well as I was able, I touched off that fine trigger. The dirt flew in all directions at the mouth of the hole. The rifle was so heavy I did not mind the recoil.

I rushed over to see the results of my shot, and my uncle on hearing the shot was coming across the meadow. At first, on arriving at the 'chuck hole, I thought I had missed entirely, since the force of the heavy ball had driven the 'chuck back in the hole. When I finally looked down into the hole, I saw a mass of blood and dirt and bone. But I was afraid to reach in after what remained of the 'chuck.

My uncle soon arrived, reached in and got the 'chuck out of the hole. The heavy bullet had struck just under the chin, taking the top of the head off. I was about the most pleased kid in the whole country, naturally, but the real pay-off came later that same evening. When my uncle asked me why I had shot the 'chuck in the head, I told him I had to do it that way for that was all of the 'chuck I could see. He didn't say anything but he looked at me sort of queer.

My uncle had a friend who used to go with him around the country, when they took in the turkey shoots every fall. That same evening while I was present, this friend dropped in for a visit. Never even giving me a glance, my uncle spoke up saying, "Jake, I guess the kid here is going to make a 'chuck hunter after all. He busted one today, plumb center, with my old turkey gun, and he only had the head to shoot at." Old Jake just grunted, but some way I had the idea that I had arrived even if it was some time before I could use the old rifle again, in 'chuck hunting.

I like to believe I really started bench-rest shooting with this fine old rifle that I still have in my possession, for, under my uncle's careful direction, I shot it many times on his own back yard range on the outskirts of town. Of course, before this, I had used a few .22 caliber rifles from a rest, but they could hardly be called bench-rest rifles. I believe I could write quite a volume in describing the rifles I have owned and used down through over seventy-five years of active shooting. Most were good, but some were better, like an old man's Irish whiskey, which he claimed was usually good, but *none* of it was really bad.

I guess I will never forget those good old centerfire Maynard and Stevens rifles with which I learned to shoot. Few are the barrels made today that will equal them.

I would like to give a little advice to the younger riflemen. Whatever happens, don't *ever* sell or dispose of any favorite rifle or shotgun. If you do, the time will sure come when you will regret it to the end of your days.

H.A. Donaldson

## The K-Hornet Story

**November 11, 1968**

Mr. Harvey A. Donaldson
Firearms Consultant
Fultonville, New York

Dear Harvey,

I have been reading your column in the *Handloader* and aware of your work for so long, I hope you won't mind the first name salutation. Your letter about my piece in the *Handloader* No. 16 on the Hornet and Kilbourn improvement is the happiest event of the month. I have known somewhat of the evolution for a long time. If I tell you that I had a Hornet in 1932 and a Lovell .22-3000 in 1935, you'll know that I was early in being quizzical about it all.

While I had known that Kilbourn did not originate the idea of the sharp-shouldered Hornet, I did *not* realize (nor had I ever been informed) the real source or correct background. This information is of great historical importance. So any additional info you wish to write about is most welcome in line with this .22 Hornet story.

My articles come out the way they do because I am an engineer with a good education and have a research inclination and background. I am up-to-date enough to be able to program computers and to understand how to use them.

I can sneak out in the backwoods, too. Time and location have never permitted real hunting. I now own a place in Maine and hope to improve upon that. The kindness of the woods has always appealed to me. Philosophy is easier where the sounds are nature's.

Sincerely,
Ed Yard

## Helen's Restaurant

**November 19, 1968**

Friend Yard,

I'm pleased to hear from you. When Dave Wolfe started *Handloader*, he got in contact with me through our mutual friend John Amber. I have known Amber for many years. A great guy if there ever was one.

John suggested that I write for Wolfe, so I have been at it since the first issue.

I note you mention that you own a place in Maine. That certainly interests me. You see I have been going up to Maine for several weeks each summer, salmon fishing. This has been going on for some thirty years. I make my headquarters at Machias, Maine. I know most everyone in that town. Maine is one state where one does not accept folks as you do in some places. They *accept you*, if you get what I mean, and this doesn't just happen overnight.

Let me give you a little illustration. Several years ago I had occasion to park my car in front of Helen's Restaurant, in Machias. Usually I park back of Helen's in the big parking lot. I walked over to the parking meter and put in my nickel. One of the only two cops in town walked over to me and said, "Harve, you don't have to do that." I asked why not; that is what the meter is for. He said, "Hell, man, I know you and I know your car number. Those damn meters are just for the use of foreigners."

Now as any Maine native will tell you, anyone, no matter who, that was not born in Maine is considered a foreigner. So I sort of figured I had arrived.

Thanks for your nice letter. I sure hope our trails will cross this coming summer. Guess I'll be busy writing for both the *Rfile* and the *Handloader*; the new editor wants a lot more on the early days of rifle shooting, when shooting was not as complicated as it seems to be today.

Sincerely yours,
Harve

Yours truly No. 18

# *Bullet Casting Is An Art*

**December 3, 1968**

Friend Neal,

This letter has to do with the art of bullet casting. Make no mistake about it, casting a bullet that is fit to shoot IS AN ART, if it is done correctly.

For quite some time I have answered a lot of questions by mail, much of it dealing with casting bullets. Some shooters complain that their moulds are no good, when the fault was with the operators of the mould.

I know that the bullet moulds available today are a lot better than those we had to use sixty years ago. In some of the old moulds the hole was so far off center that it was difficult to get the bullet out of the mould. Before we could get a mould to work properly it was necessary to ventilate it on the two faces with an engraver's tool. Others had the sprew hole larger than necessary, which forced the lead to one side, making an oval-base bullet. Another common fault was in the size of the mould blocks; they were so small that it was hard to keep them hot enough to cast a perfect bullet.

Today those errors have been corrected. We can buy a mould with both faces vented, and if it is used correctly it will cast a perfect bullet right from the start. The one thing a shooter should remember is that while he can buy a good mould, he can't buy the necessary skill to use it! I know some shooters who have been casting bullets for years, have had trouble, and all they have done is *repeat* the same mistakes they made at the start, over and over again.

When a shooter tells me his mould is no good, I have to tell him to check his operations, which are usually at fault. No one can learn to cast a bullet as it should be cast by reading instructions out of a book. You must get the proper feel, by long practice. Every operation has to be *uniform*, including the way the mould is handled.

No one can expect to make a good bullet if the dipper is full one time and only part full another. A full dipper, if used properly, will force the air out of the mould the *same* each time. But unless the nose of the dipper is held correctly to the sprew hole the *same* each time, and the mould is then turned from the vertical to the horizontal the *same* each time, good bullets will not result.

Some shooters make the mistake of enlarging the sprew hole in the cut-off, with the idea they can get more lead in the mould each time. The fact is, these sprew holes in their original state are often a lot larger than necessary, or as I like to have them. I have often made a new cut-off with a smaller hole, for certain size bullets.

If a person hurries to take the dipper from the sprew hole before the lead has had a moment to harden, and the sprew is cut off, the lead at the base of the bullet is pushed to one side and you have an oval base on that bullet. This is easy to do but hard to determine, as too few shooters take the trouble to check the bullets as they should.

One thing I have never been able to understand is why a shooter who is new to bullet casting will brag about the short time it takes him to cast a hundred bullets. I have seen a lot of these speed merchants, but sad to relate I never yet saw one of them that could cast a perfect bullet.

One time a fellow who made a business of casting bullets that were used by a police force in a large city, sent me some of his samples. He said he had cast several million bullets in his time. When I looked over the samples I wrote him that I figured it was about time, with all that experience, that he should at least send me some that were fit to shoot. I never heard from him again.

Speed in bullet casting is the last thing to consider, for anyone who expects to make a perfect product.

For years I have used a wooden club to knock off the sprew. This club is loaded with lead in one end so it makes for a better balance, and a very light tap will cut off the sprew.

With practice one can tell just by looking at the lead in the melting pot when it is at the proper temperature for making a good bullet. If the surface of the lead turns blue, the mixture is too hot. You can use beeswax as a flux and it is well to keep your mixture of lead and tin well stirred. The tin, being lighter than lead, will work to the surface, but if the mixture is well stirred and the surface kept *clean,* you will cast a better bullet.

One should never place a cold mould into the melted lead to heat it up, nor should the melted lead be poured over the mould. Never under any circumstances put any hard metal in contact with the inside of a mould. This advice should hardly be necessary, but you would be surprised how often it is done.

When you are through with the casting operations, the mould should be allowed to cool before it is wiped off with an oily cloth. My own practice is to put a light coating of oil inside of the mould, and then I leave a bullet in the cavity. This prevents a wasp from filling the mould with mud.

Never, under any circumstances, do any work around a pot or kettle of hot lead without wearing a pair of safety glasses (unless you wear glasses) at all times. The time may come when you will have a serious explosion, (as with water falling in the pot) with the hot lead flying all over the place. If you play it safe you will prevent a serious injury.

And another thing — if you add lead or tin from time to time, to keep the melting pot at least *half full,* be certain that there is no moisture on any of the metal put in the pot.

I should go into the use of the cast gas check type of bullet. They were designed to prevent the hot gases from melting or fusing the base of the bullet. I personally like the Hornady gas checks on my bullets, for they stay on the bullet better than others I have used. A lot of shooters write telling me about their experiences with the use of gas check bullets and I have been surprised that about nine out of ten insist on the use of high velocity loads with these bullets. "Why" is more than I can understand.

All of my own shooting experience has been devoted to obtaining the utmost in the way of accuracy, above everything else. Of course, I have been able to obtain high velocity in some of my own experimental cartridges, and in some instances with less powder than others had used, but this was just incidental, and not a regular practice.

One may drive gas check bullets much faster than the plain base cast bullet, but I always figured if a shooter wanted to drive them to the limit, he might better use metal case bullets. A great many years ago I discovered one fact that has helped me a lot in my own shooting. Every bullet ever made, regardless of its caliber, weight, material or design, has only *one proper velocity* at which it will deliver its best accuracy. Once you find this velocity you are on the road to accurate shooting.

Right now I am going to stick my neck out and make a statement that some of our readers will find hard to believe. My long experience in shooting matters has allowed me to determine simply by looking at or holding a bullet in my hand, just what velocity that bullet may be driven to have it give the best accuracy. The twist of the barrel, of course, has to be considered, as well as the design or form of the bullet, together with the caliber and weight.

As an instance of this, only last June at the matches held on the Pine Tree Rifle Range in Johnstown, New York, a shooter walked up to me and asked, "Harve, what load would you suggest that I use with this bullet?" It was a round nose gas check bullet in .308 caliber.

After looking the bullet over, I told him the load and type of powder to use. Some time later I got word from him that the load I had suggested had given him the best accuracy he had ever been able to get with that particular bullet.

In a later letter I will write more about some of my own experiences with different types of lead bullets.

Very truly yours,<br>
Harvey A. Donaldson

## Knocks 'Em Silly

**December 26, 1968**

Dear Friend Neal,

Just now, during the Christmas Holidays, I am more or less rushed with a lot of things that require my attention. I believe I am ahead on my letters for the *Handloader*, so after the New Year, I'll try to come up with something for the *Rifle*.

We are having a lot of real cold weather the last few days. Around 16 below this morning, and only a few miles north, up around the Fulton chain of lakes, it was exactly 42 below. We have all sorts of weather here in the Mohawk Valley. One has to be rugged to take it. A lot of folks go to Florida, but you have to go through a hard winter to really *enjoy* our summers.

I'm glad to know you got in some shooting at the Remington Farms in Maryland. We have a lot of ducks in this country, but I very seldom hunt them anymore. When my supply of duck feathers used in my fly tying gets low, I go out and get a few teal and wood ducks.

I sure hope that you and Dave have a Happy New Year. Tell Jim Carmichel that on account of the Flu Bug going around here that I am taking a very pleasant medicine. No less than Jack Daniel's old No. 7. That sour mash product from old Tennessee. If it don't kill them it will sure knock 'em silly.

Best regards,
Harve

## Mad As A Hornet!

**Date Unknown**

Dear Editor:

How you could clutter up so many pages of a fine magazine with such hogwash as Edward M. Yard's comparison of the Hornet with the K-Hornet is beyond my comprehension. The Hornet was forced out of the picture by the Remington .222 in 1950, so why not put articles in your magazine of interest to many more reloaders than a cartridge that is almost becoming obsolete?

Yard may be a fine technical man but there are still a few old-timers around that have fired just a few thousand rounds from a K-Hornet that can tell him that the regular Hornet isn't in the same league with the K. I hope that Lysle Kilbourn did not read this article before he crossed into the Great Beyond last October, God rest his soul. As a great writer of one of our leading sporting magazines once wrote me, "Lots of people here in the East throw rocks at Kilbourn but his theories and work is tops in my book."

Lysle Kilbourn chambered my Model 70 Hornet for the K-Hornet in 1940 and with 13 grains of 4227 and Sisk 41-grain Super Lovell bullets (.223), it was so far ahead of the Hornet that the Hornet couldn't see it for dust. In 1950 my Model 70 became a K-.222 Remington, the first .222 in this part of the country; had to wait quite a while for ammo before I could fire it. Some few thousand rounds went up the spout in the old 70 and it is now a K-.222 Magnum and still shoots rings around the average .222 Magnum sporter with over 10,000 rounds having blown out of this old 16-inch twist, undersized barrel.

Now, when you publish articles like Yard's, low-rating one of the finest developments for we po-boy varmint shooters and Lysle Kilbourn's developments, as a finer man never ground a reamer, it is time some of we old-timers cancel our subscriptions and start reading something else.

J.T. Stewart
Houston, Texas

# Don't Scare Easy

**January 3, 1969**

Dear Neal,

Find enclosed my letter to this character from Texas who complained about the article by Ed Yard. Hope I have covered it properly. If you can spare the time, it might be well if you made a copy of my letter and sent it to Ed Yard. I hope there will be a reply from Stewart. Some of us old-timers don't scare very easy.

Best regards,<br>Harve

# Sticking His Neck Out?

**January 3, 1969**

Mr. J.T. Stewart
Houston, Texas

Dear Sir:

I have read with more or less interest your letter. It just happens that I knew Lysle Kilbourn ever since he got out of school. From where I'm sitting I would say you are sticking your neck *way out* when you complain about the article that appeared recently in *Handloader* by Ed Yard. This man Yard knows his stuff, make no mistake about that.

For your information I used a bottleneck cased Hornet rifle some time before Kilbourn ever saw one. This rifle was made by Risley, the gunsmith from Hubbardsville, New York. This same Risley happens to be the man that made all of Kilbourn's reamers.

I note the load you used in your own K-Hornet rifle: 13 grains 4227 and the 41-grain bullet. Right here you have raised the question as to your own experience as a varmint hunter. We fellows here in the East who do long range chuck hunting would never think of shooting such a light weight bullet for long-range shooting. Sure, I know, you get a high muzzle velocity, but out where the chuck is sitting it is a different matter. Out at two hundred to three hundred yards the 55-grain bullet is the one to use. Muzzle velocity, alone, never killed a woodchuck.

Now, I doubt very much if any of you fellows out in Texas can show any of us here in the Mohawk Valley anything about chuck hunting. Mister, it was here in the East that varmint shooting was invented. I can show you some of the old records where the early settlers hunted chucks with the Kentucky rifle over two hundred years ago.

A lot of shooting was going on in our country when Texas was a howling wilderness. Our city of Albany was settled around 1612, which was before the Pilgrims landed in 1620. And this Mohawk Valley was settled right after that. Sure thing, Texas is a big state, but still it just happens to be a country where one can see *farther* and still see *less* than in any state I have ever visited. *Period.*

Very truly yours,<br>Harvey A. Donaldson

## Graphite Wad Letters

**January 6, 1969**

Dear Harvey,

Your column about a year ago on the use of graphite wads has generated more interest among our readers than any other subject. I've sent you quite a few of these letters, and there are three more on my desk. In view of the fact that you are "fed up" with all the letter writing, why don't you do a "Yours truly" column on these wads? It would save a heck of a lot of correspondence with our readers.

We are right on a deadline, so I've gotta cut this short. Longer letter later!

Best regards,
Neal

## Reprint 1936 Article!

**January 12, 1969**

Friend Neal,

Your letter of the 6th just arrived. What did you do, send it Camel Express?

Mister, all those questions about my graphite wads are getting out of hand. When I wrote about the wads in the March, 1936, issue of *Rifleman*, I had a lot of letters to answer. Why don't you just get permission and reprint that old *Rifleman* article?

As it is right now, after every issue of *Handloader* comes out I get from ten to twelve letters from your readers. Why in hell don't they write to you? It is simply impossible for me to handle all of these letters.

Enclosed is a label from a box of IPCO Colloidal Graphite Wads. The IPCO means Industrial Products Co., and the address is Box 14, Bedford, Massachusetts. Note carefully that I use .046 thickness. I now use these wads, since it is quite a job making them up. They are made to my formula.

Now, where the hell is my check for the last issue of *Handloader*?

Best regards,
Harve

*Editor's Note: This letter to Neal was found in Harvey's files. While preparing this book, we called George Martin of the N.R.A. and received permission to reprint the March, 1936, article, and a follow-up on the same subject in June, 1936, by Seeley A. Wallen. Readers will of course be aware that certain companies named are probably now nonexistent, and the products no longer available.*

**Reprinted from** *The American Rifleman,* **March, 1936**

# *Graphite Wads*

### By. H.A. Donaldson

We are told by some writers that the .22 Magnum and .220 Swift rifles have only a short barrel life, due to the erosion of the powder gases. This need not be so if the shooter will use graphite wads in preparing his ammunition; and I am surprised that the Winchester Company is not doing this in loading ammunition for the .220 Swift.

Ever since the appearance of these modern .22-caliber high-speed loads I have received from shooters numerous letters concerning the barrel life of the new rifles, and I am surprised that some riflemen are not better informed as to the use of graphite wads. I will give my method of preparing and using them, for it is just possible that more chuck hunters would use these modern high-speed loads if they knew how to control erosion and barrel wear through the proper use of these wads.

The use of graphite wads is by no means a new idea, the late Charles Newton having used them with his first experimental .22-caliber high-speed loads more than twenty-five years ago. The heavy charges of Lightning powder that he used, together with the primers of that time, gave excessive erosion in his small-bore rifles, just in front of the chamber.

There is shown herewith a picture of Mr. Newton's first — and the original — .22-caliber Krag rifle, which was made sometime between 1910 and 1911. For years this rifle was used with a load of 34 grains of Lightning powder and a 70-grain bullet, a graphite wad being interposed between powder and bullet. And at this time, after years of hard service, I find the barrel of this rifle to be in excellent condition.

In testing some new powders last fall I made several small groups with this rifle at 100 yards, using modern components, and that barrel can still make one-inch ten-shot groups at 100 yards. Which should give a fair idea of the effect on barrel life of proper use of graphite wads.

I also know of another rifle, in .25 Krag caliber, that has been used for over twenty years with Lightning powder and graphite wads, the barrel of which is in fine condition. I could mention several other .22-caliber Newton and Niedner high-speed rifles that have seen hard service in the hands of woodchuck hunters who used graphite wads, the barrels of which are even today in fine condition.

I will first give the method of using these wads that we employed when using Lightning powder back in 1910. The object then was to prevent metal fouling as well as erosion. The material I used at that time was Oildag paste, made by the Acheson Oildag Company, of Niagara Falls. Oildag is a mixture of Deflocculated

Acheson Graphite and mineral oil. Deflocculated graphite is graphite reduced to a practically molecular fineness by a process invented by Dr. Edward G. Acheson. This deflocculated graphite is believed to be in the finest state of subdivision possible to attain. There is no other graphite so fine; and I may add that it is an electric-furnace product, of the highest purity.

With our old method, before shooting it was necessary to cover a swab or patch with Oildag paste, and wipe the bore thoroughly with it. After this we would blow through the barrel a few grains of Acheson graphite No. 1340. To do this conveniently an empty cartridge case was used. The primer pocket was drilled through and a small brass tube soldered in the hole, a piece of rubber tubing being slipped over the brass tube. A few grains of the powdered graphite was then placed in the empty case, and the latter inserted into the rifle chamber. By blowing through the rubber tube a thin coating of graphite was deposited over the entire surface of the bore, in addition to the coating of Oildag. This would avoid shooting the first bullet through a dry barrel.

Then in loading the cartridges, after putting the powder into the case, one thickness of Leopold's Nitro Olio wad was placed in the mouth of the case, and was pushed down 1/16 inch with a tool made for the purpose. This 1/16-inch space was then filled with Oildag paste, and another Olio wad pushed down on top of it. This left the graphite between two wads which prevented it from coming into contact with either the powder or the base of the bullet; and the paste would keep soft indefinitely. Leopold's Olio wads contained some graphite, as does the Ideal banana lubricant now made and sold by Lyman, graphite being one of the best-known lubricants, and highly heat-resistant.

We thought that by this method the lubricant made a more perfect gas seal, and that more uniform lubrication throughout the whole length of the barrel was obtained than by lubricating the bullet. But more important still, perhaps, was the fact that the barrel just in front of the chamber where erosion usually begins, was protected by a thin film of lubricant. For it is at this point that the hot gases from the powder strike, being directed by the shoulder of our bottle-neck cases. I would not advise anyone to use a cardboard or felt wad under any high-speed .22-caliber bullet; in fact, no wad should be used that will not melt instantly. For any wad that will not melt completely has the same effect as added bullet weight, and will cause the pressures to mount rapidly. Adding weight to a bullet by means of a wad may seem to some like a small matter; however, we have found that in .22-caliber high-speed loads a very slight addition to the weight of the bullet runs the pressures up out of all proportion to the added weight.

Capt. G.L. Wotkyns and Mr. J.B. Sweany both used cardboard wads as gas checks in their development work on the .220 Swift, and they found that the use of such wads built up pressures to such an extent that powder charges had to be reduced two grains. It might be thought that this was because of the gas-check effect, but such was not the case. Wotkyns and Sweany also found that the card-wadded loads had somewhat lower velocity, and gave nearly two inches more drop at 200 yards than did the loads without card wads.

The tests made with my own .226 Krag rifle indicate that the graphite wads have not increased the pressures at all, which is accounted for by the fact that these wads melt and are blown to atoms almost instantly.

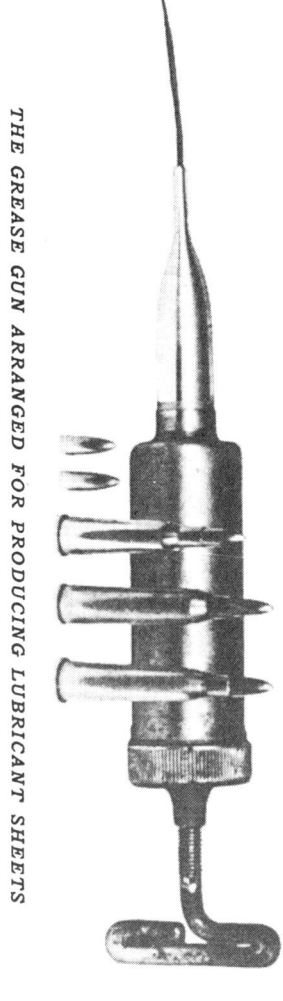

THE GREASE GUN ARRANGED FOR PRODUCING LUBRICANT SHEETS

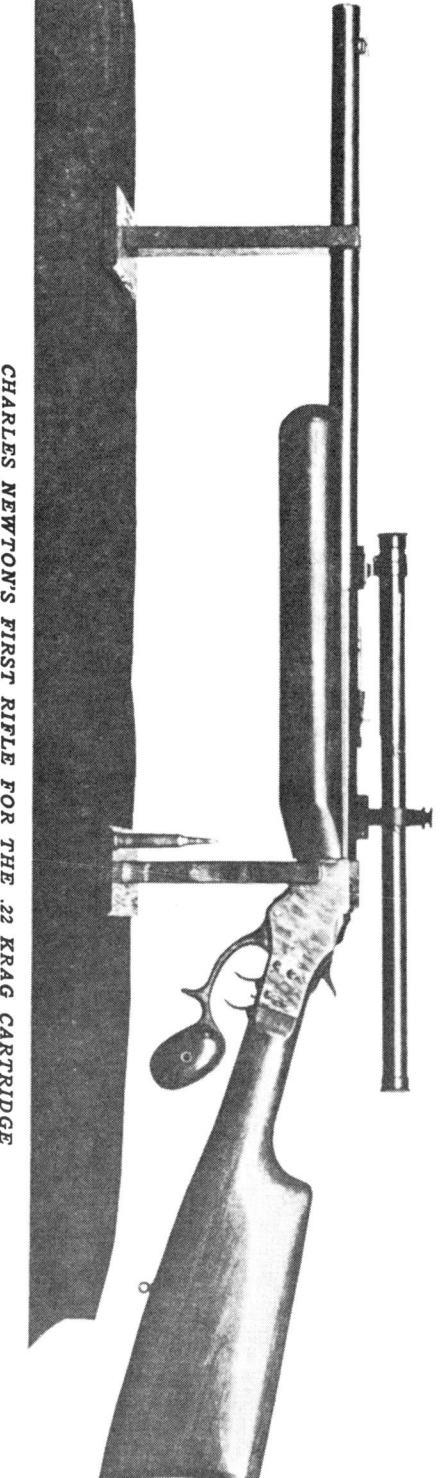

CHARLES NEWTON'S FIRST RIFLE FOR THE .22 KRAG CARTRIDGE

There are several ways to make graphite wads. One old method was the same as that used at one time by dentists in preparing dental wax. This was, first, to melt the lubricant in a deep container. A long round bottle was then filled with cold water, and the outside of the bottle coated lightly with any fine oil. The melted lubricant was then stirred up well to thoroughly mix the ingredients, and the bottle dipped into it and promptly removed; which left a coating of lubricant on the outside of the bottle. If the coating was not thick enough the bottle was dipped again.

A cut was then made with a knife through the lubricant around the ends and up one side of the bottle, and the lubricant peeled off in a sheet. This was done as soon as the lubricant had hardened enough to handle, as otherwise it would crack too much. It was sometimes necessary to fill the bottle with cold water each time it was used, to keep it cold enough to work properly.

The sheets of lubricant as made by the cold-bottle process are simple and easy to use. After the powder has been placed in the case a sheet of lubricant is pressed down over the neck of the case, leaving a wad of it in place ready for the bullet to be seated. And the wad stays in place and will not drop down onto the powder. Putting a previously cut wad into the neck of a small-caliber case is a mean job, but the above method does away with all this. There is no oil or grease in the wads that can melt and spoil the powder in any way.

Mr. A.O. Niedner, who made up some of the first .25 Krag rifles, always recommended using a wax-graphite wad in loading this fine, accurate case when Lightning powder was used. His own formula was two heaping teaspoonfuls of graphite to four ounces of Japan wax. I found this mixture quite hard and brittle, so at one time used two ounces of graphite to four ounces of beeswax and four ounces of Japan wax.

I have a dozen or more of Harry Pope's lubricating pumps for applying grease to the long tapered bullets used in several of my Schuetzen rifles. At one time it was possible to buy the lubricant for these pumps in stick form ready for use, but later it became unavailable and I was forced to make my own. I made it to Leopold's formula, and then formed it into sticks by forcing it through a round tube of the correct size, fitted to the end of an Alemite grease gun.

For some time I have been trying to devise a better way to make sheet lubricant than the cold-bottle method, and after experimenting with several different formulas for lubricant I have gone back to the use of the Alemite gun; the idea for which I really got from the tube of tooth paste. This method works so well and is so simple and easy that I am going to pass it along to the readers of *The American Rifleman*. To "tool-up" for the job a piece of 3/4-inch brass tubing was threaded to fit the end of the Alemite gun, and the other end reamed out to a thin edge with a taper reamer. This end of the tube was annealed by heating red hot and plunging into cold water; and was then put into a vise and the edges pressed nearly together. I took a piece of 1/16-inch flat stock, and closed the edge of the tube down on this. With this pump I can easily prepare my graphite wads in sheet form, the lubricant coming out in a flat ribbon 1/16-inch thick and nearly one inch wide.

The grease gun is loaded by pouring the melted lubricant into the cylinder. The lubricant should be allowed to cool somewhat, for if used too soon it will squirt out in liquid form. When of the proper consistency it can easily be forced out into a long, thin sheet that is easy to handle and use. I keep a supply of the thin sheets stored away in waxed paper; and a good supply can be made up in a short time when the lubricant is working properly. The lubricant left over from a sheet after the wads have been cut should be kept in a clean container, and later used again. One of the advantages of this method of preparing graphite wads is that it allows of more complete mixing of the graphite with the other ingredients. With the cold-bottle method the graphite tends to settle to the bottom of the deep container.

The formula that I am now using for my graphite lubricant in sheet form is: two ounces of rosin, four ounces of beeswax, three ounces of Japan wax, two ounces of tallow, and two ounces of No. 38 Grade Unctious Acheson Graphite. If the lubricant seems too hard, use one ounce less of Japan wax or add an ounce or two of tallow. Wads of this material will hold their position in the case neck, will not run in hot weather, and will not crack or crumble in cold weather.

I have used these graphite wads in my .22 Niedner Magnum, .25 Niedner Krag, .220 Winchester Swift, .22 Newton Krag and in my latest .226 Krag; and none of these barrels show any signs of wear or erosion, though my rifles are in use nearly every day.

My one idea in writing about the use of the graphite wad is to answer the many inquiries I have received concerning them; and I feel sure that more shooters will use these wads when they realize how easy they are to prepare. I see no reason why anyone should hesitate to own and use the accurate new .220 Winchester Swift through fear of short barrel life; and the same applies to the .22 Niedner Magnum. My friend J. Bushnell Smith uses graphite wads in all of his high-speed .22-caliber loads.

In the photo of the grease gun are also shown cases for the .22 Magnum, .220 Swift, and my own new .226 Krag; and I would call attention of woodchuck hunters to the bullets in these cases. They are the new Sisk 55-grain Express Magnum bullets, of the very latest design. They are made with only a tiny pin-point of lead exposed at the tip, and I have found them to be very accurate. They will not shed their jackets at high speed.

*Note — We have been advised by Mr. Donaldson that he is receiving a large number of inquiries regarding Schuetzen rifles, special methods of preparing ammunition, rest shooting, etc. All these matters will be covered in future articles by Mr. Donaldson, who asks that readers wait for the articles rather than writing him direct as Mr. Donaldson is a busy man and has no time for a large correspondence. — Editor* (American Rifleman)

**Reprinted from** *The American Rifleman,* **June, 1936**

# Concerning Use of Wads
## By SEELEY A. WALLEN

Referring to Mr. Donaldson's valuable article in the March *Rifleman* on the preparation and use of lubricated wads, the results of some experiments that I have made along similar lines may be of interest.

Experiments made prior to and during the last deer season in this state with a system like the one Mr. Donaldson describes caused me to conclude that the presence of a graphited oil in the bore during zero weather was decidedly undesirable from the standpoint of accuracy, and to suspect that it might even be dangerous if the loads used were maximum for the rifle. On a careful re-check of these notes, I consider that the experiments were not sufficiently extended to constitute proof, but they were highly suggestive. No doubt someone of the *Rifleman* family is in a position to state positively what the facts are in this case. Certainly most riflemen do not do much outdoor work in zero or sub-zero weather, but performance facts related to such temperature would be useful to Pennsylvania deer hunters.

For the few riflemen who load and reload cases that are straight, or nearly so, inside, and who use charges of powder that do not fill the case, seating a cardboard wad of about .025 inch thickness firmly (but without crushing pressure) on the powder insures much greater accuracy than can be obtained with the powder loose in the case. Certainly unless the loaded rifle is held, uniformly, muzzle-up or muzzle-down, and tapped, prior to each shot.

The use of considerably heavier dry cardboard wads will not be found to produce the results that might logically be expected in all cases. Unquestionably, lowered velocity and increased breech pressure could reasonably be anticipated in any instance, and I don't doubt that both factors would appear with some loads. However, a whole series of careful tests has shown conclusively that the same velocity with slightly decreased breech pressure is obtained by using two cardboard wads of a total thickness of .109 inch, with *five percent less powder* when using certain No. 80 powder loads in the .28-30. Using equal powder charges with the heavier wads would undoubtedly increase the breech pressure — probably to an unsafe degree with the loads in question. The wads used weigh about 1.4 grains, and the increase in velocity would hardly appear to be due to gas checking, the cast bullets used being at least .002 inch above maximum groove diameter.

These tests were made in the hope of securing improved accuracy, but the actual improvement was so slight that the practice was abandoned as an unwarrantable inconvenience. Some use might be found for the expedient as a substitute for gas checks where the load used was hot enough to call for the latter.

Subsequently a considerable series of experiments were made with the same rifle and heavy loads of No. 80 to determine the effect of using an .027 inch dry wad soaked in hot tallow (also in hot tallow and paraffin) at the base of the bullet. Object: to avoid progressive fouling of the bore, which had built up heavy pressures after the first five or ten shots with these loads and the rather soft cast bullets used. For this purpose the idea proved entirely successful. This wad, lubricated, weighed 1.6 grain; dry, .8 grain. In other respects it did not prove satisfactory. In some loads the breech pressures were noticeably (though not dangerously) increased, and, in every case, muzzle velocity was sufficiently decreased to show a higher trajectory by from 1 to 2 inches in shooting to 200 yards. Accuracy was of course greatly improved by — or with — this securing of uniform breech pressures.

The same wadding, substituting the lubricated .067 inch wad for the .28-30 gas check — weight 4 grains — ahead of a decidedly full D1204 load, gave results very similar to those of the gas-check load, but there were no indications that the lubricated wad shot cleaner than the gas checks. Considerable use of an .042 inch lubricated cardboard wad, as above, in addition to the gas check, on such D1204 loads has failed to show any measurable differences in breech pressure or muzzle velocity compared to identical loads without it. The loads using it deliver slightly better groups as to accuracy, but the improvement is barely noticeable.

Mr. Donaldson's present method seems certain to be the one best adapted to the purpose of preventing erosion from hot loads, but whether it is the plan most likely to obviate fouling in shooting cast bullets at the highest speeds and in the softest tempers practicable, I do not know. Nor do I know whether any procedure which resulted in graphited lubricant being left in the bore would be desirable in extremely cold weather.

The method used in determining approximate breech pressures in the tests I made will show a difference of less than two per cent with reasonably full charges of powder such as those used, but I have never seen it described. Cases are sorted closely as to make and number of times fired, miked one-quarter inch below rim, and separated into lots of the same diameter within .0005 inch. The average expansion of ten or more on firing will show definitely what load was used. Bad fouling in the bore shows up in case expansion, as well as in inaccuracy, of course.

While rather a nuisance, classifying cases in this way results in very definite increase in accuracy in addition to permitting determination of breech pressure as compared with other loads in the same rifle. I do not believe this would work so well in extra tight chambers. Where there is from .002 inch to .004 inch tolerance at the point measured, and a reasonably full load is used, average expansion for the same load will not usually show as much as .0001 inch variation, considering of course case lots of the same original size and quality. Naturally, smaller lots will expand more, though not up to the average after-firing size of larger ones. Comparative muzzle velocities were obtained (or closely approximated) by careful and extended rest shooting for trajectory to 200 and 300 yards.

Yours truly No. 19

# A 'Master' Crow Hunter

**February 16, 1969**

Dear Neal,

I wonder how many of our readers have heard of Ray Weeks, of Tillsonburg, Ontario, Canada. Ray was one of the greatest crow hunters that this or any other country ever saw. He was a salesman, working for an insurance company out of Toronto. I am pleased to state that I am more or less responsible for starting Ray off on his crow shooting career.

If readers will go back to the Dope Bag pages in the *American Rifleman,* edited by Fred Ness during the middle 1930s, they will learn that Weeks managed to bag from 4,500 to 5,500 crows every season.

But let's go back a few years to understand just how he started his crow shooting. Ray had read some of my articles in the *Rifleman* during the early 1930s on the results I was getting with a couple of varmint rifles. One day I got a letter from him. He said he was interested in my shooting and asked if he could visit me and see just how some of these rifles performed. This was in the middle of the winter, but I told him I would be glad to have him come at any time.

At that time I was living in Little Falls, New York, here in the Mohawk Valley of New York State. He arrived on a cold day around the middle of January. At this time I was shooting a very accurate Winchester single shot rifle with a twenty-power scope, chambered for the .22 Niedner Magnum case. It was at about this time each year that I started my own crow shooting.

The farmers would haul manure out in the fields on the snow, during January and February, and I believe they still do this. One could find crows in most every field. My method was to cruise the back roads. When crows were sighted I simply kept going for a couple hundred yards, stopped, and got out on the opposite side from the crows. Shooting was done from the top of the car with sand bags. My scope had a tiny dot in it, and was sighted to shoot dead center at two hundred yards. I might mention here that this particular rifle was accurate enough to keep ten shots on a postage stamp at two hundred yards. But that was what it took, if you were serious about your crow shooting.

As far as I know the crow is the only bird that will *always* face the wind when sitting on the limb of a tree. This gives one some idea where to hold under windy conditions. I have never seen the feathers blow up on a crow's back. A hawk or owl may face in any direction. At least this has been my experience.

At times I have killed crows out at two hundred fifty yards, even when there was quite a wind blowing. All you do is use the size of a crow's body as the measure, and hold say half the width or less of the crow's body into the wind . . . and you have a dead crow. Crow shooting, like bench rest shooting, takes a lot of practice, and one has to learn the path of the bullet. All this comes with a lot of shooting. Another thing — only have one *crow rifle*, and use it for nothing else. It is hard enough to learn *one* rifle, and just where the bullets are going; if you switch rifles you are lost.

But to get back to friend Weeks. He finally arrived on a cold day about the middle of January. Right off Ray figured it was too cold and windy for crow shooting, but I told him that crows had to eat and that we would find some of them along the back road pastures. I also told him if he learned to kill crows when the wind was blowing, he could kill them most any time.

To make a long story short, I managed to kill around a dozen crows, but what interested Ray the most was that I only had one empty case for each crow. The average shots were around a hundred fifty yards, but I got one (a sentinel sitting up in a tree) that Ray paced off at over two hundred fifty yards. I wanted Ray to try my rifle but he said it was so cold he was satisfied to just be an observer, on that occasion.

We had a good day's hunt and a long visit the same evening and I was glad to explain to him all he wanted to know about the right outfit for crow shooting.

I believe Weeks was shooting a rifle chambered for the .22 Hornet. Then he went to a rifle, or it might have been the same one, chambered for my 2-R case. Next he went to another rifle that was chambered for .219 Donaldson, and I believe it was this same rifle with which he later made his best records. When the writer started the bench rest movement, as we know it today, at Johnstown, New York, back in 1947, I invited Weeks to attend. He was on hand along with a couple other friends and we had another good visit.

After his return to Ontario I was glad to furnish Ray with whatever rifle barrels he was interested in. We both had a mutual friend in Niagara Falls, New York. I would ship the barrel to this friend and Ray would cross into the U.S. and pick it up. We exchanged letters for quite a while, and he kept me well posted. I was able to bring his crow shooting results to the attention of Fred Ness who then wrote it up for the *Rifleman*, I used to hear from him for a time, and then the letters stopped coming.

Now we come to the present time. It just happens that I drive a Chevrolet sports car. I believe it was last year, or the year before, that I was in the Chevrolet garage in the town west of here, where I buy my cars. While waiting for some minor repairs to be made to my car, I noticed another Chevrolet pull into the garage. What attracted my attention was the Ontario license. A fellow stepped out of the car and asked about getting some attention.

He then stood waiting, and I walked up and said, "I note you are from Ontario." He said, "Yes, I live in Toronto."

When I told him I only knew one man who lived in Ontario, he asked who. When I told him it was Ray Weeks, he said, "My gosh, it IS a small world, after all." He handed me his card, and I noted he was the manager of a large insurance company located in Toronto. He then told me that Ray had passed away. He said Ray was his best salesman, and he could not at first understand how I knew Ray so well.

Then I handed him my card, and he was surprised again. He said, "Why, I have often heard Ray speak about you. I believe you were the one who started Ray in crow shooting."

We then had a good visit and I managed to find out just how friend Weeks was able to kill so many crows each year. This fellow said that Ray's job was to go around the country collecting insurance payments. He spent about all of his time on the road, covering a large part of Ontario.

He carried a rifle and ammunition with him on all of his trips, and as there were plenty of crows in his territory, he was able to rack up quite a score each season. Ray kept a careful account of all of his shooting.

I was sorry to learn that he had passed away, but that did explain why I no longer heard from him. Strange things do happen now and then; the above account was one of them.

Yours truly,
Harvey Donaldson

*Harvey takes aim at a woodchuck? This photo was found in his personal effects and one of very few items not identified as to date, place or equipment used.*

Yours truly No. 20

# 6mm Cast Bullets on 'Chucks

March 17, 1969

Friend Neal,

I enjoyed the article in *Handloader* No. 18, "Cast Loads for the Sixes" by Jim Carmichel. To show you that there is little really *new* under the sun, let's go back to the year 1900.

We have before us a copy of Winchester Catalog No. 62 of October 1898. On Page 56 we read as follows, "The 6mm U.S. Navy rifle. This gun is known as the Lee Straight Pull Rifle and has been adopted as the small arm for use in the U.S. Navy. The caliber of this gun is 6mm, and it shoots a smokeless powder cartridge, with a hardened lead bullet, having a copper jacket, plated with tin, and giving an initial velocity of 2,550 feet per second. The magazine holds five cartridges, which may be inserted separately or at one time, in which latter case they are placed in the magazine in a pack, held together by a steel clip.

"The point-blank range of this rifle is between six hundred and seven hundred yards, within which the trajectory of the bullet is so flat as to make the entire range a zone of danger, and at a range of a thousand yards the bullet rises at the highest point in its trajectory only some twenty feet. At a distance of five feet from the muzzle, the bullet gives a penetration of sixty 7/8-inch pine boards or a half-inch of steel plate.

"The superiority of this rifle over all other types of bolt gun lies in the fact that the operation of opening and closing is by a *straight* pull, instead of the customary up turn and pull back."

This old catalog gives the list price of this rifle at $32.00, but I bought my own rifle in this caliber in 1900 and I remember it cost me only $25.00 wholesale. Now we turn to an old *Ideal Handbook,* put out around 1900 and on Page 97 we find listed bullet mould No. 244203. This was the correct cast bullet as designed by the Ideal Company for use with this 6mm rifle. They would furnish moulds to cast

*133*

either the sixty-five or ninety-five-grain bullets. I bought the ninety-five-grain mould, and very soon had a good supply of *hard* cast bullets on hand. I cast the bullets a lot harder than the usual type of .32-40 bullets used in my Schuetzen rifles, since for some reason or other I thought this was necessary.

Next we read what the Ideal Company had to say about this No. 244203 cast bullet: "These are the only cast bullets that are correct for the 6mm U.S. Navy rifle. The sixty-five grains for short range and the ninety-five grains for medium range." Then they go on to mention that they have made over 25,000 in the sixty-five-grain weight for the U.S. Government.

Now we turn back to this last *Handloader* article, "Cast Loads for the Sixes," and we learn that Jim cast his bullets of hard metal, and also that his handloads will be used on woodchucks.

Before we go any further on this tale, I want to give you my own experience of back around 1900, when one H.A.D. was also hunting woodchucks with the 6mm U.S. Navy rifle. My rifle had only the open sights furnished with the rifle, and I had sighted it in to shoot center at a hundred yards.

I remember the first chuck I ever shot with this rifle as if it were only yesterday. My cases were loaded with the hard cast ninety-five-grain No. 244203 bullet. The chuck was sitting up, at around a hundred yards and looking right at me. I held just under his chin, and that is where the bullet went. The chuck tipped over dead, without a move, so I was highly pleased with the first kill made with that rifle.

When one stops to consider, even a .22 Long Rifle bullet placed under a chuck's chin would kill as quickly, but I did not think about that at the time. Soon after this I killed several more chucks at from a hundred to a hundred fifty yards but these were shoulder shots, and I saw the chucks had moved some after they were hit. I returned home from this hunt highly pleased with my new chuck rifle.

To show my readers that one cannot tell very much about any rifle on simply one hunting trip, I want to record what happened on my next chuck hunt with the same outfit.

On this trip I was unable to get any shots at much under a hundred fifty yards and some were at two hundred yards. On the first chuck I had a broadside shot at maybe one hundred sixty yards. The wind was strong from the left, I held as I figured back of the shoulder, the chuck dropped at the shot, then got up and ran about twenty feet or so and got in a hole. I thought that was funny, not seeing any dirt fly at the shot. I was sure I had hit that chuck. I saw no drops of blood anywhere, which set me to thinking. I sure wanted to *examine* that woodchuck.

Near where I had shot at this chuck, I had seen part of a roll of barbed wire fencing. So . . . I had to resort to the old-time chuck hunter's trick of twisting a piece of that barbed wire round and round down into the hole until I had managed to get the barbs stuck in the hide. Then I was able to drag it out of the hole. The chuck was dead, all right, but I had one heck of a time finding a bullet hole. At last I found a tiny hole where the chuck had been gut shot. Where the bullet came out the hole was no larger than the place it had entered. This performance caused me to sit down and do some more thinking. Maybe I didn't own such a *good* chuck rifle after all, at least for gut-shot animals with a hard bullet.

I soon figured what I wanted was a softer cast bullet that would open up better, for long-range shooting. I went home and ran off a lot more bullets with the metal cast one to twenty. I also placed a piece of bank-note paper (same as used in patch bullets) across the point of the bullet, between the halves of the mould blocks, which of course divided the point of the bullet, to insure it would expand on contact — another old-timer's trick with cast bullets.

When my loads for this 6mm rifle were used with these split-nose bullets made from a softer mixture, I had no more serious trouble with gut-shot chucks. I have always been sorry I disposed of that old Winchester 6mm Sporting Rifle. It gave very good accuracy, with the open sights used at that time.

After reading over my own experiences with the hard cast bullets in a 6mm rifle, do you wonder if I question the use of those hard cast bullets friend Jim writes about in the recent issue of *The Handloader?*

Of course, if he is able to hit his chucks in the eye — yeah, either eye — he may make out all right. We have to take this matter into consideration. I'm willing to give that old ridgerunner from down in Johnson City, Tennessee, the benefits of any doubts, for who knows, he may be able to do just that kind of shooting.

With this in mind I would like to invite friend Jim to come up here in the Mohawk Valley this spring, and try some of our brand of chuck hunting. We can show him woodchucks so wild they even fight the foxes, and they don't come wilder than that anywhere.

Yours truly,<br>
H.A. Donaldson

Yours truly No. 21

# Point Shape vs. Accuracy

April 3, 1969

Friend Neal,

In my letter in No. 18 *Handloader* I mentioned that in my own experimenting I had found that each particular point shape of a bullet had a corresponding speed at which it will produce its best accuracy. In the same letter I also mentioned that I would, in a later letter, give other experiences with different types of bullets.

As an illustration of this I would like to mention a small incident that happened in the early days of bench rest shooting. This was in the summer of 1948. My friend Sam Clark, Jr., of Oakland, Maine, had written that his father was having trouble getting accuracy from some bullets he was making in a Biehler and Astles swage. It seems his dad had made up a lot of soft-swaged bullets, but the jacket was left rather blunt at the point — not as pointed as Sam and I were making them. I might mention that he was shooting them at the same velocity as Sam's pointed bullets.

When I had a chance to examine the bullets I saw right off what the trouble was, for at one time I had also tried such bullets in my own experimenting. When I wrote to Sam and suggested that they try the same bullets in loads giving around 3,200 fps velocity, they soon found that the blunt point bullets gave as good accuracy as their pointed ones.

Sam was so interested in this one feature of bullet making that he wrote an article, which was published in the first edition (1949) of National Bench Rest Shooters Association year book, *The Ultimate in Rifle Precision,* edited by Col. Townsend Whelen. I would like to quote from this book. On Page 45 we read:

"I am fully convinced that the point shape of a bullet has very little to do with its accuracy. Fred Huntington tells me that while Capt. Wotkyns was assisting him with the design and construction of his bullet dies, the matter of the relationship of point shape to bullet accuracy was quite thoroughly explored and found to be unimportant.

"Harvey A. Donaldson has, however, clearly stated that each particular point shape has a corresponding *speed* at which it will produce its best accuracy, and this is the point at issue.

"In order to fully demonstrate this matter I have shown in the illustration thirty consecutive shots fired from one of my .219 Donaldson Wasp caliber rifles, at one hundred yards. These fifty-five-grain bullets used in making the groups were formed in the same B & A swage, but in each group the point of the bullet was altered. This variation was obtained by filing the points and it will be noted that the bullet used in making group A is blunt, having in fact only one eighth of an inch of its point left. And yet *its accuracy is superb,* ten shots grouping into one-half inch. On the other hand the one used in group B has a full length point just as it came from the bullet swage, yet the result is only fair by comparison.

"Finally the bullet used in group C is the normal RCBS bullet as made in the Huntington swage, by soft swaging, and the accuracy is *less* than a half-minute of angle. The approximate velocities used in making each group are shown and this is fully in accord with Donaldson's theory as has been stated above. Therefore, in selecting a bullet swage it would be well to consider its point shape only according to the velocities at which the bullet is to be fired, and also according to its requirements in bucking the wind. The selection of a long, sharp point shape will result in far better sustained velocity over any given range and hence less wind deflection. These factors mentioned above will probably be sufficient to enable the shooter to select the bullet swage he desires either for varmint shooting, or bench rest shooting, or a combination of both."

Right about now might be a good time to tell more about my friend Sam Clark. Here was a shooter's SHOOTER, if I ever saw one. I first met Sam through correspondence in the early 1930s.

It seems he had read some of my articles on Schuetzen rifles, and shooting, in the *American Rifleman*, and he was interested in learning how to cast bullets for Schuetzen rifles. This has resulted in a long correspondence on shooting matters. Sam was then living in Trenton, New Jersey, and was a close friend of Al Marciante. This results in both he and Al paying me a visit at my home.

Soon after this Sam returned to his home near Waterville, Maine. Not many shooters will buy a six-hundred-acre farm just to have a place to shoot, but Sam did. The farm was a mile or two outside of the small village of Oakland, Maine, some five miles from Waterville, where Sam's dad had a coal business. Sam soon set up several rifle ranges on the place. Fortunately he was so far out of town that his shooting both day and night never bothered anyone.

He had one range near the house, with a bench rest right near the back door. Then another one hundred and two hundred-yard range in a patch of second growth hardwoods, out of the wind. Here he built a shooting hut with bench rest inside. This hut was heated and had a cot in it. The range could be used at night

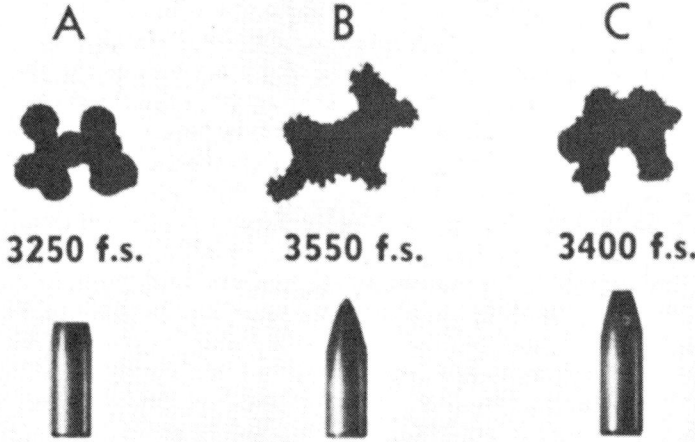

*Each particular point of bullet has a corresponding velocity at which it will produce its best accuracy. We can state the kind of powder and the weight of charge that will give a certain weight of bullet a certain muzzle velocity. But the charge that will give that bullet the best accuracy depends on the bullet form and on many other factors, and can be determined only by experimental firing at the bench rest.*

for it was rigged with lights, both in the hut and near the targets. We shot there many nights during the summer, and often around midnight we made our best groups. This is the best time to shoot — all is quiet, no wind, and when the dew is falling the powder burns at its best. Later, when Sam began shooting a rifle chambered for my .219 case, he had a one-hundred-yard range built that was all underground, including shooting bench and targets. To do this he had to sink three hundred feet of heavy thirty-six-inch tile. We had some trouble at first with the mirage caused by heat in the shooting house and near the target butts, but we soon licked that problem with some electric fans. A lot of tiny groups were fired on this range. Later still, Sam wanted to take up fifty-foot smallbore shooting. I told him that all it took was a lot of practice. With this in mind he built an indoor range right in his home.

Some of my readers may not understand just how farm houses are built in the state of Maine. First they build a house, then they attach an addition, next they attach a summer kitchen, the wood shed comes next and the barn itself is attached to the wood shed. All of these buildings are fastened together. At one time I asked an old resident of Maine just why they built houses in that way. He said, "By gad, if you lived up here and put in one of our Maine winters, you would hate like hell to go *outdoors* to the wood pile."

With this arrangement a farmer does not even have to go outdoors to feed and water his stock in the barn. Sam cut a square hole in the partitions between the rooms so he could stand in his gun room and shoot down the range to the fifty-foot target, and he used to fire fifty shots every night.

That this practice paid off is a matter of record. He made a possible of 500 out of 500 at fifty feet, a record that still stands. Those who know Sam and his shooting will tell you that he is one of the most expert off-hand shots in the country.

Sam lived only about three hundred and fifty miles from my home in New York State. I used to visit him several times every season. After working all day in the machine shop, I would take off around 11 p.m. with no sleep and drive to his house in my Corvette sports car, without stopping, and arrive at Sam's around 7:00 or 8:00 in the morning, just in time for breakfast. And what a breakfast — pancakes and sausage, with real maple syrup, country fried potatoes, and hot blueberry muffins, with plenty of hot coffee.

I have tried to coach Sam in his shooting ever since he paid me his first visit. The bench rest records show that at one time or another Sam held the world record for ten shots at one hundred yards, two hundred yards and three hundred meters.

I feel quite certain that the time spent with him was well worth-while. As I write these lines Sam is living in Florida, and putting in his time playing golf. If he does as well with golf (and I understand he does just that), his partners are going to know they are in a *ball game*.

In a later letter I will try and give some of the trials and experiments that Sam and I carried out on his home shooting range. These experiments cover over twenty years, so it will take a lot of writing.

Yours truly,<br>Harvey Donaldson

# Wife Dies at Age 82

**July 23, 1969**

Dear Neal,

I have been busy this last spring with matters that gave me little time for letter writing. I sent you a letter in April, and will get another one off later this month that you might use in the next issue of Handloader.

Sorry it took so long to get this column on the way to Peoria. It is a sort of follow-up to the last letter. Hope it will meet with your approval. When I can quote on data shown in the *Rifleman* I like to do so, as many of our readers have the old copies of that magazine. Yours Truly has *every* single copy of the *American Rifleman*.

Also, when I make any statement in my writing for the *Handloader*, you can bet I have the data to back up that statement.

Sorry to have to mention that my wife died unexpectedly last Wednesday at the age of 82. We had been married for 65 years. So you can see my own household has been more or less upset ever since. I'm feeling O.K. myself, as to health. Working in machine shop every day. Don't have an ache or pain of any sort and I am as active as ever. I don't know what it means to get tired.

I may go to Maine for my annual salmon fishing in a few weeks so I wanted to get these two letters out in time for publication.

Yours truly,
Harve

*Portrait of Harvey and his wife taken in 1913.*

**Yours truly No. 22**

# Behind the .220 Swift Design

**July 23, 1969**

Dear Neal,

This letter deals with the .220 Winchester Swift. I have read some recent articles telling about the short life of Swift barrels. All this really amounts to is that certain writers are copying data that was written some thirty years ago.

I have no fault with the young writers of today, other than that they should at least *know* what they are writing about before it is shown in print. One does not learn everything over a few weekends. I never did believe that the simple purchase of a hunting license made a man an experienced deer hunter. It takes plenty more than that. Same with writing about shooting matters.

My own experience with the use of a .220 Swift rifle has been carried on over thirty-five years. I doubt if there is another shooter in the country that has had more experience in the use of this rifle. First, let's go back to the month of May, 1935. If my readers will look over a copy of the *American Rifleman* of that date they will read the first article on the Swift, written by Fred Ness. This article caused quite a sensation among the shooters of the country. Here was a 'chuck outfit that delivered 4,000 fps velocity. It is not generally known today, but Col. Townsend Whelen had a great deal to do with the actual development of the .220. Whelen was a very modest man, as many readers know.

Capt. G.L. Wotkyns is given credit for the case design, but the writer *knows* much credit also should have been given to Col. Whelen.

Wotkyns wanted to use the .30-06 case necked down to .22, but that did not work out. Let me quote from a letter from Whelen, written to me at that time: "This long .30-06 case cannot produce the efficient results that can be obtained with a smaller capacity case. Nor will it produce uniform velocities, because high loading density is an inescapable requirement, and in this big .30-06 case such density will mean a big waste of gas, a loud report, and added recoil and muzzle blast."

Col. Whelen knew that I had designed a case for the Savage Arms Company, when they were located in Utica, New York. This was back in 1916, less than a year after the .250-3000 case was placed on the market. My case was the .228-

Two of Donaldson's designs are, left, a cadmium-plated sharp hollow-point made by chamfering the inside of the jacket and used in his .220 Swift, and, right, the two-diameter .228-250 bullet.

250, (not a .22-250). All I did was obtain a barrel from Savage in .228 caliber — the dimensions of the barrel Savage was using at that time in the .22 Hi-Power rifle. A barrel then cost only four dollars and they were good ones, at that. We used the seventy-grain Savage bullet. Later, to cut down on the pressure, I used the two-diameter bullet, in this weight, made in a swage that made a two-diameter bullet. This was an idea I had copied from Dr. Mann, but it worked out OK. Some time later, when I showed these bullets to the Savage people, they started making their own in this caliber, in two-diameter. I am sending one of these bullets along with this letter.

But to get back to my .228-250 case design, all I did was neck the .250 Savage case down to .228 caliber and have my .228 Savage barrel chambered to take the case. This barrel, by the way, was fitted to a Model 99 Savage rifle. I wanted Savage to chamber their rifles to take that case; however, they told me it was a good design, but if they chambered a rifle for it, it might spoil the sale of the .22 Hi-Power.

This is all water over the dam, so we will get back to the design of the .220 Swift. Col. Whelen knew about my experimenting with the .228-250 case, so he had a rifle made up and chambered for my early case, only it was the .224-250.

When he and his experimenter friends tried out this new design, they found that a charge of thirty-six grains of 3031 and the forty-six grain open point Hornet bullet gave *exactly* the same penetration in a steel plate, at sixty feet, as did the same slug in the .30-06 case necked down, and loaded with forty-five grains of the same powder. With the fifty-one-grain pointed bullet, it took forty-four grains of the same powder in the long case to equal a thirty-six-grain load in the shorter case. They found out, way back in 1934, that the *size* of a big case, in itself, doesn't mean a thing.

With the .219 Donaldson-Wasp, I used the small capacity case, rather than a larger one. I might have used the Zipper and left it full length, which would have saved a lot of work, but when I found in my own tests that the shorter case gave a higher velocity, I figured to let well enough alone, and have never been sorry.

When you design a case that burns *all* the powder, you have got something, but

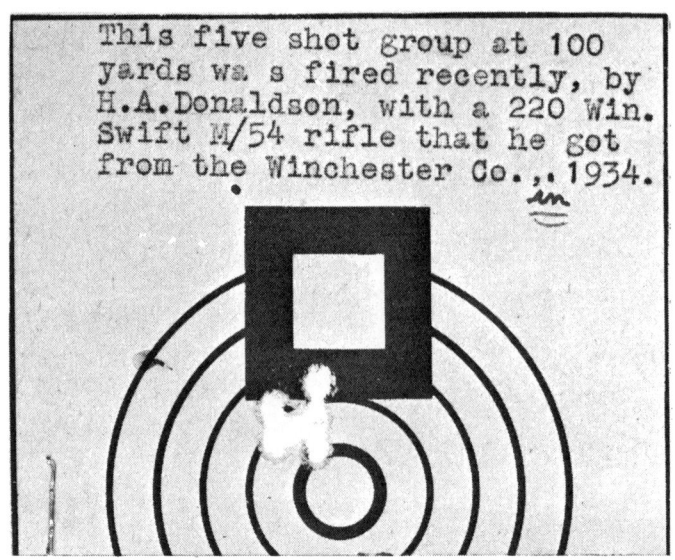

when you shoot a rifle taking a larger case, the shooter himself has one hell of a lot to learn about shooting.

Most of the above data has been taken directly from data furnished in letters from Col. Whelen, years ago.

So back again to the early .220 Swift case design. After all the experimenting was finally turned over to Winchester, they came out with their own .220 which was more or less of a compromise — and so it remains to this time.

A year or two before any .220 Swift rifle was available, and while only a few pilot rifles had been made, Col. Whelen got in touch with Edwin Pugsley, the V-P of Winchester, and suggested that a rifle be sent to me for testing from a bench and in chuck shooting. Very soon this rifle came along, made up on the Model 54 action — for this was before the days of the Model 70. Winchester later gave me this rifle, which I still use in hunting. Whelen said I was the first one outside of the factory to use the new rifle, so that is why I believe I am more qualified to write about it than someone who started shooting only last year.

I might mention that this early Swift has accounted for several thousand woodchucks. Along with this letter is a five-shot one-hundred-yard target shot with the same rifle, where only recently I managed to put five bullets into the one group.

In my next letter to the *Handloader* I will be pleased to tell how it is possible to get longer life out of any rifle barrel, and to have it give fine accuracy over the years. The life of any barrel is entirely up to the one who uses it. I mean, of course, the way the rifle is used, or misused.

Yours truly,<br>
Harvey A. Donaldson

Yours truly No. 23

# Barrel Life in the .220 Swift

September 7, 1969

Dear Neal,

This letter will about complete my series on the .220 Winchester Swift rifle. For the past thirty years most writers, when giving an account of this rifle, have mentioned its short barrel life. Actually, there is no more truth in this than in many other statements we read today in some magazines devoted to rifle shooting.

The simple fact of the matter is this: the life of any rifle barrel depends entirely on how it is used. If one insists on the use of maximum loads in the Swift, and sits down at a bench and fires a long series of shots, until the barrel heats up, he can expect short barrel life. This can be done with most any rifle, even the .30-30 Winchester.

But on the other hand, where the rifle is used for 'chuck hunting, where only a single shot is fired now and then, the barrel does not heat up. Also, if the shooter will use my own type of graphite wads in every load that is fired, he can expect longer barrel life, regardless of the caliber of his rifle.

In a recent letter of mine to the *Handloader* there was shown a five-shot hundred-yard group from my first .220 Swift, received thirty-five years ago from Winchester. This rifle has accounted for over several thousand 'chucks, so it has had plenty of service. Every shot ever fired from this rifle was protected with graphite wads.

Right from the start, the .220 Swift was given a bad reputation for a short barrel life by riflemen who knew very little about rifle shooting. Thus, down through the years this report was mentioned time and again — very often by writers who had never even owned a .220 Swift rifle, let alone had any actual use with it. As was mentioned in my previous letter, I received a Model 54 Winchester rifle chambered for the .220 Swift case some time before these rifles were available over the counter.

When this pilot rifle was received I found that it had a twenty-six-inch barrel with the sixteen-inch twist. The ammunition that came with the rifle was loaded with a short, blunt-nose open-point bullet, of forty-eight grains.

Some time after I had used the rifle, both in 'chuck shooting as well as from the bench, the Winchester company wrote and asked for a report on my experimenting. I told them that I was pleased with the performance of the new rifle, but that I had a few suggestions to make.

I told them to forget that short, fat forty-eight-grain bullet, as I had found that it did not carry well out at the longer ranges. Then I suggested that the twist of the barrel should be fourteen inches instead of sixteen. This would allow the use of bullets of fifty-five to sixty grains, having the long, sharp point for long-range hunting.

They did change the twist to fourteen inches, but they continued to use a short, fat open-point bullet, but in fifty-six grains. While this rifle and cartridge were designed for varmint hunting, the riflemen then, even as they do today, decided that it was just the rifle for long shots in the open, for both deer and antelope hunting. Very soon after this, reports came in from all over the country of instant kills being made with this rifle, even out at three hundred yards. Back issues of the *Rifleman* carry many of these reports.

I soon found I was getting better long-range accuracy from some of my own designs of the long pointed bullet, as I found they carried a lot better than the blunt nose Winchester bullet. The bullets of rather poor design that the Winchester company brought out for 'chuck hunting were a handicap in this cartridge.

As soon as the 'chuck hunters around the country began to use the better designed bullets in fifty-five and sixty grains, reports came in of four hundred and even five hundred-yard kills on 'chucks.

The .220 Swift has accounted for a very large amount of game down through the years for which it was never intended. I know personally of three different good-sized bear being killed with only one shot from this rifle. And on each occasion, the game was killed instantly. But I never could make myself believe that the Swift was a big game rifle.

It was, however, about the best all-around 'chuck rifle available, as many of my readers fully understand, and it also was in use for bench rest shooting for a number of years.

Now we come down to the more recent years. I believe it was late in December of either 1963 or 1964 that I got word from Winchester that there would be no more .220 Swift rifles available after the first of the year. Of course this meant that I really had to obtain one of them in the Model 70, with the heavy twenty-six-inch barrel. I wrote to the company but received word that they had none in stock. They advised that I contact some jobber who might still have one.

I lost no time in contacting my friend E.H. Sheldon of Norma-Precision. He reported that they still had a couple of the guns I wanted, so I had him send one at once.

This second Winchester Swift, now standing my gun rack, is a good one. It has the long heavy special steel barrel and a heavy stock of very hard, dense grain black walnut. I have a new Lyman scope in twenty power on this rifle, and it is certainly a tack driver. When I hunt 'chucks that live "way out yonder," this is the rifle I now use.

A number of years ago my friend Sam Clark and I found that if we wanted to reduce the error in the sight picture, when we were bench rest shooting, we had to use a *small* aiming point. After some experimenting we came up with the idea of a tiny round ring for hundred-yard shots. With this target we use a scope of twenty or twenty-four power having a tiny dot on the crosshairs.

It is a simple matter to center the dot in this small ring target, and it definitely reduces the error in the sight picture. All one has to do is to have the group point off to one side of the target. If you fired directly into the tiny ring, the shots would at once spoil your sight picture. We have used this type target for a number of years and have never had an occasion to change the design. Hope I have explained the way this target is used.

Years ago the old-timers used to hold on a single bullet hole in a target, to make a small group, but they used a special aperture front and rear sight. And I might add it took a man with better than normal eyesight to do the shooting.

When I first used the Model 54 Swift sent to me by Winchester, my best high speed load was with forty grains of 4064 and my own fifty-five-grain pointed bullet. This, understand, was in a barrel having the sixteen-inch twist. Bullets used were cadmium plated, to reduce barrel wear and friction. Very soon I found I got better accuracy with thirty-nine or even thirty-eight grains of 4064, and my fifty-five-grain bullet. This load has been used down through the years. With my new Swift I use thirty-six grains of 4064 powder, the No. 120 Winchester primer, and my fifty-five grain bullets in a barrel having the fourteen-inch twist.

A number of years ago I wrote up my experiences with the use of my own brand of graphite wads for the *Rifleman*. It seems I have mentioned them so much recently that it might be well if I wrote another article about these wads for the *Handloader*.

I know quite a few of the older riflemen who have used the Winchester .220 Swift on all sorts of small game with good results. They, together with the writer, were sorry to learn that the Winchester company had stopped production on this fine caliber.

It may be that the younger riflemen of today never knew a good rifle when it was available, so sales fell off and production stopped. So the .220 Swift, together with that good .358 Winchester are off the market.

I can honestly say that after over seventy-five years of active 'chuck hunting (and I am still shooting 'chucks), that the most accurate rifle I have ever used for four-hundred-yard shots, with maybe the possible exception of the .30-338 Winchester, has been with either my own .219 Donaldson case or the .220 Swift.

The time may come when some other company other than Winchester will see the light and place this very accurate rifle in production again.

Yours truly,<br>
Harvey A. Donaldson

## NBRSA Adopts Rifle

**September 17, 1969**

Dear Harve,

I've only got time for a short note. We just finished *Rifle* No. 6 — it doesn't seem possible that that one fills out a year.

By now you've heard some of the story about our visit to Kansas City and the NBRSA Nationals. Knowing that *Precision Shooting* was in financial trouble, Dave and I made a proposal to the Board that they adopt *Rifle* as the official publication of NBRSA and that we add an eight-page section to *Rifle*. We thought that we would be "planting the seed of an idea" and didn't expect anything to come of it for a year or more. However, the Board of Directors leaped upon the idea and immediately adopted us, authorizing and instructing Ray Speer as president to sever the ties with *Precision Shooting* and sign a contract with *Rifle*.

I am well aware of the stir that this has caused in the Northeast, but hope that this can be worked out without too much hard feelings. At the shoot at Hart's range last weekend, a meeting was held and apparently the majority threatened to withdraw if *Precision Shooting* is dropped and *Rifle* is adopted. It is my understanding that Ray Speer has sent a ballot to the members of the Board, asking them if they wish to reconsider their vote. If they do, so be it.

Being the official publication of NBRSA would add to *Rifle's* prestige, but the relatively small amount of increased circulation we would get as a result isn't a big financial deal. In fact, it will cost us more to produce that eight-page section than we would get out of it — at least for quite some time to come.

Our hope is that we can, through promotion in *Rifle's* relatively large circulation among advanced shooters, increase the NBRSA membership both for our benefit and for NBRSA's. The organization has stayed about the same size for several years, but we honestly think that we can help it grow. We aren't going to lose any sleep if the NBRSA directors decide to renege.

Since you are acknowleged as the Father of the National Bench Rest Shooters Assn., you might consider doing a column on the history of bench shooting. We might do a feature article in *Rifle* on the subject. Please give this some thought.

Best regards,
Neal Knox

# Col. Whelen & the .257 Roberts

**December 20, 1969**

Friend Neal,

In one of my recent letters I mentioned that Col. Townsend Whelen was largely responsible for the design of the .257 Roberts cartridge. I though I had better explain a little more about this matter, just in case some of our readers might have wondered about my statement.

To keep the records straight, turn to Page 12 in the January, 1935, *American Rifleman* — an article "Vacation Echoes" by N.H. Roberts. Quoting from this article:

"As many of our readers know, the .25 Roberts case was designed by my friend F.J. Sage, and myself, with the assistance of our mutual friend, A.O. Niedner, of the Niedner Rifle Corporation. Before tooling up for this cartridge Mr. Niedner was advised by Col. Whelen, Mr. L.C. Weldin, ballistic engineer of the Hercules Powder Company, and also one of the ballistic engineers of Frankford Arsenal to make the slope of the shoulder of the new cartridge case on an angle of 15 degrees, as this lesser angle would greatly reduce the pressure developed by the cartridge with the smokeless powder then in use. Thus it will be seen that the .25 Roberts cartridge was designed by, or in accordance with, the ideas of our best ordnance experts and ballistic engineers.

"For the first year or two after the .25 Roberts cartridge was designed, the barrels for it were made by the Niedner Rifle Corporation only. However, early in 1930 the superior accuracy of this cartridge induced Griffin & Howe to tool up for it, and furnish barrels and rifles in this caliber; and they have since made a large number of these rifles for their customers."

Now I will turn to some of my correspondence with Col. Whelen, written at the time they were working on the .25 Roberts case. At that time there were plenty of Winchester single-shot rifles available, and since this action was a favorite with Roberts he wanted to use a cartridge with a rim, so it might be used in this action. Both Whelen and Niedner advised against this idea. Whelen wrote that his idea was to use the .30-06, cut it off 1/4 inch and neck it down to .25 caliber.

I then wrote Whelen and told him as long as they were thinking of using the .30-06 case they might better select the 7mm Mauser case, which was of the proper

*Yours truly No. 24*

length, and it might save them a lot of extra work. Whelen then wrote that I had come up with a good idea and that they would use the 7mm case.

I firmly believe that most of the early experimenting on this case was done by Col. Whelen. Whelen had the experience and the time for this work, as well as the use of the Springfield Arsenal and its ballistic engineers (or was it the Frankford Arsenal?). Our old friend Whelen at different times was in charge of both of these arsenals.

Now let's go back nearly seventy years. I first met Ned Roberts when he was teaching school in a business academy, located in Gloversville, New York, only a few miles from my home. This was around 1900. He had heard from a mutual friend that I was a rifleman, so he called on me at Fultonville. Thus started a friendship that continued up until his death. He used to come down from Gloversville and I would take him chuck hunting.

Ned Roberts, like Teddy Roosevelt, was bothered all his life with poor eyesight. On these early hunts I could never get him to shoot at a chuck. I would do the shooting and he would lie down beside me and check the shots through my spotting scope. For many years when he took his vacation in the summer months he would visit me and we spent many days chuck hunting, or shooting on my range. He was very interested in my collection of Schuetzen rifles, and in his writing for the *Rifleman* during the early 1930's he wrote about my rifles and showed prints of some of them.

He had the free use of my files when he wrote his book on "Cap Lock Rifles." Ned made a few errors in this book, for there were a number of things about these guns he did not fully understand.

In the early days Ned attended a number of important rifle matches, but this was as an observer since his poor eyesight prevented him from doing much actual shooting. In the early days of bench rest shooting on our Pine Tree Range at Johnstown, New York, Ned was usually on hand. I remember he would pass down the line looking at the targets posted on the Wailing Wall, and he would tell me how sorry he was that Harry Pope was not around to witness some of the targets the fellows had made when shooting a rifle chambered for my .219 Donaldson case.

When I lived in Little Falls, New York, Ned and his wife spent a couple of weeks during summer vacation at my home. Ned and I spent many days chuck hunting, and at the range. His interest was more with the old Schuetzen rifles than with the more modern rifles I was shooting at that time. I well remember one instance at my range, involving a very accurate .32-40 Schoyen-Ballard Schuetzen rifle that was once owned by Charles Rowland. At the hundred-yard range I had a pile of railroad ties with wall board on the front to hold the targets. Directly in front of my targets were several daisies in full bloom. I had already started a group when Ned, who was looking through the spotting scope, spoke up quickly. "Let's see you hit that honeybee on the daisy directly below your target."

All I had to do was place the crosshairs on the bee; the next shot spattered the bee on my target. Ned jumped up and said, "Wait till I tell Abel Merchant that I saw you pick off a honeybee with your Schoyen rifle at a hundred yards. He will never believe me."

Abel Merchant was a mutual friend living in Nassau, New York. If Roberts could have seen some of the shooting I was doing with my .219 Donaldson Wasp a few years after this, he would have been more surprised. On several occasions, with the use of my good .219 Wasp, I managed to hit an ordinary house fly that walked along the face of the target at a hundred yards.

When my friend Sam Clark was doing the shooting, these flies were really in danger, for it was very seldom that Sam ever missed a fly. If some of my readers will note the small groups that are today posted on the Wailing Wall of most any bench rest match, they will understand that hitting a fly at a hundred yards is a very simple matter.

During his life Ned Roberts witnessed many rifle matches, and he reported these matches for the several magazines that were at that time devoted to shooting matters. Since his passing I have missed his pleasant visits every summer, but I still have the memories of the many days we spent together chuck hunting.

Yours truly,<br>
Harvey A. Donaldson

Yours truly No. 25

# *The Bigger, the Better?*

February 1, 1970

Friend Neal,

This letter has to do with some of the wonderful things we read about today in the various magazines devoted to shooting. The *wonderful* part is the simple fact that much of the information is far from accurate. I have often wondered what such riflemen as Col. Whelen, A.O. Niedner, Dr. Mann and a host of others I might mention, would have to say if they could read some of the articles that have appeared recently.

About all I have been able to learn is that most modern writers on shooting matters seem to have the idea that the larger the cartridge, the better it is. This isn't true, never has been, nor do I believe it ever will be.

The young shooter of today, in reading the magazines, gets the idea he should start with a MAGNUM rifle, so of course the bigger it is, the better. The simple fact that no beginning shooter would be able to handle such a rifle never enters his mind. Next, after he obtains such a rifle, he starts his reloading operations, and not being satisfied with factory ballistics, studies the maximum loads as shown in the handbooks, and goes UP from there.

About the time this shooter gets around to sighting in his new magnum from the bench, he learns about something we call recoil. This matter of recoil will usually prevent him from getting any sort of accuracy, and if and when he starts to do any offhand shooting, he finds that he is unable to hit anything with his new rifle.

I have always believed that one had to learn to creep before he learned to walk, and I believe this certainly applies to shooting. If more modern-day riflemen would buy their first rifle in such a caliber that they could handle successfully, their progress in shooting matters would have a much better result.

But let's get back to this idea of a big cartridge, or one having the maximum charge of powder, regardless of caliber. It is what any cartridge of any caliber will do with a *medium* amount of powder that counts. The shooter of today will have a hard time learning this simple fact from reading the data as shown in our modern books or magazine articles on shooting.

It takes considerably more than a few years experience in shooting matters to learn about this. I know a number of riflemen with twenty to thirty years of rifle shooting who have yet to discover this simple fact. I had to learn it the hard way, in my own shooting.

A lot of so-called experimenters, who should know better, will take a factory cartridge, change the chamber with the help of a new reamer, so as to change the shoulder angle or to shorten the neck, so the case will hold a couple of grains more powder. He calls the result an "improved" case. But does he really *improve* the original design?

Now, if this same experimenter were really smart, with many of the cartridge designs now available, he would have the new reamer made for a design that would hold *less powder* than the factory product. This, in most cases, would produce more efficient performance.

Maybe right here would be a good time to tell my own experience back around 1930, when I was working on the design of the case known as the .219 Donaldson-Wasp. I had been shooting a very accurate rifle made by Niedner and chambered for a rimmed .22 caliber case. At first I experimented with a couple of designs that were made up from the .25 Remington rimless case. I had several good Winchester single-shot double-set trigger actions, with the Pope speed action (and still have them), so when the Zipper case appeared, I started working with this case.

My first design called for a case having only a twenty to twenty-four-grain capacity. This worked out okay, but then I decided I should try several case capacities to see which one was really the best. My next step was to get a new reamer made for a case holding from twenty-six to twenty-eight grains of 3031 powder. The new reamer was run in the chamber, and this called for considerably more shooting. When testing this rifle by shooting into steel plates, I found it would shoot through more steel than the first design.

But the most remarkable thing about this second design was that it gave the finest accuracy I had ever obtained. Then again I got to thinking: while I am at it, why not see if a case with more capacity would be better still. But something told me not to change, in any way, this rifle that gave such remarkable accuracy. So I left it as it was. This rifle now stands in my gun case, the first .219 Donaldson-Wasp ever made.

I took another Winchester action and fitted it with a .22 barrel chambered for the Zipper case left full length and expanded the same as the Improved Zipper. Again, all this called for a lot more shooting and experimenting.

I had had no trouble shooting through half-inch steel plates with the twenty-eight-grain capacity case, so you can imagine just how surprised I was when I found the larger case, holding several grains more powder, would not shoot through the same steel plate!

This bothered me until I realized I had *not improved* the second design at all. The few grains more powder that was used in the larger case were not fully burned behind the fifty-grain bullets, so I had really reached the limit of powder that would burn properly with the twenty-eight-grain capacity case. Finally, when all the tests were finished I was able to fall back on the second design as the finished product, knowing it was the most efficient design of the three I had tried, and so it remains to this day.

It all simmers down to the fact that the Improved Zipper design was no improvement over the second design simply because it held more powder. So with this experience in the medium capacity case we are able to say that at times it is not extra grains of powder that count, as the average shooter would easily believe. What counts is the case and charge that proves most efficient. When you arrive at this point you have obtained a load that will give the best in *accuracy*. I might add that only when the modern-day handloader understands this matter fully will he begin to produce accurate shooting ammunition.

There are hundreds of riflemen who have had a good accurate rifle chambered for the .219 Donaldson-Wasp case, and then with the idea of making it even better, have had it made over into the Improved Zipper. All they have done is spoil a good rifle. But when you contact these same riflemen, you usually find that their own experience in these matters is so vague that they do not know the difference. I might also add that such shooters do very little testing on their own. Shooting into or through steel plates has opened the eyes of a lot of experimenters.

Just to give one instance, I was visiting a gunsmith friend that lived in a small town some thirty miles south of my home, here in the Mohawk Valley. I had my good .219 Donaldson-Wasp rifle with me at the time, since it was a chuck hunting trip. This friend also owned a fine-shooting rifle chambered for my .219 Donaldson case. Before I entered his gun shop he came out with this rifle and handed me a cartridge. I saw that he had enlarged the chamber so it would take the Zipper case left full length.

He said, "I have improved on your own case." I only laughed at him, and I told him to dig up a piece of half-inch cold rolled steel so we could *check* on his improvement. He did and when he had placed the steel tight against his chopping block, I invited him to try a shot with his Improved Zipper rifle. He fired three shots and not one of them went through the plate. Then I fired a couple of shots with my own .219 Donaldson-Wasp and both bullets went entirely through the plate, as well as driving the piece of punched out metal well into the chopping block.

He examined the plate and stood shaking his head. "Hank," I said, "you have just learned that when you design a case that will burn all the powder, you have the most efficient design." We had both used fifty-five-grain soft nose bullets, but my bullets were cadmium plated, and I used graphite wads.

If Hank had used a case that held twice the charge of mine, it would have made very little difference. Unless one adds to the weight of the bullet, one can only burn a portion of the powder charge. The powder we use today does not act like the black powder we used to use. Trouble is, some of our shooters are still back in the black powder days. Some day they may learn that it takes more than just a primer to produce a loaded case that is both accurate and efficient; and usually where you have one of these, you have both.

Guess this will wind up my letter for tonight. I may have more to say in my next letter along the same lines.

Yours truly,<br>
H.A. Donaldson

## 'Donaldson' Barrel

**Date Unknown**

Dear Harvey Donaldson,

Your letters are the most enjoyable feature in *Handloader*. Being an old smokepole addict, I've always got to see "what's new" in the older ones. So, I look at your letter and generally find that nothing's new; somebody has just raked over the old coals and found an unburned chunk.

I've recently acquired a practically new .32-40 Winchester barrel, a No. 3 round takedown. It's marked "H.A. Donaldson" on the bottom, near the breech. I have installed it in a heavy-walled action which I obtained from Jim Serven years ago. This action was new when I got if from Jim and I've never used it until now.

Can you tell me anything about this barrel? It's unmarked except for your name and the usual Winchester stampings. No screw holes for scope blocks. There was a front sight on it at one time. The rear dovetail slot looks unusual.

I would like to find a Winchester lower tang with set triggers like the one in a Winchester later-model Schuetzen I once owned. That was a nice gun. It had an interchangeable .22 Long Rifle barrel and breech assembly. It was bought new from the German-named store in Chicago, Lenergerke, I believe. An old gentleman traded it to me for a marlin game fishing rig. I must have been nuts to have let it get away from me. So it goes.

Can you help me out with info on the barrel?

Dan Dwyer
San Diego

## That Barrel's A Good One

**February 4, 1970**

Dear Mr. Dwyer,

I have just received the letter from you that was mailed to *Handloader* in Peoria some time ago. They take their own time in sending along these letters, and the fact is that I am so far behind in my letter writing that I will never get caught up. Evidently this man Knox thinks all I have to do is to answer mail they are unable to do at headquarters.

Now in regard to that barrel you mention that has my name stamped on it: If my name is on it you can *bet* it is a good one. From before 1900 up until around 1920 I was doing a lot of off-hand Schuetzen shooting. At that time I owned twenty or more fine Schuetzen rifles. I sure wish I had kept them. But I was interested in the .22 caliber varmint rifles, and since most of my old buddies in the off-hand rifle shooting had passed away, or given up shooting, I gave it up myself. Now, at the age of 87, I am still shooting varmint rifles.

Your barrel is probably one that I took off one of my own Winchester actions to replace with another caliber of barrel. If no scope block holes are in it, it is one I used with a target front sight way back when I had eyes like a hawk. You see I had so many good barrels it is hard to pin down any one in particular.

It is almost impossible to get any of the old tangs with the double set triggers you mention. Those who have them just keep them, if you know what I mean.

Sorry I have not been of more help but glad to know you enjoy my letters to the *Handloader*. If anything turns up about the triggers you want I'll let you know about it.

Sincerely yours,
H.A. Donaldson

Yours truly No. 26

# A Good Gunstock Finish

**February 12, 1970**

Friend Neal,

Some time ago I got a letter from a doctor friend up in Maine. He has a wonderful collection of fine target rifles and he wanted to have the stocks of some guns refinished. He knew that I had an old-time formula for stock finishing, so he wrote for it. Recently I got a nice letter from him and he suggested that I have the formula shown in the *Handloader,* where anyone could have the use of it. When I wrote to Doc I had no idea it could be used for publication, but after reading it over it may be of benefit to other shooters. Many years ago I gave the same data to Clyde Baker, who wrote a book on gunmsithing, and I believe it was shown in his book.

With this in mind I am forwarding this letter for your own approval:

Dear Doc,

In one of your recent letters you asked about the sort of red finish that the old-time stock makers put on their gun stocks. This method seems to be a lost art among the modern stock makers. It is very old and a variation was used by the violin makers of centuries past. It was also used by some early U.S. gunsmiths, such as Billinghurst, Brockway, Morgan James, A.O. Zischang, etc.

In my own files of data on gunsmithing I happen to have considerable of this old stuff that might well be used in modern gunsmithing. Also, being old enough to know just how some of the old-timers produced the fine finish we see today on some of the old guns, and having also known some of the early 1900 gunsmiths, I will try and explain just how this finish was produced.

When I was a whole lot younger than I am today, I was taught considerable about gunsmithing from probably the very finest gunsmith on shotguns that this country ever saw. This was the late Frank Lefever of Ilion, New York. He was related by marriage to my brother's wife. Frank was the son of old Dan Lefever, the master gunsmith who invented and made the Lefever shotguns. Frank worked for years in the Remington factory in Ilion. He could trace his ancestry directly back to the first riflesmith by the same name that settled in Lancaster, Pennsylvania, very soon after 1700. I might mention that Frank's son is still doing gunsmithing.

This method of finishing a gun stock that I am about to tell you about is the same method used by Dan Lefever. Considerable of the finish put on any stock has a lot to do with the quality of the wood itself. For instance, a soft wood like butternut requires a different method than that used on a very hard, dense piece of black walnut. I have made a number of gun stocks down through the years, and I have always found it took a lot more time to put on the proper finish than it did to make the stock. This may well be the reason why we do not see more stocks today finished with the old-time London oil finish. The modern workman cannot put the time in on a gun stock that this finish requires.

Time, itself, with plenty of linseed oil applied now and then, and then plenty of hand rubbing, will in time produce a beautiful finish. One that can also be renewed from time to time with little effort, and no harm to the original finish. Personally, I don't go for the glossy finish put on with a spray gun that we so often see today. They look fine in a show case, but after they are used awhile, they look a lot different.

Most of the old-time gunsmiths had a sheet iron tank in which they placed enough linseed oil to cover the stock completely. They also used to heat this oil, as well as the stock, to assist the oil in penetrating the wood. One should leave the stock in this tank for a day or so, according to the density of the walnut. A hard dense grain takes longer than a more porous grain wood.

The next operation is to remove the stock from the tank and stand it up to drain off, leaving it alone for several days, at least. Complete drying will take place quicker when the oil is applied in this manner. Now, the next step is very important, and has a lot to do with the final finish. Let your stock dry completely! If you make the mistake of applying more oil before this first coating is completely oxidized by the air, you will about double the amount of work actually necessary. Remember that too much oil, or rapid application, is worse than none at all. The fact of the matter is simply that this complete drying of this first coating is really the secret of the perfect finish.

Now, the next operation is to stop any more penetration of oil into the wood. When your stock was first placed into the metal tank and completely covered with oil, the oil had penetrated the wood for 1/16 inch, or so. But again, if the wood is soft with a more open grain, this oil penetration will go on indefinitely, which will then result in an oil soaked stock, and one which will never take a good finish. Also, when the time comes to checker such a stock, you may find that this excess oil will ooze out under the checkering tools, making it almost impossible to get clean sharp diamonds.

There are several ways of stopping the oil penetration. If your wood is very soft with open pores, you should apply a coat of the following mixture, with a small wad of cloth. Take about four ounces of boiled linseed oil and mix it with about three ounces of white shellac that has been cut in alcohol, one ounce of spar varnish, ten drops of Venice turpentine, 20 drops oil of cedar leaves, and enough of the oil of Soluble Red to get the required color. This oil of Soluble Red is a dark reddish powder, sold by some large drug stores or a chemical company. You only require a very little of this powder. You see, a lump of this stuff not much larger than the head of a match will color a full half pint of oil to a bright red, so go easy on this red powder stuff. Try only a small amount at first, until you get the required shade of red to your mixture.

This red powder puts a slight reddish glow to the wood without actually staining it red, if you obtain the proper amount.

Some of the old-time stock makers did not use this red at all, or only if their customers asked for it. Again, if the grain of the wood you are working on has a reddish cast, you can use Alcanet Root instead. This is a very vile smelling powder, and it should be well mixed with the linseed oil before the other ingredients are added. Warm the oil, let the powder remain for two or three hours, and then strain. Venice turpentine is a very thick substance, and hard to pour. The old-time violin makers used to add or mix it with the special varnish they used, to prevent the finish from cracking on a violin.

If my reader will use only a few drops of this stuff in any stock mixture that calls for varnish, it will help a lot to close and seal the pores of the wood.

This above mentioned mixture will soon penetrate and sink into the grain of your stock, and should be allowed to dry for 24 hours or more, before any more finish is applied. Some of our modern-day stock makers have been known to simply apply a very thin coating of shellac to the wood, after the first oiling operation had dried. This might be O.K. on any open grain wood. After it is well dried this should be well but lightly sanded from the surface, before you follow with any more oiling.

Now, for any hard walnut having a close grain with small pores in the wood, it may be sealed with the following mixture: One half pint of raw linseed oil, three ounces of spar varnish, one ounce of turpentine, ten drops of Venice turpentine, and one grain oil of Soluble Red. One can also omit the red stuff and use Alcanet Root, if that is desired. Warm the stock lightly and apply the above mixture with a swab, once over. Pay some attention to the time it takes to sink in properly. If your wood takes it up at once, it might well be necessary to use the first formula again. But again, if a lot still remains on the surface it is going to be O.K. This mixture should be allowed to dry for several days. Now comes the oiling for the final finish. With the pores below the surface pretty well sealed, we can now expect results from our work, from now on. My own method has been to use raw linseed oil, or if I want a red tint to the stock, the red oil mixture is added.

Just apply a light coat with a rag or swab and then let it stand for an hour or so. Next, rub briskly with palm of the hand for about ten minutes. Then set the stock up with a thin coat of oil on it, but not enough for running or dripping. You can repeat this treatment every 12 to 24 hours. Say, 12 hours if the surface still looks dull, or 24 hours if the oil remains on the surface that long. Next, after four or five treatments, allow the stock to stand for a couple of days. Then apply another coat of raw oil, or use boiled oil in case you want to hurry the job; next set the stock away, out of sight somewhere, and forget all about it.

In several days this last coat will be hardened and also somewhat gummed over the surface, just the same as a coat of varnish would appear. The next operation is to take a small wad of rags or waste, coat the stock with hard auto cup grease, then sprinkle with powdered pumice. Scour off this hardened coat of oil, right down to the bare wood, as you cannot hurt the finish.

After this, simply rub with the bare hand and you will have a finer finish than is ever turned out by any factory, and your gun is ready for use. Of course, this finish might still be a little green, so it will do no harm to let it dry a few days before the gun is used.

Again, after this, take up the stock every so often and go over it with a hand full of cup grease, and rub well with the hand until it is dry, each time. From now on after the gun is used in hunting, rub it over with raw oil until it is wiped dry.

Now, if you want a super fine smooth finish, just follow the pumice rubbing with fine powdered rotten stone. Use this on a hard piece of felt, held in the hand and rubbing across the grain. This will put on a firm hard finish that will stand up under many years of actual use.

The chances are good if you have followed me thus far in trying to explain in my rather crude way just what it takes to produce a real *London Oil Finish,* that you can travel many miles before you can run across any firearm that has this particular finish.

Only the fine English shotguns that take a long time to produce are made in this day and age with the London Oil Finish.

Best regards,<br>H.A. Donaldson

## 'Major' Roberts Story

**March 6, 1970**

Friend Neal,

I've been thinking recently about matters concerning my old friend Ned Roberts. On the last visit Col. Whelen made to the Pine Tree Club to attend one of our large matches at Johnstown, I asked the Colonel about when or where Ned Roberts had been a member of the National Guard. The good Colonel seemed rather surprised at this question, and he told me that he had known Roberts all his life and to the best of his knowledge Roberts had never been a member of any National Guard, in any state.

I wondered if Ken Waters would have any data on this. Then I remembered a time when both Roberts and his wife had visited me, when I lived in the country near Little Falls, New York. I had asked Mrs. Roberts about Ned being in the National Guard, and she laughed and said, "Why Ned never was a member of the National Guard." Then I asked her how he got the commission of Major. She laughed again and said, "Oh, he got that from Phil Sharpe."

So here is the story. It seems that at one time Roberts was a teacher or professor in a military school up in Poultney, Vermont. Now if you are familiar with military schools you will know that any teacher in such a school is always called Major. I should know about this, for around the last few years of the last century I attended a military school in Peekskill, New York.

It seems Phil Sharpe wanted some favor from Ned, and somehow learned that Ned was once a teacher in Poultney, and ever after that in all of his writings, Phil called Ned "Major Roberts." Ned was so pleased with the name that ever after that, he let it ride. So he became Major Roberts up until the time of his death.

What sort of a commission would you like? I can cook up one in a short time, if I knew what branch of the service interested you most. How does *Commander* Knox sound as a sample? Ask Dave. I'm just telling you about this for the record in your own private files.

Ned was a good friend, understand, but he certainly was an odd cuss.

Sorry to learn my old friend Sisk has passed away. I knew him from the very start of his bullet making. Guess this will be about all for tonight.

Yours truly,
Harve

## New Cartridge

**March 7, 1970**

Friend Neal,

You might be interested to know that I have designed a new cartridge that could be used for bench rest shooting from 100 up to 300 meters. You will learn more about this later, but I thought you should know I am still on the job and hep to the very latest in rifle shooting.

Yours truly,
Harve

# On Seating A Bullet

**March 8, 1970**

Friend Neal,

I have just been reading *again* the data that Ken Waters gave in the last *Handloader* in regard to Schuetzen loading. Here is what he has to say: "When bullets were seated from the muzzle by the use of a false muzzle, a dummy solid case could first be chambered, providing a uniform stopping place for the bullet base to bottom against."

Most anyone should know that the length of the seating rod would determine the seating depth of the bullet. Nothing to it.

Suppose you pick up in trade or otherwise an old Pope muzzle-loading .32-40 rifle, with the barrel in good condition, but the last inch or so of the barrel at the rear is worn so much that the heavy bullet will not stop where it should, but drops down onto the face of the breech bolt. What does one do about this?

Mister, this is a simple matter. All you do is insert a dummy case in the chamber, then push your bullet down the barrel, and the dummy case holds it in proper position. You lay the rifle on the bench top, remove the dummy case, and then insert a loaded case.

Now, one other thing one should know about seating a bullet in a Pope barrel. Never have the seating rod so large that it fills the bore of the rifle. In a barrel that is badly worn at the breech, if you withdraw this seating rod too fast, it will by suction draw the bullet part way up the barrel. A few of us old-timers *always looked* into the breech of the barrel *before* we ever inserted the loaded cartridge, to see if the bullet was in the proper position.

You can use this data in the *Handloader* at a later date. There are so few of the old-time shooters still around, that you had better use the data while it is still available.

Yours truly,
Harve

# Cartridge Efficiency

**Date Unknown**

The outstanding efficiency of the .22-250 case that I designed way back in 1916 is readily evident on Page 177 of the N.R.A. *Handbook on Reloading*.

Here we find that 35 grains of 3031 powder, when used with the 50-grain bullet, gives a velocity of 3,926 foot seconds, with a pressure of 50,190 foot pounds. Now if you turn to Page 180, data is shown for the .220 Winchester Swift case.

With this larger case, it requires 40 grains of 4064 powder to give the 50-grain bullet a velocity of 3,935 foot seconds, and pressure of 50,570 pounds.

This should show any interested rifleman that the .22-250 design is far better than the Swift, which has a larger case capacity. In all of my own cartridges I have tried for accuracy above everything else, and I found this could only be obtained with a case that would burn *all* of the powder.

Look at some of the magnum cases of today; most of them hold much more powder than is necessary. But then take the .30-338 cartridge. Here is a design that gives better accuracy than any of the others, and gets the results with from ten to twenty grains *less* powder than any of the others.

There is a very good reason for this, and I found it out many years ago. But this sort of reasoning is entirely foreign to most modern-day writers.

H.A. Donaldson

Yours truly No. 27

# It's the Primer that Counts!

May 2, 1970

Friend Neal,

The writer has been reading that good little book by Col. Whelen, *Why Not Load Your Own*, which has good basic information for everyone. I will quote the colonel, my buddy for many years: "The bullet is the most important part of the cartridge. Indeed today it is the most important part of both gun and ammunition." Now the writer is about to take exception to such statements. My own experience will not allow me to agree.

I have always understood that the *primer*, and not the bullet, was the heart of any loaded ammunition. I have found that when the primer was defective, resulting in its failing to function, we have a misfire. The good Colonel gives plenty of thought to the fact that the bullet is what puts the hole in the target. This may be true, but he has neglected the point that if the primer fails to function properly, that bullet will not put any hole in anything. Nor will it even leave the barrel.

Before we go into this matter of primers any further, it will be necessary to go back to my early days of handloading. Back in the old days, from say 1890 to up around 1915, primers were not as carefully made as they are today. The greatest fault was that usually when we opened a box of 100, we found several primers had no anvil in them. The anvils were loose in the box.

If any of the old-timers are still around they will understand what I am writing about. It was quite a job sorting out the good ones, for when the primers were handled, more anvils fell out. This trouble with early primers is what made it necessary for me to devise a new idea in loading tools. While there were a lot of the old Ideal tong tools around, I wanted a tool that would do everything. The tool I made at that time is still in use, and I have never been able to improve on it.

My readers can see a print of this arbor press tool on Page 220 of Phil Sharpe's book on handloading. First I made a drawing of what I had in mind, then made the wooden pattern (this was my trade at the time). Next the casting was made from a certain kind of material, to have it tough and strong, then the dies to use with the tool were made up. We used what one might call a stripper to locate and hold the cartridge exactly under the center of the ram. Another plate was made to hold two different stems that a .22 Krag case could slip over. One was to hold the case so the fired primer could be removed, the other had a flat top so the cartridge was

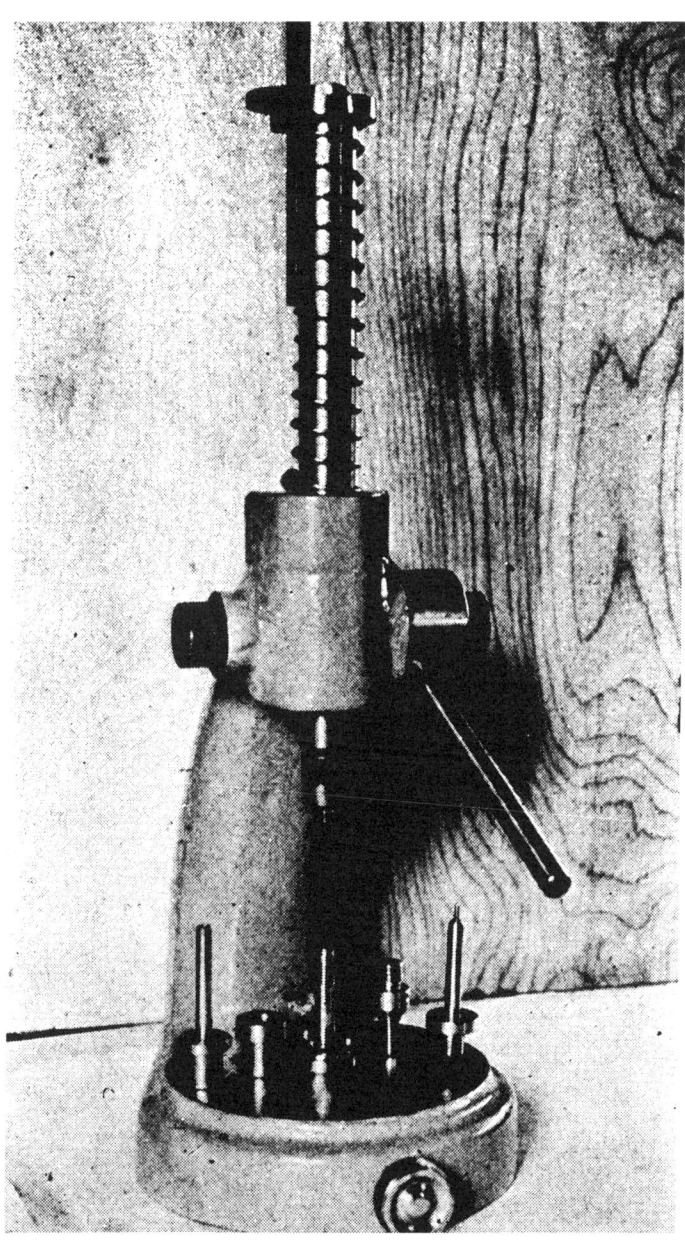

Photo reproduced from Sharpe's Complete Guide To Handloading. It was captioned: Special homemade straight-line tool designed and manufactured by H.A. Donaldson, Little Falls, New York. This is a revised version of the old Perfection. The stock screw at the top center accurately controls this modernized "arbor press" type of tool. Various units such as the resizing dies, priming stakes, decappers and bullet seaters are securely held in position on the flat-base table by screwing into a properly aligned and threaded hole. Other units are screwed to the spring-retracted straight-line plunger operated by a rack and pinion gear.

placed on it with the primer partly inserted, and then seated properly by feel with the hand lever. Very little pressure was required for this and each primer was seated the same each time.

But the really slick part of the operation was the way the primers were handled. I never had to handle any primers with my fingers. My method was as follows: first I would empty a box of primers on the top of my loading table near the press; next, with a pair of tweezers, each primer was turned so one could see at a glance if every primer contained an anvil.

Instead of picking up the primer and putting it in the cartridge, I simply picked up the cartridge and pressed it lightly over the primer, thus the primer stuck in the case. Then the case with the primer partly inserted was turned over and placed on the stem of the sliding base, under the ram, and the lever would seat the primer with very little effort.

Primers with no anvils were discarded; at that time they only cost ninety cents to a dollar a thousand. With this method the primers were started into the cartridge perfectly flat, and not canted one way or another. If any of my readers should visit me tomorrow, they would find me seating primers exactly the same as when I made up this press. Habit does strange things, at times, but I was taught when I found something good, I had better stay with it.

With this press I am able to neck size or expand the neck of most any case. One can even seat bullets without any die, if one is careful. Also, for years I seated the formed cores in the jackets when I was making my own metal case bullets. I'll bet there is hardly another handloader in the country who can honestly say that he is *sure* the primers in his handloads all contain anvils. Today, with better primers, the lack of an anvil is not likely to occur, but it can happen.

Long ago I found that it did not pay to take any chances in handloading operations, so with my system of handloading I am sure of every single operation as it is performed. Nothing is ever left to chance.

Another feature of this old press I nearly forgot to mention. And this feature, by the way, is not seen in any other loading press. With my method of seating primers I can either extract or seat a new primer, in any cartridge, regardless of size — from a .22 Hornet up to an 8 gauge shotgun shell — without any change in the press. I can place either on the bench, place it on the .22 caliber stem and remove the primer, then lift the case up on the other stem and replace a fresh primer. This is done with no change of any sort, and with no dies to handle.

The idea I had was to work from the center of each cartridge, to do away with shell head holders. When you get around to the fact that every cartridge you ever saw had the primers seated in the center of each cartridge, you will understand what I mean. My stripper device does away with a lot of extra case holders. What one saves here goes into other components.

As near as I am able to figure out, this press was made around 1905 or 1906. It has been in use constantly since then, but it still continues to function as well today as when it was made up so long ago.

I believe it is important to seat your primers carefully. I doubt very much if a young or inexperienced handloader can seat the primers properly with the powerful loading presses in use today, which is why I cannot understand why any experienced handloader would use such a press for primer seating.

Another thing I have to use for is any tube or magazine device that is supposed to speed up seating primers, though this may pay off for loading handgun ammunition. Some time ago a friend was telling me how fast he could prime cases, but I told him to figure out how long it took to fill up the long tube, and see how much time was saved. This particular shooter was putting the primers in the tube one by one. He was quite certain they were all the proper side up, but that was about as far as it went.

With my method I can seat primers a lot faster than if I had to pick up each primer, one at a time, and then start it into the cartridge. And another thing, I want no grease, oil, or ever the perspiration from the hands to touch any of my primers. Years ago primers were made from both copper and brass. Either metal was rather soft, compared to modern primers, so they were easily deformed, or crushed if one got careless in placing them in the cartridge. Today we find most primers are flat on the top, the way they should be made.

I would suggest to the young handloader to use *only* rifle primers for use in rifle ammunition. One might think such advice hardly necessary, but you might be surprised at how many shooters believe a primer is a primer, as long as it will fit the cartridge in hand.

There is much more to be said on this subject of primers than can be covered in one letter. It also requires some experience to know the proper primer to use, in any certain situation. One can change the results of almost any powder by the proper selection of the primer. This has little to do with the make or name that may appear on the box.

The larger amount of powder required in magnum loads and the slower-burning powders used in such large capacity cases call for a primer better suited for that purpose. But I understand some handloaders believe they get better results with magnum primers in medium capacity cases, which I doubt very much.

Very often one can obtain improved accuracy from certain cartridges with the use of a mild primer. When I was working on the design of my .219 Don-Wasp case, I had 3031 powder in mind when I determined the capacity of the case. At first I used the Remington $9\frac{1}{2}$ primer. Then later, when I tried the milder No. 115 Winchester primer I found that accuracy of the case improved, so I use it at the present time in this particular cartridge. All this proved was that with this fast-burning powder in the medium capacity case, a milder primer was required.

Today, when I load for my .22-250 Remington, I use the Winchester 120 primer, but in this rifle I use 34 grains of slower 4064 powder, with the Sierra 53-grain bullet. I'm still shooting a balanced load, and an accurate one as well.

Yours truly,<br>
Harvey A. Donaldson

## We're Worried

**July 14, 1970**

Dear Harvey:

You've sure got us worried. We haven't heard from you for many weeks and we're afraid that you may be in ill health. I would like to have just a postcard saying that you are O.K.

Fond best regards,<br>Dave Wolfe

## Tough Customer!

**July 17, 1970**

Friend Dave,

I have just returned from a month's salmon fishing trip up in Maine and New Brunswick, and found yours of the 14th waiting for me. *I am O.K. and feeling fine.* Wish you had followed me for the past few weeks. You see, I travel alone on these trips simply because I am unable to find anyone who can keep up with me.

My local fishing friends claim I am a tough customer to follow on a trip, so I have to go it alone, but that never bothers me. Just as an illustration, on this last trip, after working all day in the machine shop, I came home at 5:00 p.m., packed my bags, took a shower, wrote a couple of letters and then took off *at midnight*, without any sleep, on the 550-mile trip to Machias, Maine, where I arrived in around eleven hours, without even getting out of the car. After lunch I spent the rest of that day fishing. Now, after you have digested the above, you may see that I must be in good shape physically, and also why I have trouble finding someone who can follow me on such a trip.

Since along in April I have been doing considerable shooting. Guess I have killed at least 200 chucks. Our country is full of them. They get killed by cars along our roads. One can go out most any night after supper, and bag a dozen or so before dark. Bill Ruger gave me one of his new varmint rifles, the Model 77, in .22-250 caliber (my own old design), and it is a tack driver. I know Len Brownell, who is at Ruger's factory in Newport, New Hampshire. I see him quite often, so Len — who knows my car license number (MY 777) — put this number 777 on the receiver of my new rifle.

This job has a special French walnut stock, and it sure is a tack driver. I got the new rifle back in May so have used it in my recent chuck hunting. I knew Len when he lived out in Wyoming. As you may know, he is one of the best stock makers in the country, which may account for the fine design of the Ruger Model 77 stock. They are now bringing out the 77 in the longer action so it will take the longer .30-06 and .25-06 case.

Another old friend, Joyce Hornady, sent me a supply of his new 120-grain .25 caliber bullets to try out in the .25-06 rifle. Since they have no chucks out in Nebraska, he wanted me to try out these bullets and then report my results. I found this long, slim open-point bullet opened up fine on chucks, so it should be O.K. on antelope, or deer. In fact, with a mid shot, the new bullet just about cuts a chuck in two.

Thanks for your letter. It was nice hearing from you. Sorry I have caused you folks to do any worrying, but I have been so doggone busy the last few months I have had little time for writing. My letters for the *Handloader* will be coming along soon.

Yours truly,<br>Harve

## More on New Case

**July 24, 1970**

Friend Neal,

I have been busy all summer — actually since early spring. I wrote to Dave a short time ago and explained the situation. Have been shooting lots of chucks. One of my correspondents in Scotland cannot understand how I can go out in the evening after supper and bag some twenty chucks before it gets too dark to shoot. This guy evidently has the idea that killing a chuck is about on a par with killing a bear. Evidently they have no chucks in Scotland.

I have been testing a new cartridge of my own design, strictly for bench rest shooting. It is simply the .308 Winchester case necked down to .270 caliber, with no other change. It has a fourteen-inch twist, and very accurate up to four hundred yards or so. Beyond that, *who cares*, in bench rest shooting.

Yours truly,<br>Harve

## I Think She's In Love

**July 27, 1970**

P.O. Coalville<br>Transvaal, South Africa

Dear Mr. Donaldson:

On reading your articles in each issue of *Handloader*, I find them terribly fascinating, and also you as a person. I would dearly like to know how you have kept so active, healthy and alert over all these years, as you have been writing articles for at least seventy years.

Please give me your secret, for I think you are a most admirable person.

Yours faithfully,<br>Mrs. Hazel Shaw

*Editor's Note: When Neal Knox forwarded this letter to Donaldson, he scribbled on the envelope, "No perfume on this letter, Harve, but I think she's in love!" Evidently Harvey failed to see any humor in Neal's statement, nor did he take Mrs. Shaw's words as a compliment. The letter was found in a batch of unanswered correspondence.*

# Front Page News

### August 13, 1970

Friend Neal,

Just received your letter and note that you will be moving out to Arizona. I think you are making a big mistake. You might better move east to New England, or even New York State. We have got *everything* out this way . . . even taxes.

If you go to Arizona you can throw away your rain coat. I have been out that way, and know my way around. When it does rain, if ever, it is front page news in all the papers. I once knew a fellow who lived down around Tombstone. The damn cuss lived in one mud hut *several years* before he found out that his roof leaked. No fooling.

We have a big match coming up at Johnstown in September, on the Pine Tree Range. The club is doing O.K.; our membership is steadily growing. We have a lot of shooters this side of the Mississippi River!

I want to give a little advice to JUST JIM (Carmichel). If he does migrate West, he wants to *tread lightly.* Any Tennessee hillbilly had better learn the ropes before he tells the town boys he has just arrived in town.

I wish you all the luck in your new location. Best regards to Dave.

Sincerely,
Harve

## Arizona 'Snow Belt'

### August 14, 1970

Friend Neal,

You asked for another "letter" for *Handloader* so here it is. I sort of had an idea that your readers would be interested in the early development of the .25 caliber rifle. The chances are very good that yours truly has the only data on this subject. Later I will have more to say on this subject, for it has long been a favorite with me. Then, still later I will write about the 7x57 caliber as well as the .270 Winchester caliber.

I sure wish you would let me know when you receive these letters. I now know nothing 'til I read them in the *Handloader*. You may be busy, but mister, so is yours truly, and no fooling. My last three letters should take care of everything 'til the end of 1970. Is that correct?

If you think you will get out of the *snow belt* in Arizona, you may be surprised. I have seen snow in that part of the country that would equal any you ever had in Peoria. But you will have to find this out by yourself.

Be sure and give my best regards to my old friend John I. Moore when you go to the bench shoot in Midland. He was the one who developed the Permian Basin oil country. You may even see my friends from Big Spring, Texas. I sure know a lot of shooters from out that way. I kind of wish I were going with you. Tell my old friends I am *still shooting,* and enjoying it the same as ever.

Best regards,
Harve

Yours truly No. 28

# A Look Back at the .25's

**August 14, 1970**

Friend Neal,

I have noted considerably more interest recently in .25 caliber rifles, perhaps because of Remington bringing out a rifle chambered for the .25-06 case.

In writing about the .25 caliber rifle it is interesting to go back to the very *first* rifle made in that caliber. Looking over some old copies of The *American Field*, dated in 1884, I noted several letters from F.J. Rabbeth, the rifleman who should get the credit for the design of perhaps the first wildcat case. This particular case was later known and standardized as the .25-20 Single Shot. These letters throw considerable light on his early experimenting.

The reader should understand that at the time this cartridge was produced in 1884, no metal case bullets were available, so one and all used only cast lead bullets.

"J. Francis," as he was called by the Walnut Hill riflemen, had first worked on a .28 caliber case, the present .25-20 S.S. case being the outcome after his .28 caliber rifle was in use. Perhaps we should say that his .28 caliber case was really the first real wildcat case. Mr. Rabbeth was a woodchuck hunter, and was interested in developing a cartridge that might be used in chuck hunting with the components available at that time — one that would give better accuracy and velocity than any then on the market.

For the modern shooter to fully understand the situation as it stood some 86 years ago, one should realize that there were no jacketed bullets, everyone used cast lead, and there were no rifles available for small game hunting other than the .32-20-115 Winchester, as used in the old Model 1873 Winchester rifle. This particular cartridge, while fairly accurate, had a low velocity and high trajectory, and thus was hardly suited for either squirrel or chuck hunting. Back in the old days chuck hunters were looking for higher velocity — the same as today.

I have often wondered if the shooters of today ever give any thought to the simple fact that *most* of the improvements in rifles and their ammunition, since about the time of the Civil War, were brought about through the combined efforts of the woodchuck hunters of this country.

The excellence of the modern varmint rifle is due to the untiring efforts of such experimenters and fine riflemen as F.J. Rabbeth, Dr. Henry Baker, Major Hinman, W. Milton Farrow, Dr. Skinner, Dr. Mann, A.O. Niedner, Horace Warner, Rueben Harwood, E.A. Leopold, Harry M. Pope, Charles Newton, N.H. Roberts, Capt. G.L. Wotkyns, Col. Townsend Whelen, and a host of others I might mention.

At one time or another I personally knew nearly all of these fine riflemen. It was from the association of such men that I learned the art of rifle shooting. My files are full of correspondence from each of the above named shooters. They have all left the range, and I doubt very much if this country will ever see their equal again.

In working out the design of his .28 caliber case, Mr. Rabbeth proceeded as follows: first, in order to avoid the expense of an entirely new case, he selected the longest .32 caliber shell then on the market. This was the Frank Wesson .32 cal. centerfire case, which was 1 5/8 inches long. He then had his barrel bored for a bullet that was the size of the *inside* of this case so he could use a bullet of a uniform diameter and seat it to any depth in the shell. Thus the bore of this rifle was of approximately .28 caliber.

For the benefit of the modern shooter who has never seen a .32 centerfire extra long case, as used in the Frank Wesson rifle, I should explain that the bullets for this case were really around .30 caliber, and were held in the case only by a heel the diameter of the inside of the case neck, .28 inch, the rest of the bullet being about .30 caliber. You are familiar with this system, for it is about the same as in the .22 Long Rifle ammunition in use today. Thus the outside diameter of the case was the same as the caliber size of the rifle.

With this .28-caliber case Mr. Rabbeth used a charge of 25 grains of fine black powder behind a cast bullet of 85 grains weight. The twist of the barrel was one turn in fourteen inches, which my readers will note is exactly the same as used in the .250-3000 rifle of today. This twist was found to be correct after several other barrels had been tried and discarded.

Mr. Rabbeth did some remarkable shooting with this .28 caliber rifle. The April 1884 issue of The *American Field* shows some ten-shot groups that he shot at 150 yards which measure only 1-1/4 inches. One can easily understand why the small game shooters of 1884 were very much interested in this new case design.

How many modern riflemen can equal such shooting today when shooting black powder and cast lead bullet ammunition? Also I believe the shooting was done with iron sights, such as vernier and pin head sights. There is little wonder that the experimenting with this new caliber rifle aroused a great deal of interest.

This rifle was given considerable testing on small game as well as on the range. For chuck hunting it was the best outfit available at that time. But when he tried it on ducks and gray squirrels, he found it tore them up so much that he decided the bullet was too large for his purpose. With all of his data available on the performance of the .28 caliber rifle, he decided to go to the smaller .25 caliber.

But back in 1884 there were *no* .25 caliber rifles in existence. After considerable delay, writing the several barrel makers of that time, unsuccessfully trying to get them to make up the unheard of .25 caliber barrel, Mr. Rabbeth decided to contact the Remington factory in Ilion, New York. In due time an order was placed with E. Remington & Sons Arms Company, calling for a barrel in .250 caliber with a groove diameter of .256 inches, in the fourteen-inch twist.

There was quite a delay before this first .25 caliber barrel was delivered. Now, note well, there is little doubt that this was the *very first .25 caliber barrel ever made*. At one time Harry Pope claimed to have made the first .25 caliber barrel in 1888 or so. His may have been the first hand-made barrel in this caliber, but the records show that the Remington factory made the very first .25 caliber rifle barrel, and it is appropriate the company is again making .25 caliber barrels.

Mr. Rabbeth had this barrel chambered for the case we know today as the .25-20 Single Shot. He used the same 1-5/8-inch Frank Wesson case, but reduced it to .25 caliber with a slight bottleneck. This was another first in case design. This new design met with the instant approval of the more expert riflemen of the country. The tests and experiments that Mr. Rabbeth made with this new rifle were given plenty of space in both *Shooting and Fishing* and *The American Field*.

Loaded with 22 grains of Hazard's No. 3 powder and a 67-grain cast bullet, quite high velocity was obtained, together with remarkable accuracy. In shooting in competition at two hundred yards, ten shots *off hand*, at the Walnut Hill Range, Mr. Rabbeth made an 86 on the Massachusetts decimal target, or 48 by Creedmore count. In his rest shooting on the same range, he very frequently put ten shots into 1-3/4 inch or *less* at two hundred yards.

The hundred-yard mid-range trajectory height of the .25-20 S.S. rifle with its 26-inch barrel, shooting the above load, was only 1½ inches, and 9½ inches at two hundred. The corresponding data for the .32-20-115 Winchester case then in use was 3½ inches and about 15 inches. These trajectories were obtained on the same day at the Walnut Hill Range by Mr. Rabbeth and Mr. Hinman by shooting through tissue paper screens placed at intervals of twenty-five yards over the two-hundred-yard range.

Here is a little more early case history, not generally known: Remington not only made the first .25 caliber barrel but they formed the first .25-20 S.S. cases used by Mr. Rabbeth. As can well be imagined, expert riflemen all over the country, after hearing about the tests made by Mr. Rabbeth, were anxious to obtain both this new rifle and ammunition for the new case design. But for some reason, Remington was rather slow in tooling up for this new rifle. From some of Mr. Rabbeth's old letters it seems Remington was waiting to see just how great a demand there might be for the new case.

However, at about this time, the Massachusetts Arms Company of Chicopee Falls, Massachusetts (later to be the Stevens Arms Company), was busy making the Model 1882 Maynard rifle and was quick to see the advantages of the new rifle and cartridge. So, they were the first to make a .25, adapting the Maynard rifle to take the new .25-20 Single Shot case. The writer has one of these fine old rifles in this new caliber standing right now in his gun case. Like most Maynards, mine is a tack driver.

When this new Maynard was announced back in 1884 it was received with the same enthusiasm as was the .220 Swift some 50 years later. These rifles had barrels with 15-inch twist, though barrels could be ordered in 12, 14, 15 or 16 twist. Considerable experimenting was being done with bullets from 60 grains up to 90 and even 100 grains. These were all made of lead, cast in several types of moulds. The pages of *Shooting and Fishing* for the years of 1888, '89, '90 and '92 all give loading data as well as reporting tests with different weights of bullets in the Maynard .25-20 Single Shot.

Where a low velocity load was used it was found that the 77-grain bullet gave better accuracy than did the 86-grain. But when a higher velocity was used, it was found that the 86-grain bullet gave the best accuracy out at two hundred yards.

These find old Maynard rifles are hard to find today, but now and then I have seen them at gun shows around the country. Surely such a rifle in good condition is really a museum piece. My own old Maynard was the first rifle I ever had in .25 caliber, and it has been used since before 1900. Since that time I have used about every rifle in .25 caliber that was available, and one might say it is still one of my favorite calibers.

Yours truly,<br>
H.A. Donaldson

## Weather's Good!

**September 1, 1970**

Dear Harve,

I just got back in the office this morning from my trip into the Southwest — stops in Oklahoma, Texas and Arizona. I didn't receive your letter in time to give your regards to John I. Moore, though I did get to chat with him a bit. I was in Midland three days, shot the Light Varmint, but couldn't stay for the Heavy Varmint.

The area we're planning to move to in Arizona, Prescott, is about halfway between Phoenix and Flagstaff — and has the better weather of the two cities. The hottest it got last summer was eight-six degrees, and didn't get below eight degrees during the winter, and those cold temperatures are only early in the morning, with things warming up rapidly as soon as the sun comes up. I'm really looking forward to prowling and hunting that rugged country out there.

The letter you just sent in on the .25 caliber gives us one extra (above the column that we're starting to put in the next *Handloader*) so I'll be needing a couple more before Christmas. I must get back to the stack of correspondence on my desk — it's really a pile. Thought you would want to know about the shoot.

Best regards,<br>
Neal Knox

## The .270-308 Don-Ace

**September 4, 1970**

Friend Neal,

You are doing O.K. in your shooting, so keep at it. One does not learn bench rest shooting over a weekend. It has taken me most 80 years to be able to sit down and put five shots into one hole, but only when conditions are right. On the other hand if you keep trying to shoot under bad conditions, you will learn things about holding that you can learn in no other way. It takes a long time to judge either wind or mirage, and this is what pays off in competition.

I told you in a post card that I have designed a new bench rest cartridge. It may be some time before it gets out your way. This is simply the .308 Winchester case necked down to .270 caliber with no other change in the case. It is working out O.K. My barrels for this new case call for a fourteen-inch twist. This is only for 100 to 300-meter shooting. Have been testing the 120-grain bullet so far — bullets made in my own B&A swages. The barrel was made and chambered by Douglas. With this light bullet we get away from heavy recoil, and accuracy is good.

Give my best regards to Dave, and I will write again and try and give you a few tips that may help in your holding. First I should know just what rifle you are shooting, weight, caliber, etc.

Best regards,
Harve

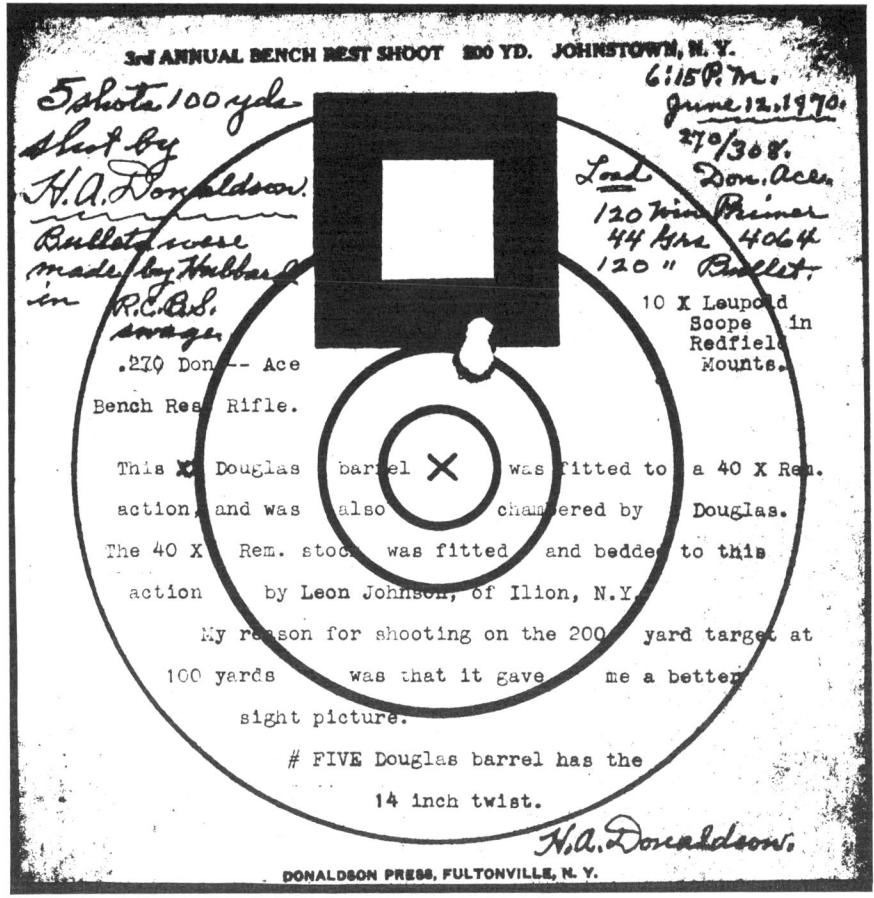

**Yours truly No. 29**

# Case Life Is Up To You

**September 5, 1970**

Friend Neal,

I would like to discuss cartridge cases that we use in our reloading operations. In my time I have used plenty of factory-made empty cases, and I still have the quaint idea that the factory who makes these cases understands more about them, and just how they should be made, than some shooter who started a month or so ago with his handloading operations.

When I started handloading well before the turn of the century, I used empty cases made by the old U.M.C. Company. These were in .25-20 S.S., .32-40, and .38-55 caliber. No doubt some of our modern riflemen never even heard of these cases. Since these cartridges were used with black powder, I had my cases plated inside and out, which was a real help in cleaning. After years of use I still have a good supply of this brass.

Soon after 1900 I purchased a Stevens single-shot rifle in .28-30 caliber. This gun has the *breech loading* barrel that was made by Harry Pope. With the rifle I got two hundred empty cases, which are just about indestructible, made by U.M.C. I still have this fine old rifle together with the ammunition. Recently in looking over this ammo I note that the purchase price of a box of twenty, loaded with a 120-grain lead bullet, was forty-five cents per box. Date on the box was 1905. Quite different from the cost of 1970 ammunition!

This particular rifle was used for years in chuck hunting, and for this hunting the bullets were seated in the case — same as modern ammunition. But for testing and bench rest shooting, we would seat the bullet in the breech with a ball seater, and then place the loaded cartridge, with a wad on top, into the chamber. In such loading we used only the *one* cartridge, and loaded it over and over.

Of course, the neck of the case was *never* neck sized, for it did not have to hold the bullet, with the result that one cartridge would actually last for years. In case one of my readers has occasion to try this kind of loading, and has no bullet seater, all that is necessary is another cartridge with a piece of wood fitted into it, with 1/16 inch of wood sticking out of the case. In seating, just drop the bullet in the rifle chamber, place the dummy case in the chamber and close the action. This will seat the bullet properly in the barrel when the dummy case is removed and the case loaded with powder is then put in the chamber. This is a lot easier to do than it is to explain. One should remember that this method was used with a plain cast lead bullet.

Around 1900 I purchased a Winchester single-shot hunting rifle chambered for the .30-40 Krag case. When I bought this rifle I got a supply of Winchester empty cases (all of the same lot number). This started me using Winchester ammunition, and now at this late day, I am still partial to Winchester ammunition.

This old .30-40 caliber single-shot rifle was made to order for still-hunting deer, and down through the years it accounted for a number of them. Next, I got the idea I had to own a repeating rifle, so I got a Model 95 Winchester in this same .30-40 caliber. This was a good rifle, but rather mean to carry over the arm due to the box magazine. I sold my old single-shot Winchester soon after that, and I have been sorry ever since. So . . . I would give this advice to young shooters: if you ever obtain a rifle which gives good service, and which you are used to shooting, never part with such a gun. If you do you will live to regret it.

But to get back to the empty cartridge itself, the life or use one may obtain from any empty fired case is entirely up to the one who uses it. First, one should understand that no cartridge will ever give the accuracy in a particular rifle as will the case that has been fired and thus fitted to the chamber. This is why I never full-length size my cases. Also, I never resize the case necks more than, say, half the length of the case neck. Thus your fired case *fits* the back part of the chamber. This is just common sense.

Nor do I ever subject any loading tool to *full-length* resizing of fired cases. The reason for this is that I have a screw press that will give some twenty tons pressure, the amount used when the time comes to full-length size any cartridge, but one will find that the *less* you work your brass the longer service you will get from it.

I want clean brass, and especially on the case necks, and I have found that the use of my graphite wads sure helps in keeping clean cases. Another thing — we often find a shooter spending more time in useless checking over his cases that might better be spent in his other operations. I know one fellow who will spend hours going over his cases checking the size of the flash hole. If he would do as I do, simply buy one brand, and then see that they are all from the same lot of brass, he could forget all about the size of this flash hole.

When it comes time to clean the primer pockets in your brass, *never* use any tool that may remove any of the brass itself. A small screw driver with the sides rounded over, so it does not scrape the sides of the primer pocket, is about as good as anything one can find. Most of the dirt found in any primer pocket is in the bottom. I have known shooters who used power tools to clean primer pockets, and then they wondered why they got short life from their brass.

Again, I would remind my readers that the life of your cases is determined by how they have been treated. If you use hot loads, your case life will be short. One should keep the cases clean at all times. Very often sticking cases will be found *dirty*. Get in the habit of keeping your cases as clean as you do your rifle, and *never* fail to try your reloads in your rifle chamber before you leave camp on a hunting trip.

Way out on a stand miles from camp is a poor time to discover that the case you have just fired cannot be extracted. This is when a fellow needs a friend, or rather a good stiff cleaning rod.

A lot of books on handloading devote a chapter or so on chamfering case necks. This is a simple operation, and quite necessary on new, never fired cases. This may be done with a pocket knife or any reamer made for that purpose. But even this operation may be over done, if more brass than necessary is removed from the case mouth.

One will sometimes find what we call season cracking at case necks, usually in ammunition that has not had the proper neck anneal, or has also been stored for some time. Some say that the grain structure may change and the brass will become brittle and crack. It is well to examine cases carefully every time they are reloaded, and to destroy any that show defects. Again just common sense.

Recently, I had occasion to try and slow down the burning rate of No. 3031 powder, in a medium capacity of case. But I tried in this particular instance the old No. 115 primer and found I got the desired results. If any of my readers desire to try the slower burning powders (such as No. 4320) in a case such as the .22-250, they should try a magnum primer such as the CCI No. 250.

After considerable experimenting I was able to get the best results in my .22-250 with the use of the Winchester No. 120 primer, and with 34 grains of No. 4064 powder and the 55-grain bullet. This is only one way in which different primers may be used for some special purpose. You simply balance the burning rate of the powder used with the known characteristics of your primers.

Yours truly,<br>
Harvey Donaldson

## Bench Rest Advice

**September 7, 1970**

Friend Neal,

Now that you are into bench rest shooting, I may have some ideas that might be of help.

First, you should understand that *tension* on the stock or the way it is applied, has considerable to do with where bullets land on your target. During the last twenty years or so, I have coached many shooters in bench rest shooting. At first, most shooters have their own way of holding the rifle on the bench, and they pay more attention to "sighting" than they do to the way the rifle is held. I can tell just by looking at a shooter as he sits down at the bench, how much experience he has had.

If you have formed the habit of holding your rifle with a tight hold on the stock, the tension should be uniform from shot to shot. Long ago I stopped using a tight hold on the stock, and my shooting steadily improved. Of course the type stock used, as well as the recoil, has something to do with the amount of tension.

At the present time, I put no tension whatever on the stock. I simply put the rifle up on the sand bags, front and rear, and align the outfit so it is on the bull. Then I sit down and again check the sighting. The only part of the rifle that is then touched is the trigger. If you saw me shoot, you might think that I was holding the rifle, but no part of my body touches the stock. The butt plate may be as much as an inch from my shoulder. With this method I get away from putting any tension on the stock itself.

Understand most of my bench rest guns are in .22 caliber with little or no great amount of recoil. I figured if tension on the stock had any effect on bullet impact why not remove the tension *entirely*, and get better results. Just common sense.

Even with a rifle in .308 caliber, with more recoil, one is easily able to touch the trigger with the left fore finger, (if right handed), and then catch the recoil with the right hand held just back of the butt plate. The next time you attend a match pay plenty of attention to some of the experts and how they hold their rifles on the bench. You may be surprised.

All my rifles have light trigger pulls — usually the 40X triggers. When shooting, stocks are *well bedded* into the bags. Don't put too much sand in your bags. The front bag should be made to exactly fit the fore-end of the rifle, and I might add that the fore-ends on my varmint rifles are exactly the same shape. When my rifles are bedded down into the bags, they *don't move*.

When you watch the wind or mirage, you have to fire when you believe it is the correct time; this is one thing you learn from lots of shooting. Many fellows hold off for certain conditions, and they quite often find that is exactly where their bullet went.

My own varmint guns have Leupold scopes, in ten power with the C.P.C. cross hairs. I have used everything up to 25 power but like ten the best. I used to think the high power was best, so as to check mirage, but I then found the lower power showed less mirage, so gave me less to worry about.

Best regards,
Harve

## O. Henry & Wootters

**October 31, 1970**

Friend Neal,

Enclosed is another "letter" for the *Handloader*. In almost every mail I get letters from your readers telling me how they enjoy my articles. Why in hell don't these jokers write to *you* instead of to me. Some write and ask why it is that certain of your writers can fill several pages without really saying anything.

For instance, read over what John Wootters has to offer in the last *Handloader*. His article covers five or more pages when it all might have been said in only a single page.

O. Henry never made his reputation as a writer by taking up a dozen pages when only one would do the trick.

Now read over this last letter of mine, as per my own method of handloading. I have tried to give information that most anyone can use, and I found it was hardly necessary to use up several pages to do it.

Maybe I should lay off writing letters and write a book. No one should sit down and write to the editor unless he has something to offer. To date some of your own writers simply hash over time and again the same old stuff that has been shown for years. Ken Waters is O.K. and you can quote me on that, but some of the fellows who wear the big Hollywood cowboy hats usually give the impression that they are talking through their hat. Some of your readers even rate the data by the shape of the author's hat. But I have them all buffaloed; I never wear a hat.

A magnum owner recently showed me his rifle together with only a single box of loaded ammunition. When I had opened the box I found two empty fired cases. This was the extent of the use of this particular rifle. Will this sort of practice keep our country a "Nation of Riflemen?"

As I understand it, all correspondence from now on goes to Arizona, right?

Best regards,
Harve

## New Varmint Stock

**Date Unknown**

Friend Neal,

I have been thinking it over and since you and Dave will be heading West before very long, I believe you fellows should take off in your plane some weekend and fly East. You could land at the Johnstown airport and stay in Johnstown, the home grounds of our Bench Rest Association. I could arrange to meet you at the airport and show you around. We have a club house valued at over $140,000 and the very finest 200-yard range in the U.S.A. bar none.

You would have a chance to see and examine a new type of varmint bench rest stock. There is nothing like it out in your country. It is made from a Remington 40X Match rifle stock, but changed in many ways to make it *perfect* for our purpose. A good friend of mine who works for Remington in Ilion makes up these stocks. As yet only a few of our local shooters have seen it. The barrel is glass bedded, and *stays put!*

I know you fellows will be crowded for time when it comes time to move West, but anyway, think it over.

Best regards,
Harve

**Yours truly No. 30**

# Expert Tips on Reloading

**October 31, 1970**

Friend Neal:

I am receiving a lot of mail — far more than I can answer — from all over the country on reloading matters. The questions these fellows are asking! They could obtain the answers in any loading manual. One fellow writes in that he is having trouble with sticking cases in his No. 1 Ruger rifle, chambered for the .22-250 Remington case. I had a chance to examine some of his fired cases, and I hardly wonder that they were sticking. It was simply a matter of maximum loads.

This shooter was loading 37 grains of 4320, with the 55-grain bullet. The primers were really flat and the heads swelled. My own load for this same cartridge is the No. 120 Winchester primer, with 34 grains of 4064 powder, and the 53-grain Sierra bullet. This is my best chuck load for long-range hunting, say up to 250 yards. For any shooting up to 350 yards I use the 55-grain Nosler bullet, with same powder charge. I have found in my own testing that 3031 is too fast and 4320 is too slow, so 4064 is exactly correct for this case (among Du Pont powders).

My reason for the use of the above load is that it gives the best accuracy, even way out to three hundred yards. I load for accuracy first of all, and I was never able to get the best accuracy with *any* maximum loads. I am at a loss to understand why a young shooter should look for velocity over accuracy in chuck hunting. The writer has been handloading for so many years that some of my friends claim that I have reduced it to an exact science. I would hardly say that, myself, for quite often you learn something new, or else you learn that what you used to know is hardly so at all.

It might do no harm if I gave our readers some of my own methods in handloading. My own shooting started way back in 1890, so I have been handloading for eighty years. Time sure flies for it hardly seems that long. What pleases me most is that I am still shooting, and looking forward to this fall's deer season.

During these years I have worked out some methods in handloading that you do not read about in the loading manuals. It might be that your readers would be interested in some of these ideas. At the present time I load for nearly a dozen different rifle cartridges. Also I have a shop full of loading tools, and many of them are left set up for some particular rifle. The same holds true with my powder measures, but I don't leave the powders in these measures for any length of time. I just slip a note in the powder hopper that tells the charge in grains of the kind of powder that particular measure has been set for.

The first thing I would advise any young shooter to do in handloading is to take pains to keep his fired cases clean, even to the primer pockets. It takes but a moment to wipe off the outside of the necks of your fired cases, and it is a good plan to also examine closely each case as it is put in the loading block, for possible cracks or flaws. I keep the loading dies and tools for each particular caliber in a box by itself. This box also contains a slip of paper with the proper loading data for that caliber as well as the particular rifle it will be used with. Mark the caliber on the front of each box for easy reference.

I am still amazed at the way some of my friends load their ammunition. For instance some fellows will use the same powder (not the charge of course), no matter what bullet weight they are using. As I have it figured out, the first thing a handloader should consider, before he does any reloading, is to learn the burning rate of each and every powder he expects to use.

Before we go any further in this matter I will list the approximate burning rate of several of the powders that are most used by the average handloader. At least this is about the order that I find them.

First comes Bullseye, which is the fastest powder I have ever used. Then comes a number of shotgun powders, in which we are not interested. Then, Unique, which can be used in a number of reduced loads with cast bullets. Next, No. 2400, which was developed for the .22 Hornet case. Next comes 4759, then 4227, 4198, Hi-Vel No. 2, 3031, 4895, 4064, 4320, H-375, H-380, 4350 and 4831.

To be accurate we might have listed fifty or more different powders, but the other powders will be listed in most reloading manuals.

Before we go any further in this matter it might be well for me to show just how I go about handloading for my favorite deer rifle, which happens to be in 7x57 caliber. Way back around 1900 when I started to use such a caliber for deer hunting, about the only weight of bullet one could buy was the 175-grain. Now it is possible to buy bullets in nearly a dozen different weights.

In my system of handloading the first thing to consider is the proper choice of powder, as well as the proper charge that will be best for the lightest bullet I will use, which in this case happens to be the 100-grain bullet. We do a little experimenting until we find that a fairly fast powder like 3031 is the best to use as it gives the best possible accuracy, together with normal pressure, with a charge of 45 grains. So . . . we set our powder measure to throw 45 grains of 3031 powder, and lock it. I want my readers to understand that this measure will not be changed, or in other words the bulk content of the other loads, with other IMR powders, is the same as the first charge.

The next load we use will be for the 120-grain bullet. So we use the next slower burning powder, which happens to be 4895. Without a change in the measure we find the bulk of this powder as thrown from the measure weighs 46 grains. Suppose we wish to shoot the 139-grain bullet; we fill the measure with 4064, which is the next slower powder. Again with no change in the measure we find we have a load of 4064 powder that weighs the same as the 3031, or 45 grains. With the 154-grain Hornady bullet, which I prefer for deer hunting in this particular caliber, we use 4320, as it is the next slowest powder. Here we find due to the small grains of powder, the load, with no change in the measure, weighs 48 grains.

Again, we wish to use a heavier bullet, for use in real heavy cover as found up in some parts of the Maine hunting country. For this load we again select a Hornady bullet, but of 175 grains. For this weight bullet we fill the measure with 4350 powder, and find that the charge as thrown weighs 47 grains.

Now, my readers, if they have followed me thus far, have found that I have loaded five different weights of bullets with no change in the powder measure. All I have done is to use the same bulk of powder for each load, but in each case I used a slower powder as the weight of bullet was increased.

I was very much surprised to learn that with my system of loading, out at one hundred yards I could shoot any one of the different loads with no regard to the bullet weight, into practically the same group.

Now, if any of my readers doubt the above statement, all they have to do is to get in their car, and pay me a visit. They can do the same shooting, with this same rifle. I will mention that this particular rifle has a far different twist than the old military 7mm rifles. My rifle was designed for a hunting rifle, and when you find one that will keep five different weights of bullets into the bottom of a tea cup, out at one hundred yards, you had better hang on to it.

*(Editor's Note — Some of the above loads are excessive for standard 7x57 rifles and are not recommended! Though this system undoubtedly works for Harvey Donaldson in certain rifles, we caution against using this technique without checking each load/bullet combination in a reliable handloading manual. All of the loads mentioned are maximum, or up to five grains above maximum for the standard 7x57mm, according to the* Hornady Handbook.

*(If this technique is used, bear in mind that it is valid only with IMR and other powders with similar characteristics, and then only if the progression in bullet weights is similar to the progression in relative burning rates of the powders used. — Neal Knox.)*

Common sense in loading operations should prevent one from the use of maximum loads in most any caliber. If you are looking for accuracy in your handloads, you will never find it in any maximum loads. Your handbook will not know your particular rifle. And remember it is the loads that will be used in your own rifle that should interest you most.

One can learn plenty about handloading if he follows it long enough. Maybe that is what makes handloading, for me at least, so interesting. Only recently a fellow shooter asked me just what it took to be a handloader. I told him right off I figured that a fair amount of good common sense, with more or less patience, was all that was required. He laughed and said, "Yeah, that's all it takes for most any worthwhile project."

Maybe he had something, at that.

Yours truly,<br>H.A. Donaldson

## All Balled Up!

**November 10, 1970**

Hi Dave,

Our friend Neal has got me all balled up! Last word I had I was supposed to send mail to Prescott. So on October 31 I wrote him at Prescott. At the same time I sent in an article for his approval.

Now this morning I get a letter from him saying he is still in Peoria. What in hell is the matter?

I know you are a busy guy at present, but please find a moment to drop me a line, in reply to this letter. I am busy as usual, have done some deer hunting but so far have only seen does, no bucks. Soon as snow comes, hunting will get better, as the bucks will be moving around more. Will be waiting to have some word from you.

Yours truly,
Harve

P.S. Is Neal's secretary, June, going to move to Arizona? Sure like that gal!

## Wanna Buy A House?

**November 16, 1970**

Dear Harve,

I'm sorry for the foul-up. I have moved to Prescott, but Neal has not sold his house in Peoria as yet. We're hoping to get him out here before the end of the year, but even that may not take place if the economy doesn't improve considerably. It seems no one wants to buy a house these days.

Anyway, for the time being, write to Neal at the Peoria address. I'm busy here in Arizona training gals to handle circulation, and at the same time trying to sell advertising. Have found that it's not a simple matter to move a company half way across the country.

Cordially,
Dave

## Stranded in Peoria

**November 24, 1970**

Friend Neal,

How come no answer to my last letter? I have had a couple letters from Dave recently. I do not know yet if you received my last "letter" for *Handloader*, regarding my methods of preparing loads. I sent this letter to Prescott. Did you ever receive it?

Last I heard from Dave you were still stranded in Peoria. That should make your job rather difficult I should imagine.

I have several ideas for letters to *Handloader* but I have hesitated to write 'til I found out the score. I have been doing considerable deer hunting but to date have seen nothing with horns. Will hunt Thanksgiving and over that weekend.

You seemed pleased with my letter giving the data on the early design of the .25-20 Maynard single shot case, so I though it might be followed up with the designs of several more cases. I have the data on every case that has been designed since the .30-40 Krag came out.

I have often wondered what ever happened to Hervey Lovell. Do you know? Last I heard he had left Indianapolis, and that he was holed up on a houseboat off the coast of Oregon. Try and find time to drop me a line and let me know about any more letters.

Best regards,
Harve

## A Husband Problem

### December 7, 1970

Dear Harve,

I am sorry for the delay, but things have really been in a mess with me here and Dave in Prescott — as you guessed. For the present, continue to write me in Peoria. I don't have time to check right now, but I *think* that we have one or possibly two "letters" from you. I do like those letters on the .25 calibers — more will be appreciated.

Been meaning to tell you that June is staying in Peoria. Her husband frowns on the idea of her going off with us.

Still no news on my house. We may have to winter here. I will write again as soon as I can get a breather.

Best regards,<br>Neal

## Is He Still Alive?

### December 9, 1970

Friend Dave,

I have not as yet had any word from Neal. What the devil seems to be the matter? I have prepared a couple more letters for *Handloader*, but I am more or less at a loss to know *where in hell* to mail them. Do I send this data direct to you, or simply hold it 'til I hear from him, if ever!

Would like to know if he could use any stuff for his Reader By-Lines column. I could send him plenty of data from my own shooting experiences. At one time I mailed him a hunting story or two, but he fired them right back to me.

As a sample of what I have in mind, I am enclosing a short piece about a chuck hunt I thought he might be able to use. Look it over and then fire it along to him. I am getting mail in three days from Australia, but it seems to take forever to get mail from Neal. By the way, you might like to know you have a lot of readers in Australia.

Send my data along to Neal, if he is still alive. Best regards and a Happy New Year & Christmas Season to you and yours.

Yours truly,<br>Harve

## 'Barking' A Woodchuck

### December 9, 1970

A few years ago I was chuck hunting with a friend in country south from my home. This hill country was covered more or less with shale or loose slate rock. I wondered how a chuck could make a home in such country. We had never-the-less managed to find quite a number of chucks.

I remember particularly one shot that I made that afternoon. I was shooting a good single shot job chambered for my .219 Don-Wasp. My friend was shooting a Model 70 Winchester chambered for the .270 case. A very accurate rifle, by the way, with a Lyman 20X Targetspot scope on it.

It was my turn to shoot. I soon spotted a chuck looking right at me from about 150 yards. A piece of sharp shale was directly under and right in line with his chin. It made me think of another chuck I had killed under similar circumstances long ago.

We were in a meadow, way below the chuck, so it was an up hill shot. I told my buddy to let me have his rifle and I would show him how to kill a chuck without hitting it with the bullet. He laughed, but handed over the rifle. I got in an easy prone position with my chuck stick, and I held on the piece of rock directly under the chuck's chin. At the shot he seemed to explode and flopped over backward.

We walked up and found exactly what happened, just as I had it figured. The bullet hit the under side of the shale, which drove it upward so it nearly cut the chuck's head off. And sure enough, my buddy dug out what was left of the bullet from the hole *under* the piece of shale.

My friend said it was the first time he had seen anyone *bark* a chuck the way we used to bark squirrels in the long ago. Having done this before, I was quite sure what would happen.

Harvey A. Donaldson

## Harve Was Not Amazed By Vom Hofe Article

### December 12, 1970

Dear Dave,

I've been reading over the article on the "Amazing 5.6 x 61 Vom Hofe" rifle and cartridge that appeared in the latest issue of *Rifle*. I was not *amazed* by this account because I had a rifle that gave about the same ballistics back in 1935. Fred Ness wrote about this rifle in the *American Rifleman* in the Thirties.

My rifle was made up as an experiment; I was looking for .228 ammunition that would give a velocity of 4,000 fps velocity. The reason I wanted a barrel in .228 caliber was because I already had a swage of .228 caliber that Niedner made for me back around 1912, when I was shooting the Savage .22 Hi-Power rifle. This particular swage, by the way, makes a two-diameter bullet.

First off I obtained a barrel blank from Savage before it had been rifled. The boss of their barrel department was a good friend of mine so he selected a blank that they called a "natural" — one that did not require straightening. The blank was thirty inches long. It was then sent to Niedner, who cut the rifling. I remember he said it was as straight a blank as he had ever seen.

It was cut with only four grooves, with rather wide lands and quite shallow grooves. The idea was to cut down on pressure and to prevent the jackets from tearing apart. The throat was quite long, also to ease pressure. After the barrel was made it was fitted to a Winchester Model 54 action.

When it came to the cartridge, I selected the .270 Winchester case. This was necked down to .228 caliber with a 30 degree shoulder to prevent case stretching. The case forming dies were made up, as well as the loading die. The body of the case was blown out a little larger than the factory .270 cartridge.

When I started my loading operations I selected a powder that the modern rifleman never heard about — No. 10 Du Pont. This was a special powder that was made up especially to load some of the large capacity cases used in the Newton line of cartridges. I used to do considerable handloading on a number of experimental cases for Newton, so I had a fair supply of this powder on hand.

It had about the same characteristics as No. 4831. At first I used the regular 70-grain .228 Savage bullet, but when I tried some maximum loads with this bullet, I ran into trouble. The bullets simply blew to pieces — not one so much as reached the fifty-yard target.

Then I started to make my own with my Niedner swage. This swage formed the two-diameter bullet, the front part riding on top of the lands while the back part takes the grooves. This was an old idea worked out by Dr. Mann.

I went up to Middlebury, Vermont, to visit my friend J. Bushnell Smith, so he could chronograph some of my loads. But before I did this I made up a supply of bullets with *double* jackets. This happens to be one hell of a job, but it works.

It was well that I had these double-jacketed bullets as they were the only kind that gave the results I was looking for.

Smitty found that my top loads with a 70-grain bullet registered around 4,200 feet per second. We decided to cut the loads a little and arrived at a load that gave a velocity of 4,000 fps, and this gave good accuracy, and no trouble from stretched cases. We got a long life from those good .270 Winchester hulls.

This rifle was used only for long-range chuck hunting, and I still believe it was the best rifle I have ever owned in that respect. It took over about where the .220 Swift left off. The only drawback was in forming the bullets, and before long I found that it was a lot more work than it was worth.

After reading over this data you'll understand just why I was hardly amazed after reading the article on the 5.6 x 61 case.

We find very little that is really new now days, for most of what we read has been done before. But it sure brought back pleasant memories of long ago. Anyone could easily have a rifle made up as I have described, but one might have trouble obtaining the barrel. I have the reamer that chambered my rifle, and I might be able to dig up some of my fired cases. I know I still have the dies. I am still making my own metal case bullets in .22, .25, and .270 caliber, with the same dies that Niedner made for me so long ago. And these old swages are very simple to use.

I am not so positive as to the date this rifle was made, but I do know that I was shooting the rifle before the .220 Swift was available. You see I had been tipped off by friend Col. Whelen that Winchester was working on a new high speed case development, but Whelen said they were going to use a light .22 caliber bullet to get the velocity they wanted.

This information from friend Whelen was what really started my own experimenting with the .228 caliber.

I had it figured that most anyone could get high speed with a light bullet, but my own idea was to use a bullet of at least 70 grains, and finally I was able to do exactly what I had started out to do. All of my varmint hunting experience has proved that I got far better long-range killing power with the use of a heavier bullet. Common sense should show any hunter that the lighter bullets lose velocity very fast. Also, a light bullet is more affected by adverse wind conditions.

A fellow learns a lot of things as he grows older, so it is wise to cash in on what you may have learned through long experience.

Yours truly,
H.A. Donaldson

## Data from Pope?

**December 13, 1970**

Friend Dave,

No word as yet from Neal. What the devil is the matter? I'm holding several letters 'til I hear from him. It has occurred to me that our readers might be interested in data taken from very interesting letters I have received in the past from old Harry Pope. Would it be O.K. if I wrote up some of this stuff for *Handloader?* I do know that plenty of early shooting data, still in my files, will probably be lost for publication after I pass away. So, with this in mind I wonder if Neal would be interested? As I get no answer to my letters, I hardly know what to think!

Last week I had a phone call from some man in Michigan. He wants to visit me soon after the New Year to obtain some data for a book he is writing. He said he wanted to visit me so he might take down on a tape recorder some information about the old 200-yard Schuetzen matches that were held from 1900 up to around 1920. It seems the fellow who wrote the book on Harry Pope also mentioned some of my rifles and the shooting I did soon after 1900, so this chap read that book and now he wants to visit me.

Yours truly,
Harve

## New Hornady Bullet

**December 14, 1970**

Dear Harve:

The 7mm caliber 154-grain bullet illustrated in our ad in the current *Rifle* magazine is not a new bullet in our line; we've had it for a number of years and it is one of our most popular 7mm bullets. However, recently we have redesigned this bullet, giving it a longer point radius so the ogive will come a little closer to the crimping cannelure which will also improve the ballistic coefficient slightly. This new design is not yet in production; it will probably be 90 days before the tooling for this bullet is completed, bullets made and tested, ready for delivery.

I can send you a box of our present bullets or, if you prefer, you can wait for the new one, or both. Enclosed is a sample of the current 154-grain bullets.

The way we make them, our pointed bullets expand just as dependably as the round nose, only in the deer woods a pointed bullet is more apt to be deflected than a blunt one. For long-range antelope hunting, don't overlook that 139-grain bullet.

I'll be looking for your letter in the forthcoming issue of *Handloader*. I always look forward to your message in the back of that magazine and figure I've just read a letter from an old friend.

Best regards,
Joyce W. Hornady

## Call from Detroit

**December 15, 1970**

Dear Harve,

Greetings from the Sunshine State! Your letter early this month mentioned snow in New York — frankly, I don't miss snow at all. Guess it's just my "old age."

I'm sure the reason you haven't heard from Neal is simply a heavy workload. He is still in Peoria, hasn't sold his house yet, and has been doing all the editorial work by himself. This includes editing, layout and paste-up, including all production problems. That's a night-and-day job, seven days a week. I'm sending your letter on to him, and I'm sure you'll be getting a note from him shortly.

Also, I will have Jim Carmichel write to you. He is moving to Prescott, and will be here in a few days to look for a house.

Too bad you don't still have your Chevy sportscar. I got a call from Detroit the other day, and GM wanted to do another feature story on you for one of their magazines. I guess they found out you sold the Corvette a couple of years ago.

Fond best regards,
Dave

## Offers from Magazines

**December 16, 1970**

Dear Neal,

Yours of the 7th arrived today. I thought I had lost touch with you entirely. I have had several nice letters from Dave.

I am sending along a "letter" for *Handloader*, which will be followed in a day or so with one for *Rifle*. Have another for *Handloader* that will follow shortly.

I am getting letters from all over the world, it seems. Have had several letters from Australia. They all seem to like my material. I have had offers from different magazines to write for them. But as things go right now, my writing for you and Dave takes up about all of my time. You guys must have worked up quite a circulation, as word is getting around about my "*Yours truly*" column.

Hope you have a nice holiday season, even if you are away from Dave.

Sincerely yours,
Harve

## Brand New Wife!

**December 21, 1970**

Dear Friend Joyce,

I have checked my supply of 7mm Hornady bullets and find I have some in both the 134-grain and 154-grain. So there is no real hurry about your *latest* design. When they are available, just send along a box.

Together with your letter I got a nice long letter from Fred Huntington. He writes that he has a brand new wife. Now isn't that something.

I can see where your long, stream-line bullets are O.K. for long shots, where the country is plenty open. Mister, you should see some of the deer cover we have in this state, as well as up in Maine. When you try to bust into some of our cover, you don't get through. You *back out*. So, your round nose bullet for our type of hunting is just what is required. And mister, they really do the job.

Just got a letter from my publisher, Dave Wolfe. He said that he had a long phone call from General Motors, who it seems, are doing a feature article on me for publication in their magazine. They claim I am the *oldest* sports car driver in the U.S.A. Dave claims I have data on shooting matters not available from anyone else. How did you like that letter on the .25-20 case?

All the best for the Holiday Season.

Sincerely yours,
Harve

Yours truly No. 31

# More on the Beloved .25's

**December 16, 1970**

Friend Neal,

I have used several .25 caliber rifles for many years. You see, along with the 7x57mm and the .270 Winchester, these are my favorite rifles. My hunting seldom calls for any caliber larger than the 7x57 Mauser and I have used it for deer hunting since around 1900.

My first .25 caliber rifle was an old Model 83 Maynard in .25-20 Single Shot caliber. This was given to me by my shooting uncle when I was only eight or nine years old. Guess I am as old as this rifle for I was born in 1883. For years I used the old black powder loads and this old rifle accounted for a great many gray squirrels. Then later I used it with the 75-grain Lyman gas check bullet and five grains of Unique powder.

This load gave wonderful accuracy. I believe it was in the March 1936 issue of *The Rifleman* that the Hercules Company had an ad showing one of my targets with five shots in one hole with this load.

My next .25 caliber rifle was made for me by Niedner back around 1909 or so when he was in Malden, Massachusetts. This was in .25 Krag, made on a nice Winchester Single Shot rifle. This rifle also killed a great many woodchucks, but it also was one of the most accurate single shot rifles I have ever owned. Of course I had one of the early .250-3000 Savage rifles, for I happened to have something to do with the design of this case.

When I heard that Winchester would stop the manufacture of the Model 70 in this caliber, I sent in a Winchester action and had them put on a barrel chambered for the .250-3000 case. This rifle had a nice close chamber, and it is one of the most accurate factory products I have ever seen. With my own 85-grain bullets made in one of Fred Huntington's fine swages, and with 36 grains of 3031 powder, it will put five shots into one hole at one hundred yards.

Along in the 1950's I was experimenting with a new case in .25 caliber which I called the .250 Don-Ace. Sam Clark, Jr. shot a world's record at three hundred meters with a rifle chambered for this case, down at DuBois, Pennsylvania, some fifteen years ago. While I used 36 grains of 3031 and the 86-grain bullet in my regular .250-3000 rifles, with this larger case, made from .250-3000 brass, I was able to use 42 grains of 3031 with the same weight bullet. When I used the 100-grain bullet in the .250 Don. case it made a very fine deer rifle. I understand that there are quite a few of these rifles still in use around the country.

When friend Whelen and Ned Roberts were working on the design that later was called the .257 Roberts, I had a similar design based on the 7x57 case, but with a 30-degree shoulder. When friend Whelen shot my rifle he said it was better than the first Roberts design. Later, when the case was used in the Remington rifles, they also changed the design of the shoulder, but they used 20 degrees.

I was sorry to see this case taken from production as it was a good one, and it *still is*. And speaking about taking cases from production, I am wondering what has happened to Winchester. First, Winchester took .220 Swift rifles out of production, next it was the .348 Winchester, then the .358 Winchester and now I understand they will no longer make rifles in the .225 Winchester caliber.

All of these rifles were good calibers and they still are, if one can find a rifle chambered for one of them. Could it be that the magnums are making this change in rifle shooting? I was hunting back in the days when all we had were black powder rifles, and whenever we killed anything with them they were *dead*.

Also it was an easy matter to hit with the old rifles. No trouble from recoil. I have seen many of this younger generation shooting magnum rifles, and the trouble seems to be that they don't do enough shooting to get used to their rifles.

This extra recoil seems to take their minds off the fact that you have to hit something before you can kill it, no matter what sort of rifle you use. I don't go for magnums. But again, everyone to his own notion, as the old lady said when she kissed the cow.

Some time ago my friend Joyce Hornady sent me a supply of his new 120-grain .25 caliber long spitzer bullets for trial in my rifles. It was some time before I got around to shooting them, but one day last fall we had a perfect day for shooting. I went up on the Pine Tree Rifle Range, near Johnstown, New York. Of course, I had a couple of my most accurate .25 caliber rifles with me. I had loaded up some cases in both .250-3000 and .250 Don-Ace. For this heavier bullet I went to a lower charge of 4064 powder.

I can hardly remember when I was more surprised at the results I got, not only at one hundred yards but at two hundred. Friend Hornady has certainly come up with *something* with this new bullet. But the chances are good that I am not telling anything new to those shooters who have been shooting this bullet. It was made to order for the .25-06 Remington rifle, and I believe it will go a long way in bringing back the .25 caliber rifles' popularity.

I have always had excellent results with Hornady bullets in my hunting rifles, and his .22 caliber bullets are hard to beat in my chuck rifles. Recently I have been shooting chucks with the new Nosler .22 Zipedo bullet (now called the Solid Base) for long-range (three hundred yards or more) chuck shooting with very good results. I was pleased to learn that the firm of Leupold & Stevens had purchased Nosler. I have used Leupold scopes ever since they were available, and they are the finest scopes I have ever used. When a person gets to my age a good scope is everything. I have them in 10X on several of my chuck rifles. What surprises me most is that they have so much light gathering power that I can see and kill chucks later in the day than with any other scope I have ever used.

And make no mistake about this, in a long lifetime of chuck shooting I have used about every scope it was possible to buy.

I have been making my own metal-jacketed bullets since back around 1909 or 1910, when I started making them with swages I got from Niedner. Dr. Mann really got me started in bullet making, when we were experimenting with some early .22 and .25 caliber cases. We had to make them ourselves as it was the only source of supply. I have a lot of fine swages; some of the best were made by

Niedner, as well as Fred Huntington, who runs RCBS. As it is easy to see, Fred is still going strong.

I have no apologies for writing about these products. I have the idea that if anyone turns out a good product there can be little harm in telling the world about it. I feel quite certain my readers have had as good results with the items I have mentioned as I have had.

My readers may also get the idea that I am making some rather strong claims for the .25 caliber rifles. Well, all I can say is that after some 80 years of active rifle shooting, I have found that for all-around use, no rifle in either .22 or even in 7mm caliber will equal a good .25.

One will notice, for instance, that with the use of the new .25 caliber 120-grain Hornady bullet the .25-06 Remington case will give long range results very close to that of the Winchester .270.

The writer was shooting a rifle in 6mm caliber long before most of the modern day riflemen were born. This was back before 1900, and it was called the 6mm Navy case. The only bullets available were the long slim metal case bullets, and I can still hear them hum, as they ricocheted off the hard ground when we used them in chuck hunting. There is nothing one can do with any 6mm rifle that cannot be done a lot better with a .25.

And I really believe that most of the experienced riflemen of this country will agree with me in this matter of caliber.

It takes years of active rifle shooting before one can form solid opinions on rifle shooting, but once certain facts are known and remembered, they add up to a total that will bring results in your own rifle shooting ever after.

Yours truly,
H.A. Donaldson

P.S. My No. 30 issue of *The Handloader* has just been received. It is a good issue as usual. I note your comments in regard to the loading technique and loads I use in 7x57 rifle. Guess I should have mentioned that my rifle has a barrel with a twelve-inch twist, instead of the usual eight or nine-inch twist of the old military barrels.

The 7x57 loads mentioned in the manuals are often way under what may be used with safety in a modern 7x57 rifle. At one time the Winchester Company chambered the Model 54 rifle to take the 7x57 case, but after sales of a lot of war surplus Model 93 Mausers that were chambered for the 7x57, both factory ammunition and listed loads had to be conservative. These low velocities had a bad effect on the sales of the Model 54 Winchester in that caliber, so it was soon taken out of production.

But a modern rifle, particularly one with a slow twist like mine, can safely handle loads much more powerful than the published loads. So, while my loads are far above maximum published loads for this case, they aren't maximum loads in my rifle. I don't use maximum loads. I hope this clears up the matter.

Harve

Harvey in his easy chair, summer of 1968. Photo was taken by Jean Streeter while she was interviewing Harve for a biographical article that appeared in the January-February issue of Handloader. Harvey said this picture made him look as if he were a hundred years old.

# On Super-Accuracy

### Date Unknown

Dear Neal,

I have found that good bullets are required to produce the super-accuracy we look for in our modern varmint and bench-rest rifles. I would even go so far as to say that good bullets represent 90 percent of the results obtained.

As a case in point, I will mention two different .250-3000 custom-made rifles as well as a .250 Don-Ace that stand in my gun rack. Any one of these rifles will give one-inch groups of ten shots at one hundred yards with factory bullets, but this is not my idea of super-accuracy.

Wishing to obtain better results, several years ago I had Fred Huntington make up a swage in .25 caliber that would produce bullets of from 75 to 115 grains. Bullets from this swage will in the above mentioned rifles produce groups that will *average* a half inch at a hundred yards, if I do my part in holding properly.

I was fortunate to obtain a large supply of Sierra jackets, from about the first batch they produced. At first I tried bullets in the 75-grain weight, and while they were O.K. in a special barrel of 16-inch twist, in my regular rifles having 14-inch twist they were too short. Next I tried an 80-grain bullet, then the 85 and 90. Balancing the load to these different weights, I began to get good results. While different powders may be used in the .250-3000 case, I happen to know that when Du Pont brought out No. 3031 powder, they had this case in mind, so this is my own choice of powder for this medium-sized case.

In my powder magazine is a ten-pound can of No. 3031 of Lot No. 1 that was furnished me by Du Pont for experimental purposes about a year or so before it was available to handloaders. Even my friend J. Bushnell Smith, of Smith's Custom Loads, had to borrow some for his first testing. The date on the can shows it was received in the fall of 1935. I have used many pounds of this powder since Lot No. 1 was produced.

Another factor in obtaining accuracy is to have the powder charge fill the case. As many shooters know, this has been the one feature that has been connected with my own experimenting in case design. I'm still strong for the 30 degree shoulder, and will continue to use it until I find something better. It seems the factories have trouble with sharp shoulders, but fire-forming does away with all that. Years ago I learned the hard way that powder position is important, so I undertook to design cases having *no air space*, or nearly so. And this feature has produced better accuracy. Now today I read that *zero* air space is the ideal. How a man learns as he grows older. Or does he?

With my own swaged .25 caliber bullets in the .250-3000 I have had the best accuracy with those of from 83 to 85 grains with 34 to 35 grains of No. 3031. For a long-range load I use the ninety-grain with a case full of No. 4350. I have never found any load in the .257 Roberts to equal it. It would take a good-sized book to tell all the important features required to produce accuracy, so I have only tried to bring out the most important ones in this short letter. I note that most modern cartridge designers seem to run to large capacity cases. They may look well on paper, but I doubt very much if any of them will take a load of powder that will fill the case to the base of the bullet.

I am still shooting and experimenting, but the sad part is that most of my old correspondents have long since left the range.

Very truly yours,
Harvey A. Donaldson

Yours truly No. 32

# The Importance of Twist

December 19, 1970

Friend Neal:

When the Winchester Company was working on the .220 Swift cartridge, I received what I believe to be the first rifle that ever left the factory. My buddy Col. Whelen suggested to Edwin Pugsley of Winchester that they send me a pilot rifle for experimental purposes.

When J. Bushnell Smith found out that I had a new rifle in this caliber, he made a trip down to my home so he might shoot it. Well, after I had given the new rifle a good workout I wrote to Mr. Pugsley suggesting that the twist be changed from sixteen inches, which was the twist on my pilot rifle, to fourteen inches. I also suggested that they bring out a good 55-grain spitzer bullet instead of the short stubby 48-grain bullet.

A number of years after this, when I got to thinking more about this twist proposition, I was sorry that I did not suggest a fifteen-inch twist for the 55-grain bullet.

While shooting a Schuetzen rifle long ago I learned that the proper thing was to use a twist that was correct for the weight of bullet used at the range the rifle would be used. In other words why select a barrel, say in .30 caliber, with a twist that was correct for 1,000-yard shooting if the rifle would only be used for two hundred or three hundred-yard shooting. Just plain common sense. Later in some correspondence with Harry Pope, he wrote that I had the right idea.

For a number of years in experimenting with several varmint rifles in .22 caliber, this idea of the 15-inch twist kept popping up. When Vernor Gipson chambered my first .219 Don-Wasp he used a barrel having the fourteen-inch twist. I made a slight change in the design of the original case, and when the barrel for this particular case was made up it had the fifteen-inch twist. I still have this fine-shooting rifle and I might add it is the most accurate rifle I have ever used.

After my friend Douglas started the manufacture of rifle barrels down in Charleston, West Virginia, I suggested that he make some experimental barrels in

.22 caliber with this fifteen-inch twist. But for some reason or other he never took much interest in such a barrel.

Douglas made up a number of very accurate .22 barrels that were used in bench rest shooting by Sam Clark, Jr. These barrels proved so good, when Clark was doing the shooting, that then continued to make them in fourteen-inch twist. I have found that being contented with past accomplishments will very often stifle future achievement.

When Winchester brought out the .225 case a few years ago, I thought it a good time to again try out my fifteen-inch twist idea. I selected one of my good Remington Model 722 actions with a 40-X trigger and sent it down to Douglas to have him fit one of his stainless barrels, twenty-six inches long in his light varmint weight, but this time I wanted a barrel in the fifteen-inch twist, and no fooling!

In due time the outfit arrived and it is the most accurate varmint rifle I have ever seen. I own six or eight good varmint rifles, but my favorite, and the one that is used the most, is the Remington 722 action with the fifteen-inch twist barrel. With it I have made numerous ten-shot groups at one hundred yards with nine shots into one hole and the tenth shot touching the others. My readers may get the idea that I own a very accurate shooting outfit.

Recently a shooting friend asked why I used the fifteen-twist and how I had arrived at that figure. His first question was easy to answer: I had found that twist gave the best accuracy; his second question might be answered with one word, experience.

I have seen strange things happen in rifle shooting which at the time were hard to explain. One can take out a certain rifle, usually one with a rather quick twist, work out a load that should perform, then start shooting. The hundred-yard groups look sort of hollow.

Next you move the target out to two hundred yards and the group will tighten up, and you wonder what the devil is going on. Next if you will take the target out to three hundred yards you get another surprise, for the group you are looking at is even better, when this longer range is taken into account, than the one you made at one hundred yards.

The explanation is that your bullets, usually of a light weight, gyrate to a certain extent, quite close to the muzzle of the rifle before they have had a chance to stabilize. This action of the bullets in flight can be seen in spinning a top. When the top is first thrown it will gyrate, more or less, and then when it has slowed down to the proper velocity it will run true.

Bullets act in about the same way. The factories that make the barrels for hunting rifles have to use a twist quick enough to stabilize at long range the heaviest bullet that can be used in that particular caliber. Of course we may use that rifle in woods hunting where the range usually is shorter, or we may use bullets of a lighter weight. During my own experience in bench rest shooting, which started soon after 1900, at ranges not over two hundred yards, I found that the slowest twist that would keep the bullets point-on out at that range gave the best accuracy. Even if the bullet showed a slight tipping as shown by holes in the target, I was getting tight groups.

My readers may by now understand why I use a fifteen-inch twist in my 22 caliber varmint rifle.

The old issues of *The American Rifleman* show that around 1923 Harry Pope made barrels for the .30-06 Springfield, and these barrels had either the fourteen or fifteen-inch twist, rather than the usual ten-inch. These barrels were made up for the Free Rifle International Team of 1923. I believe the 150-grain metal case bullets were used and the ranges were one hundred to three hundred meters. Pope found he got the best accuracy in these slow twist barrels with his special cast bullet design, Lyman No. 308403. These barrels very soon held all the records, up to two hundred yards.

Many years later a friend of mine from Buffalo, New York showed up on the Johnstown range with a bench rest rifle with a bull pup stock and a short heavy barrel chambered for the .308 Winchester case. The owner asked me what I thought of it. I told him that I figured that he was trying to shoot at one hundred yards with a barrel twist correct for 1,000-yard shooting. He sort of shook his head and walked away.

The results he got in that match were exactly as I had suspected. Before this fellow was ready to return to his home, he walked over to say goodby. While we stood visiting I said, Bruno, if you insist in shooting a .30 caliber bench rest rifle, why not do as Harry Pope did back around 1923. I then related what Pope had done with his slow-twist .30 caliber barrels, giving him the data that would allow him to look up the old records. He said maybe old Harry had something at that, and it was worth giving it a try.

The next year, at our next match in Johnstown, I happened to be on the range when this same friend arrived. In fact I walked over to his car before he got out. This time, my friend was all smiles, and said, "Stick around awhile, I have something to show you." He opened up the trunk of his car and brought out what looked like the same rifle he had the year before, but I noted the barrel was shorter and heavier. He kept the rifle in his hands while we were talking, but I reached over and said, "Let's see the new job." When I took the rifle I took out the bolt and looked up through the barrel, where I noted at once this barrel had the fourteen-inch twist. So I said, "Well Bruno, you are getting smart." With that, he only laughed and said, "Keep it quiet." Well, to make a long story short, from that very match friend Bruno made bench rest history, winning not only at Johnstown, but at every match he attended, including the NBRSA National Championships in 1962. This was the start of the use of the .308 case in bench rest shooting, where it has made many records.

Yours truly,<br>
Harvey Donaldson

## Rattlesnakes!

### December 21, 1970

Dear Dave,

Your nice letter of the 15th just received. Have also had word from Neal and I have sent him a lot of stuff for *Handloader*. We are having a real winter out this way, and the fellows with Snow Cats are having a ball.

That General Motors outfit gave me a write up in the Corvette Magazine several years ago. If they want any more data have them contact the Hubbard Chevrolet Garage, St. Johnsville, New York. I have been buying my Chevrolet cars from this place for over thirty years. Reason I had to get a bigger car than my last Corvette was because one can't carry much stuff in such a small car. I still drive a Model 1970 Sports Car — a Malibu Chevelle.

Will be glad to hear from Jim. You see, years ago I was down in his country. I used to do a lot of bird hunting, and I had a string of bird dogs, English Setters. Field Champions, too. One time I was down in Grand Junction, Tennessee, at the Field Trials. There I met "Uncle Jim" Avent of Hickory Valley — the *best* damn field trail dog handler this country ever saw. I also knew Nash Buckingham, who was a field trial judge. A great guy, that Nash.

Only thing I find fault with hunting quail in Tennessee is that you want leather pants and leggins to hunt in that country — RATTLESNAKES, and how. I'm having a fine Christmas Season, so far. Best regards and write again soon.

Sincerely,
Harve

## 88 and Feeling O.K.

### February 3, 1971

Dear Dave,

I suppose Neal is in Prescott by now, but I am not sure about this. Our local bench rest magazine, *Precision Shooting*, gave me a write-up and had my picture on the cover of the February issue. They got the data inside more or less balled up. In a day or so I will send you a copy of this magazine, which has a picture made last fall of an *old cuss* who is still shooting.

Month after next I will be 88 years old, but that don't mean a thing. I am feeling O.K., without an ache or a pain, and still working every day in a local machine shop. I wonder if I'll live long enough to get a write-up in *Rifle* magazine.

I'm rather proud that yours truly started the bench rest movement in Johnstown, New York, back in 1947. Sure, a lot of bench rest shooting was done long before that, but what yours truly developed into a national organization, has now become international.

Best regards,
Harve

## Solid Gold Card

**February 7, 1971**

Friend Neal,

How come no word from you? Have been looking for a letter from you for a month, but no luck so far. They put my picture on the February issue of our *Precision Shooting*. I am sending you a copy for your files. Our I.B.S. is doing O.K. We have chapters all over, and still growing every year. I happen to be an honorary life member of the NBRSA and I have a solid gold membership card that the fellows gave me to prove it.

I am busy as ever, and out shooting foxes over the weekends. We have plenty of snow in this part of the country. You can walk *over the wire fences* in most of our fields. I use snow shoes and walk the critters down.

Have no idea how far ahead I am with my "letters" but you must have several letters on hand. I have had offers to write for other magazines but I am too damn busy. I get letters from all over about my stuff in the magazine. You must cover a lot of country.

Get busy and write to me.

Sincerely,
Harve

## A Good Picture

**February 16, 1971**

Dear Harve,

I finally made it to Arizona and I'm in love with this country. It's dry and rugged, but the climate is great — February weather beautiful.

Congratulations on the cover picture on *Precision Shooting*. I always did like that picture; I thought it was a good one when we ran it with your column a few months back. Speaking of columns, I think we only have two on hand. I'm trying to get a little better organized out here and hope to get a little further ahead with all the writers, so why don't you sit down at the trusty typewriter and bat out a few more while the snow is so deep. Then I won't be pestering you for more during the summer and fall shooting seasons.

I'm glad to know that you're getting a lot of letters from all over, as a result of your writing in the *Handloader*. However, I understand that you don't have the time to answer them so I've been heading off the many letters to you that come in here. Unless it's a letter that I think you will find particularly interesting, I either answer it myself, or if it's simply a technical question, send it to one of the other boys.

Best regards,
Neal

## Telegraph Poles!

**February 22, 1971**

Friend Neal,

Yours of the 16th just received. I figured it was about time I had some word from you. Glad to learn that you like that Arizona country. I have been out your way several times. My own favorite western country is in New Mexico, around Taos.

We are having the worst winter here in some seventy years. Right now the snow is three to four feet deep. Did you ever see snow drifts as high as telegraph poles? Well we got 'em.

I am getting lots of exercise with my long-range fox hunting. The month of February is when they are running and breeding, so I get out after them on snow shoes. I pick up a track and then follow it 'til I find the fox asleep, under a drift. Then I lay down and shoot prone with a sling, and most of the shots are long ones, over two hundred yards.

Guess I must be in good shape for I can't get anyone to follow me all day on snow shoes. Best regards to Dave and tell him to drop me a line.

So long,
Harve

## He Sure Gave Us Snow

**February 22, 1971**

Friend Neal,

This is the *second* letter I have written you today. Guess my pep is still going strong. At any rate this extra attention should deserve another letter from either you or Dave. How is that ornery cuss, anyway? No word from him in one hell of a while!

I have wondered if Jim Carmichel is with you in Prescott. Write soon and give me all the news. Will send you some snow pictures when I get the prints back. There is a saying in this part of the country to the effect that the Good Lord looks after the people who live in this Mohawk Valley. If this is true, He sure gave us plenty of snow this winter!

But spring will soon be here. The chucks are already out, as I have seen their muddy tracks on some of the snow drifts out in the country. Pussy Willows will also soon be out, so spring is only a short way off.

Yours truly,
Harve

## Sit Right Down, Neal!

**March 9, 1971**

Friend Neal,

I wonder if either you or Dave will attend the 100th convention of the N.R.A. in Washington, over April 2nd to 7th? My friend Frank Hubbard, who helped me start the National Bench Rest Association, and I are going to attend this convention. There will be several hundred shooters on hand that I know personally, so I am planning a real good time.

My 88th birthday comes on April 6th and I hear some of my friends are planning on giving me quite a birthday celebration. I was simply wondering if you two fellows might be on hand.

When you get this note, *sit right down* and answer it at once! You might just as well be in China as far as any word from you. Tell that cuss Dave to write also!

Now that I have given you hell, I had better close.

Sincerely yours,
Harve

## Lost in Skull Valley?

**March 11, 1971**

Dear Dave,

I have had no luck writing to Neal, so figured I had better write to you. Could it be that Neal is lost some place west of Skull Valley? First off, why in hell have I never received the last issue of *Rifle?* Also, here it is March the 11th and still no issue of the *Handloader.* Why this hold up?

My purpose in writing today is simply this: Will you attend the big *doings* in Washington? If all goes as planned I will attend the convention. My buddies Fred Huntington and Joyce Hornady will be on hand, as well as a lot of my old shooting friends.

My 88th birthday comes on April 6th, and some of my friends have written that if I show up they will throw a birthday party for me that I will long remember.

Will be looking for some word from you soon, so *get busy and write!*

Sincerely yours,
Harve

## Will Miss Celebration

**March 12, 1971**

Dear Harve,

Just time for a note. Since we can't seem to get caught up from the move, Dave and I aren't planning to go to the NRA meetings this year. We have reservations just in case we can get time, but right now I just don't see how we are going to be able to make it. I sure hate it, since you're going to be there — I would certainly like to take part in your birthday celebration.

Best regards,
Neal

## Mailman Likes Guns?

**March 16, 1971**

Dear Harve,

Neal has read your letter and says he's written you several letters in the last couple of weeks. I wonder if you're getting all your mail.

It appears neither Neal nor I will make it to the NRA Convention this year. We have attended regularly for the last 10 or 12 years but it's just too far away from Arizona. Also, we have to kind of watch our pennies for a while. I'm sorry I won't see you there but I know you'll have a good time.

Glad that you are still in good health and high spirits and I'm sorry the last two magazines didn't reach you. Maybe you have a mailman who likes guns! Replacements are on the way.

Cordially,
Dave

## Hasten To Answer

**March 18, 1971**

Friend Neal,

Yours of the 12th came a day or so ago and I hasten to answer at once. I am unable to figure out this mail situation. Usually it takes at least six days to get a letter mailed from Prescott. At other times your mail comes thru in *three days*. How in hell does that happen?

Now about the N.R.A. Convention. I am not sure as yet if I can make it myself. My buddy and I had planned to drive down to Washington, that is less than a day's run from here. But this friend is sick, and unless he makes a recovery by April first, the trip is off. Thought I had better let you know at once. I hate to pass up that trip, myself.

Thanks for your note and best regards to Dave. Will write again soon, but wanted to get this off to you promptly.

Yours truly,
Harve

## Surprise of His Life

**March 19, 1971**

Friend Neal,

I enjoyed your article on the *"Inside Story of Nosler Bullets"* in *Handloader* No. 29. Also noted Jack Slack's picture, as well as the one shown with John Nosler. Jack is a good friend of mine and I have known him for quite some time.

I would like to write a letter for *Handloader* telling of my own experience with Nosler bullets. It is a funny thing about those bullets. I bought a box of .22 caliber Zipedos several years ago, mostly out of curiosity, then put them on a shelf in my gun room. They sat there for some time; then one day I took down the box, and loaded up twenty for trial in my tack-driving .225 Winchester Model 722 Remington, with 10X Leupold scope.

Now, with my own 53-grain bench rest match bullets, this rifle will put five shots into a quarter inch at one hundred yards, if I hold right. Well, along last spring I loaded up those twenty cases for trial and I got the surprise of my life when I examined the targets I shot with them at one hundred and two hundred yards. They went into a half inch at a hundred and less than an inch at two hundred. I sure wondered what in hell was going on, as no hunting bullets should do that well.

About then I tried to buy more Zipedo bullets, and I had one hell of a time before I located any. Now I must have a half dozen boxes or so that will last me for some time to come.

Best,
Harve

## Of Course, He's Young

**April 2, 1971**

Friend Neal,

Today I received the May-June *Rifle*. I got a great kick out of our friend Jim Carmichel's article on barrel cleaning. That hillbilly has much to learn about rifle shooting, but of course he's very young!

For instance, I am *still shooting* the very first .220 Swift rifle that left the Winchester factory. This was way back in the early thirties. How many bullets have passed down this barrel I will never know, but I can say that *today* the barrel of this rifle is in perfect condition.

Way back before 1910 I started making my own metal cased bullets, and in the beginning we had some trouble with metal fouling. First we learned never to shoot any bullets in rapid fire off the bench. Let the barrel cool between shots. Next we learned that if we had our bullets cadmium plated, no copper was ever left on the lands. Finally, we learned that the use of graphite wads sort of lubricated the bore, and all of this resulted in *long barrel life,* but of course friend Carmichel does not know about our early methods. Guess I will have to send him a letter telling about this early experimenting to reduce metal fouling.

Understand one thing — cadmium plating does not foul the lands of a rifle bore like a copper jacketed bullet. Why the devil the bullet makers have passed up this feature is more than I can figure. Instead, it is sort of a greasy metal, and it sure adds to barrel life. I'll bet neither Jim nor you has ever even heard about this.

Sincerely,
Harve

## No Extra Writing

**April 14, 1971**

Friend Neal,

Have had no word from you in some time. How about a letter? I'm enclosing an article on Schuetzen rifle matters.

Now, I have had some good offers from the *American Rifleman* to write for them, but the chuck hunting and fishing seasons are coming along, so I'm not sure I want to take on any extra writing. Bud Waite, who is Technical Editor of this magazine, is a personal friend of mine. I have known Bud for years.

While this magazine pays pretty well for articles, I would much rather see my data shown in *Rifle* and *Handloader* magazines.

If you read *Precision Shooting,* you may know that some of the Schuetzen shooters out Missouri way have run into trouble in trying to get their Schuetzen rifles to perform with *modern* powders. All they did was to ruin some good barrels. Now yours truly has all the data on this matter and the article I am sending covers this fully.

Sincerely yours,
Harve

# 'Blue Boy'

### May 6, 1971

Friend Harve,

Dave just got his gun back last week from Chet Brown of San Jose, California, who sleeved it (it's a 40X with factory barrel) and installed one of his lightweight fiberglass stocks — painted *baby boy blue*. Naturally we call it "Blue Boy." Also, naturally, it brings a lot of snickers from the purists. Dave didn't have time to work up a good load before the Casa Grande shoot last Saturday night, and the load he was using performed very erratically. Sometimes the flash would light up the countryside, and most of the shots sounded as if they had been fired down a rain barrel.

One hundred-yard groups ranged from an inch down to .249, which was the smallest group in light varmint class. He was using Ball C-2 powder, and may have gotten a bad lot, or else the Remington primers weren't doing their job properly with that hard-to-ignite powder. He had previously used the same load with Ball C-1 with good results.

I've been having troubles with my gun. The bedding went sour, probably due to the stock shrinking in this dry climate. Bill Atkinson of A&M bedded it in Devcon three times before he got a good scald. Loosening the front screw with the rear one tight results in only .004 movement of a dial indicator at the fore-end. However, the gun still isn't shooting as it should — possibly because it has had many rounds down the tube. It acts like it wants to shoot, but I'm getting unexplained fliers.

During the heavy varmint shoot I tinkered with the screws on my gun until I got it shooting, and managed to win the first match with it — but after that one, bad fliers occurred in each group on the record target, putting me way down in the standings.

A local gunsmith is building an experimental bench action for me to try — right-hand bolt, left-hand ejection port. It will be interesting to see how it does.

Must get at some of these other letters.

Best regards,
Neal

**Yours truly No. 33**

# Loads for Schuetzen Rifles

**May 12, 1971**

Friend Neal,

From what I hear some of the shooters of the Schuetzen rifles are running into trouble trying to use modern powders in the old soft steel barrels. Back around 1900, when the Schuetzen rifle was a popular firearm, the old-time riflemen learned it wouldn't work. At one time even Harry Pope tried some Pyro D.G. powder in one of his good barrels. He ruined it and gave up any more experimenting along those lines.

Those of us who used the Schuetzen rifle around the turn of the century used either Fg black powder or King's Semi-Smokeless with soft lead bullets and we got results. The barrels of these old rifles were made of a rather soft mild steel and they had to be used very carefully. Harry Pope used a thin cardboard wad over the powder, the powder completely filling the case. Some used a thin wad of asbestos to try to protect the soft lead bullet base from fusion, but the writer used thin graphite wads. They worked out okay.

One cannot make a racing car out of a Model T Ford simply by filling up the tank with high octane gas. It simply does not work out that way. If some of our modern Schuetzen shooters want more velocity, they might better turn to the use of a modern varmint rifle. If they prefer the balance and hang of the old rifles they could have one made up on that plan, but chambered for a modern varmint cartridge. If our modern riflemen are unable to use the old rifles with the proper components, why shoot them at all? It may be that those who have already ringed the barrel or chamber of one of these priceless old soft steel barrels will understand what I mean.

At the time I gave up the use of the Schuetzen rifle, and went over to the varmint rifle, around 1925, I had over a dozen of the finest Schuetzen rifles ever made in

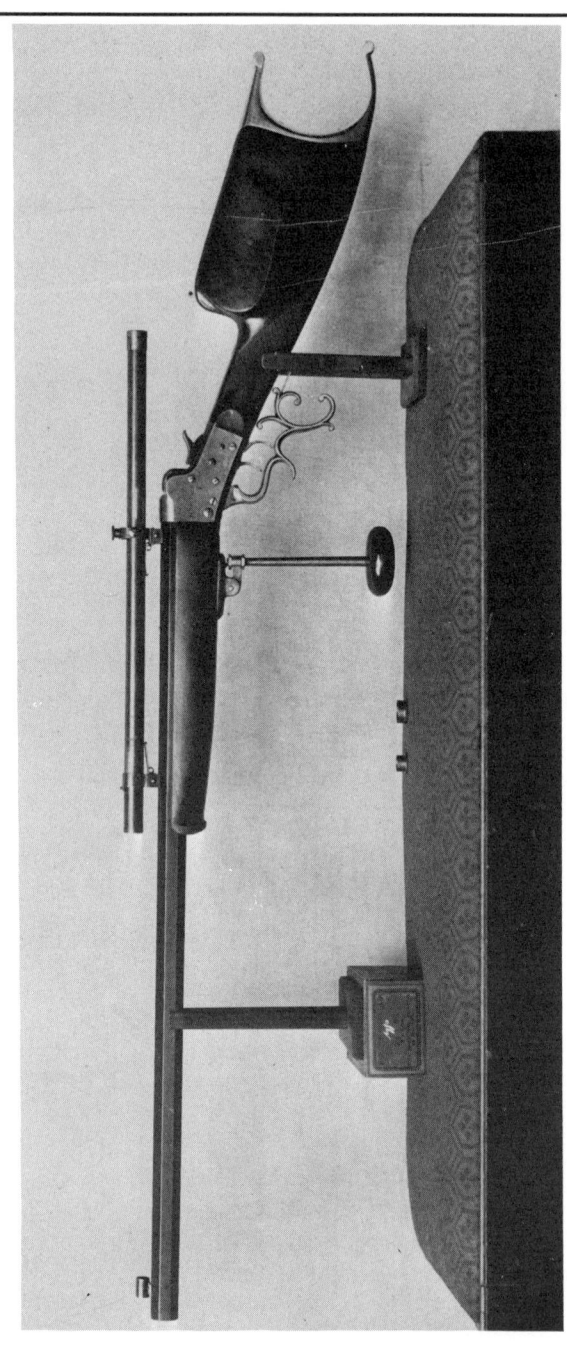

Donaldson once owned this .38-55-310 Remington-Schoyen rifle, Serial No. 4. Back of this photo, which was found in the boxes of old correspondence, has a notation, "Dr. Hudson used this fine rifle." It is probable that it is the gun Dr. Hudson used to set the world record, mentioned in Harvey's text. Scope is a six-power Peterson, and the rifle weighed 13 pounds.

this country. Most of these were made by Pope, but I had some from Schoyen, Zischang and old George Schalck, who taught Harry Pope how to make a barrel.

At one time I owned the rifle with which Dr. Hudson made a world record back around 1901. This was a .38-55 Remington-Schoyen special rifle with double set triggers of Dr. Hudson's design. This fine rifle is now owned by a friend living in New York City.

Another of my fine target rifles was the one used by Lt. Henry Fulton when he turned in the highest score made in the first of the international matches held on the Creedmore Range on Long Island, New York, back in September of 1874.

This rifle was later owned by Charles Rowland of Boulder, Colorado, who at one time owned more than sixty fine target rifles. We corresponded from around 1900 until he passed away and I still have all this correspondence in my files.

During 1935 and 1936 Ned Roberts wrote about my rifles in *The American Rifleman*, which published pictures of some of them.

But to get back to this matter of some of our modern Schuetzen riflemen and the trouble they are having in ringing the bore or chamber of their rifles, I note that some of these shooters report they were acting on advice found in the writing of Ned Roberts.

This writer first met Ned early in this century when he was a teacher in a business school in Gloversville, New York, about eight miles from my home. I was more or less closely associated with Ned until he passed away. For several years he and his wife came to visit me during his vacation, and we also had an extensive correspondence.

During all those years, if he ever did much Schuetzen shooting, I never knew it. All of his life friend Ned was bothered by poor eyesight which affected his rifle shooting and caused him to have to rely upon others for much of his experimental shooting.

I suspect the reason Claude Roderick and other modern Schuetzen riflemen have reported coming to grief while following Ned's loading advice was because Ned was publishing data someone had given him. If Ned had tried those loads and had trouble with them, of course, he would never have put them in his books. I have autographed copies of every book Ned wrote, by the way.

Modern Schuetzen riflemen might be interested in the loads that some of us used in our .32-40 Schuetzen rifles more than half a century ago. Harry Pope's best load for his .32-40 muzzle loading rifle was five grains FFg King's Semi-Smokeless, 19 or 20 grains of Du Pont Schuetzen powder, one post card wad, Pope's 190 bullet cast either 1-27 or 1-30. He first used the No. 2½ Peters primer, but later told me the No. 8 UMC was better.

Old Harry's next best load was No. 8 UMC primer, three grains of No. 1 Du Pont Smokeless, a shell full of FFg Semi-Smokeless, one post card wad, his 190-grain bullet, cast 1-30.

One of my best loads I used in my .32-40 Pope muzzle loading rifle was the No. 7 Western primer, three grains FFg Orange rifle (black), 14 grains No. 80 powder,

This 5 shot group was made from a bench rest at 100 yds., by H.A.Donaldson at 4:00 P.M. Feb.12.1931. A warm day, no air stirring, the light was poor. 32/40/200 Schoyen-Ballard 6" black bulls eye used, Martin .116" size aperature globe front, and Martin .032" aperature cup disc rear, as prescribed by C.W.Rowland. Load used as follows;
#8½ Western non-cor. primer
9 grs. Dupont white shotgun powder
200 gr. Pope bullet, cast 1-25 selected Leopolds banana lubricant, 1 greased wad, but powder loose in shell. Bullet seated in barrel 1/16" ahead of shell, charges thrown by an old Ideal # 5 measure.
This shooting was witnessed by the following members of the National Rifle Association.

*L. L. Root*    # 6435    1/31/31.
*F. K. Blissell*    # 14909    3/31/31.

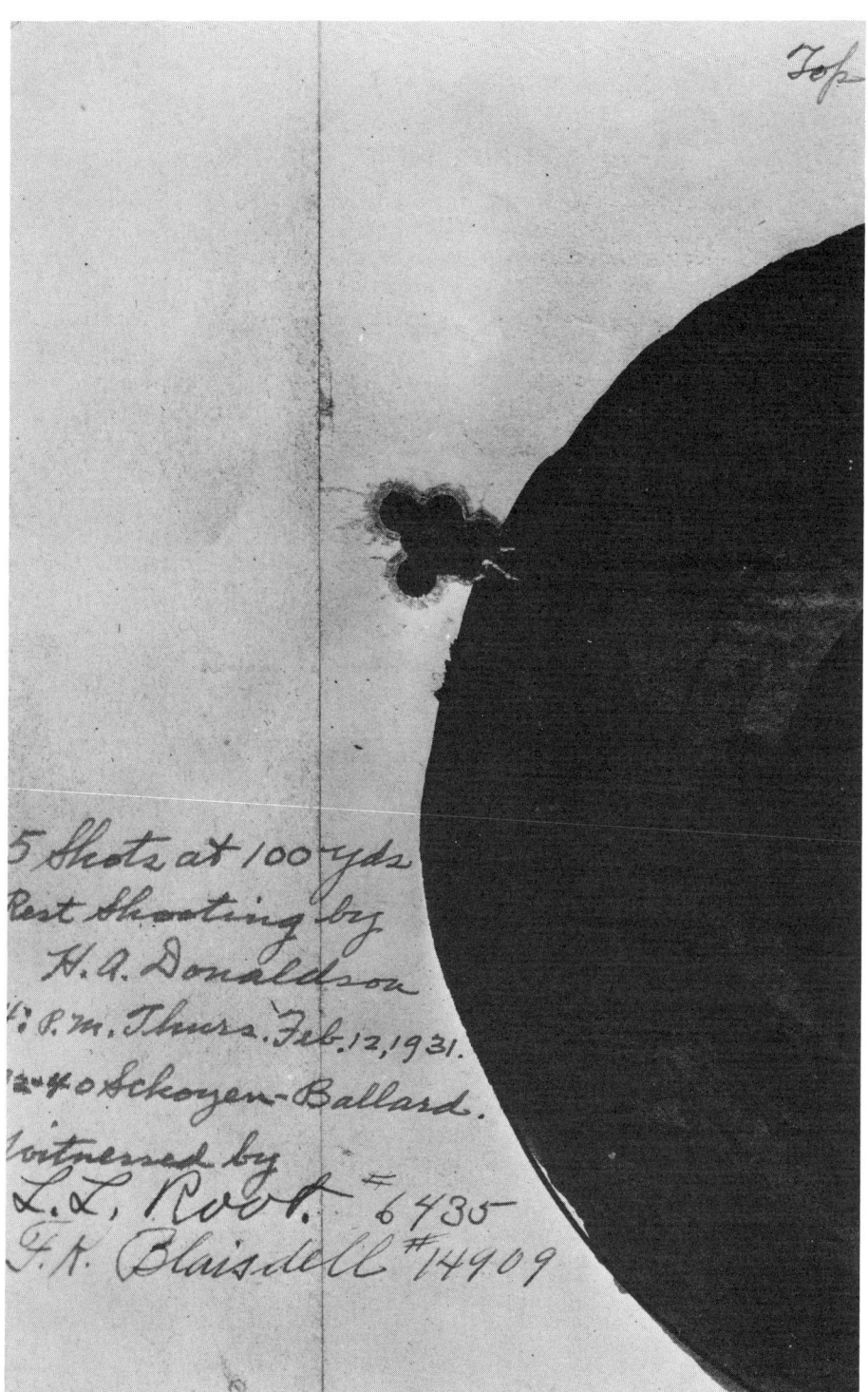

190-grain Pope bullet cast 1-30, blotting paper wad. Another good load was No. 8 UMC primer, four grains Du Pont No. 1 powder, 30 grains FFg Semi-Smokeless powder, 190-grain Pope bullet, cast 1-30 and my graphite wad.

C.T. Westergard's load, used in his .32-40 Pope-Ballard, was the No. 2½ Peters primer, five grains King's Semi-Smokeless, 15 grains Du Pont Schuetzen powder. I believe he used the same 190-grain bullet as mentioned above.

Of course you can't buy these old components any more, but there is some of it around. The writer still has several cans of No. 80, Du Pont No. 1 black powder and Du Pont's old Schuetzen powder, as well as the old primers.

With the components they were made for, these old rifles would shoot forever without any trouble. The lead building up on the lands that Roderick and the other modern Schuetzen shooters are having trouble with was absolutely unknown with the loads we used in the old days.

In loading a Schuetzen rifle, every one was a problem in itself. Often times we found that a load that was okay in one barrel would not do as well in another. A little experimenting was necessary to find the best load. And we had lots of things to experiment with — primers, powders, (usually two at a time), bullets, bullet alloys, lubricants, wads, seating method and other things as well, besides varying the way the gun was held. But when the right combination was found, that was the load we used ever afterward.

Yours truly,
Harvey A. Donaldson

Left to right, John T. Amber, editor of **Gun Digest** and **Handloader's Digest**, Fred T. Huntington, founder of RCBS, and Harvey Donaldson at a Johnstown shoot in 1965.

Yours truly No. 34

# A History of Bench Rest

**June 13, 1971**

Friend Neal:

    This letter to *The Handloader* has to do with the history of bench rest shooting in this country. One might say that bench rest shooting really started down around Lancaster, Pennsylvania, from around 1720 to 1730, when fine riflesmiths such as Lefever, Charles Leman, and a number more I might mention, were building the early rifles that were later known as the Kentucky rifles.

    These were of smaller caliber, with long octagon barrels, and shot either the round ball or what was later called the picket bullet, from slow-twist barrels, with the bullet patched by either linen or buckskin.

    Naturally there was considerable rivalry among the several gunsmiths as to who produced the most accurate rifles. It was customary for each gunsmith to demonstrate his own product at what were at that time called turkey shoots or beef shoots. At first this shooting was done from a prone position, with the barrel rested over a folded blanket placed on top of a log. The ranges were generally at 60, 80, 100, or 110 yards, though for some time 60 yards was the favorite distance. Every shooter made up his own target, which consisted of charcoal marks on a shingle. The rifleman whose bullets came the closest to the V or X on the shingle won the match. Even at that early time these old riflemen did some remarkable shooting, as I have seen copies of these targets in an old magazine published before the Civil War.

    When the country west of the Allegheny Mountains was opened up by these old-time riflemen, they carried the Lancaster rifles, and the good use they made of these rifles in Kentucky was what later gave the name of Kentucky Rifle to this particular firearm.

    Around 1830 the false muzzle was invented by one Clerk or Clark, then living in Boston, Massachusetts. Soon after, the early gunsmiths of the Eastern states started building heavy muzzle loading target rifles that used this false muzzle. Wm. Billinghurst of Rochester, Morgan James and George Ferris, of Utica, New York, as well as a number of other gunsmiths made up these fine old rifles, which were used in a form of bench rest competition.

I own a muzzle loading rifle made before the time of the false muzzle by J.J. Hill, of Johnstown, New York. This rifle is in fine condition, even after all these years of active service. It is of .40 caliber, with the slow twist, as it was made to use the short, pointed picket bullet.

The barrel of this particular rifle was made by no one less than E. Remington, Ilion, New York, and as near as can be determined it was made around 1830. The barrel is marked, by the way, on one side "cast steel." The story is that this man Hill walked the tow path along the Erie Canal, all the way from Fultonville, New York, to Ilion, New York, (a matter of at least 70 miles) carrying the heavy barrel on his shoulder on his return to Johnstown, New York. At that early date the packet boats were running on the Erie Canal, but evidently this old-timer would rather walk than ride. (He should see today's traffic on this route.) If one will read on Page 14 in Horace Kephart's book *Sporting Firearms*, he will read all about a barrel exactly like the one I own, on a gun made by Morgan James of Utica, New York.

It was during the half century preceding our Civil War that the muzzle loading rifle reached its highest development. After a lot of testing the riflemen of this period discovered the peculiar sugar loaf or picket bullet. These bullets weighed around

> Joe
>   Harvey A. Donaldson.
> With my best wishes. You started all this. Had it not been for your efforts there would not have been any bench rest shooting.
>   Townsend Whelen
> August 29, 1954.

Col. Townsend Whelen pauses for refreshment during one of the early bench rest matches at Johnstown, New York. At left is a card to Harvey that was found tacked to a wall in his shop. It was nearly overlooked during the search for early correspondence.

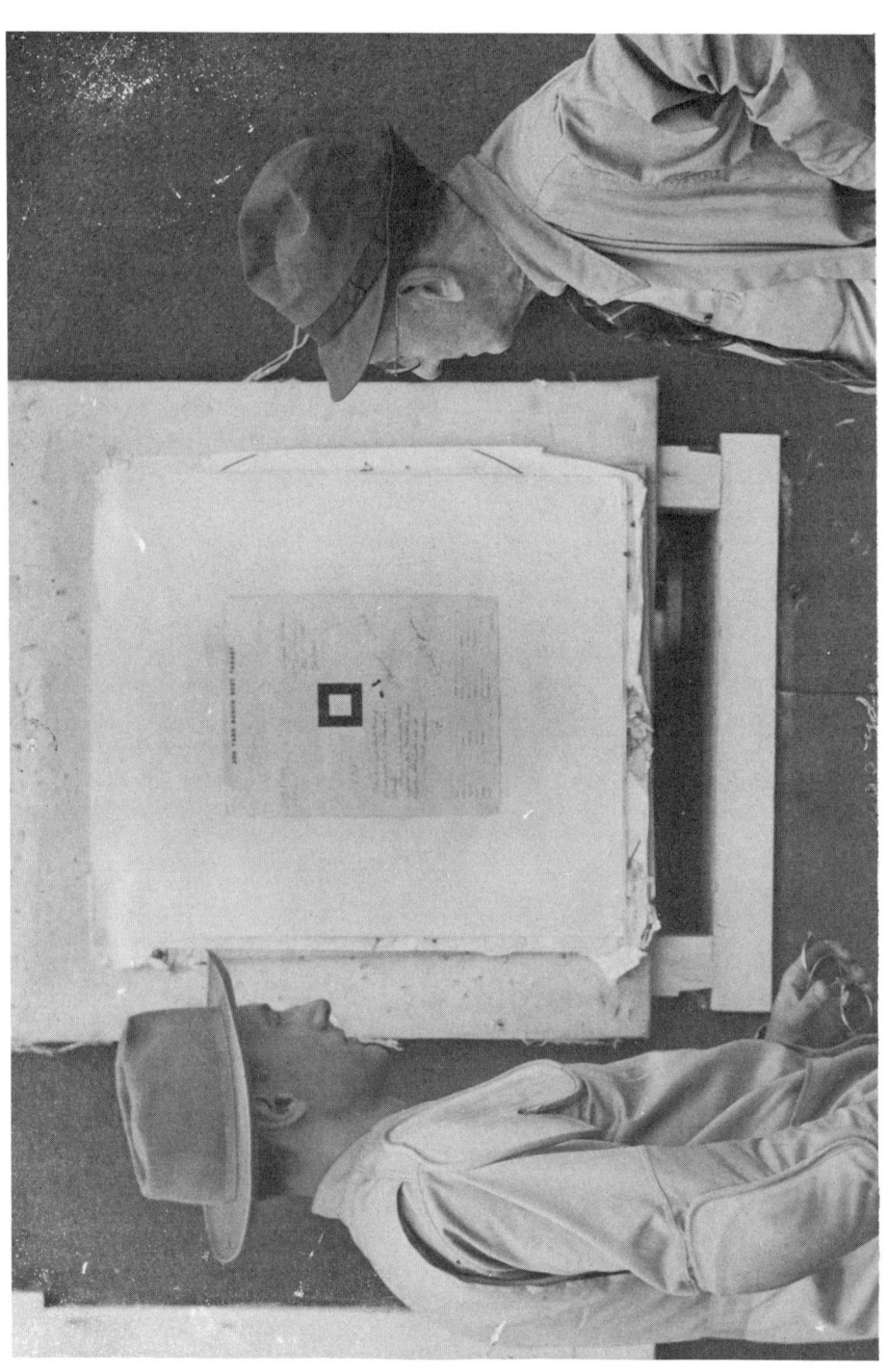

Mike Walker and Donaldson look over Mike's new world record. This was a 200-yard target, fired June 13, 1948. Mike was using the .219 Donaldson cartridge.

240 grains in .40 caliber, and gave the best accuracy in old rifles. Mr. Kephart gives a complete test of these old bullets.

This old .40 caliber rifle of mine was used for years by both my mother, as well as my shooting uncle, before and after the Civil War. If my readers will turn to Page 24 in the first issue of The *Rifle* Magazine, January-February, 1969, he will find an article by this writer which gives my first experience with this rifle, when I killed my first woodchuck. This was back around 1890 when I was only seven years old. Now, it just happens I was out chuck hunting only yesterday, so I can say that I have been chuck hunting for over 80 years. I sort of wonder if there are many active chuck hunters around this country who can beat this record.

Back before the Civil War, when my mother was only around 16 years old, my shooting uncle taught her how to use both the rifle and the shotgun. By the time she was 18, she could beat him at any sort of shooting, and in the fall she used to go around the country with him taking in the turkey shoots that were held each fall from around election day until after Thanksgiving.

While my mother taught me to stand up and shoot offhand, like a man, as she said, my early testing of rifles and loads was with the use of a shooting bench that my uncle had in his back yard. This uncle at that time lived on the edge of town so one could shoot at any time. I would test loads and sight in my rifles from this bench, where I gathered plenty of experience that helped out in later years.

My mother told me if I ever wanted to obtain any data on shooting matters that I should contact the best riflemen in the country. Sort of sound advice, to this day, and which I have tried to follow. Soon I had a close correspondence with such old-timers as Harry Pope, Charles Rowland, John D. Kelley, Kephart, and a host of others. A lot of this correspondence makes very interesting reading, even today.

It was back around 1900, about the time that I first met Pope, that I got interested in offhand two hundred-yard Schuetzen shooting. I eventually owned rifles made by Pope, Schoyen, Zischang, George Schalck, and others. My favorite rifles were made by Harry Pope, but to this day, I am not sure if my Schoyen or Zischang rifles were the most accurate.

I followed the use of the Schuetzen rifle until along in the middle '20's, when I gave up that rifle for the more modern chuck rifles. I was in close touch with Niedner from the time he was experimenting with Dr. Mann up until the time he passed away. It was really my association with Niedner that got me interested in the modern high speed chuck rifle.

When Niedner brought out his .22 Niedner rifle I had one of the first ones he produced. This, by the way, was a fine shooting outfit. I used such a rifle 'til along in the '30's when I got the idea I might design an even better case. After testing several designs, I ended up with the case called the .219 Donaldson-Wasp.

The few rifles for my .219 Don-Wasp case, owned by friends and me, gave such remarkable accuracy that I got the idea that the only way to improve on the modern chuck rifle was to get into some competition, shooting from the bench, where any new ideas in shooting might be worked out together with other bench rest shooters.

About this time, out in Seattle, Washington, my old friend Dr. Rod Janson had gathered a few shooters together to form an outfit called the Sniper's Congress,

Shooters at the 1948 Labor Day Matches in Johnstown include (top, left to right) Frank Hubbard, John Unertl, Harvey Donaldson, Col. Townsend Whelen and Clair Taylor. Bottom, Joe Rich, Manly Butts and Sam Clark, Jr.

mainly using high-power target rifles. This was during the war. Out in Monett, Missouri, another group under the leadership of my old friend Claude Roderick had gathered together a group of shooters who were also interested in shooting from a bench, with varmint rifles.

When I got the idea of starting a bench rest movement that would take in the whole country, about 1945, I was a member of the Pine Tree Fish & Game Club, located in Johnstown, New York. This was mostly a social club, with only a few members, where clam bakes were held in the fall. We had no rifle range of any sort on the club grounds. Several members in this club were interested in chuck hunting, and they all shot rifles chambered for my .219 Don-Wasp case. These shooters included Frank Hubbard, Bill Buchner, and Bill Van Nostrand.

For some time I talked over this matter of starting some sort of a bench rest movement, and the chuck shooters thought it was a good idea, but that was as far as it went. This meant that I had to convince the few members that ran the club that we should cut down a lot of trees, dig out the stumps, level off the ground, and lay out the range on about the only spot on the property where a range could be built.

The fellows thought I was crazy to think anyone would visit our range to simply sit down and shoot a few shots from a bench. But today, with a new club house, both one hundred and two hundred-yard rifle ranges, with fifty covered benches as well as skeet and trap ranges, our property is valued at over $200,000. The boys now tell me that the .219 Don-Wasp case design brought it all about.

But before anything could be done, my friend Frank Hubbard and I had to agree to make good any loss that the club sustained before they would let us start the rifle range.

I planned the range so we would shoot toward the north, which would allow sun on the targets all day long. Next was the job of clearing and preparing the range grounds, building target frames and benches, and formulating some sort of plans for running a match. Here is where I got plenty of help again from Frank Hubbard. Just what we had planned had never been done before on a large scale, so it took considerable hard work. I'm told that the bench design I used at the first match is still used all over the country.

At that first match on the Johnstown range, the Eastern Bench Rest Shooters Association was formed, with Frank Hubbard elected secretary-treasurer, Sam Clark, Jr., executive officer, Col. Townsend Whelen, vice president and H.A.D., president. In 1949 the name was changed to the Bench Rest Shooters Association and in 1951, after a meeting at Denver with the Western shooters, the National Bench Rest Shooters Association was formed.

But I'm getting ahead of my story. One of these days I'll tell about that first match.

Yours truly,<br>
Harvey A. Donaldson

Sam Clark, Jr. and Harvey Donaldson receive the Townsend Whelen trophy at a banquet following the National Bench Rest Championship matches in Johnstown, New York. The date was September 1, 1955.

Yours truly No. 35

# *Understanding Trajectory*

**September 2, 1971**

Friend Neal:

I suppose anyone who writes on matters pertaining to shooting will sooner or later receive some strange and curious inquiries. I know that I have had my share.

I am constantly surprised by some of the crazy ideas in these inquiries. Many shooters seem to have only a vague idea of what trajectory is all about. Where they get such "theories" one is at a loss to understand.

The average, well informed shooter of today has a pretty good notion as to the course a bullet takes after it leaves the barrel. But what about the fellow who writes in that his rifle shoots flat way out to one hundred yards or so. Now he wants to know how to load his ammunition so it will shoot flat at two hundred yards!

As I understand the situation, trajectory of a bullet is the curved path of its flight from muzzle to target. Since a bullet will start to drop the moment it leaves the barrel, the sights are adjusted to bring the bullet on the point of aim at whatever range it is sighted for. Every bullet, no matter what speed, has a curved flight, since it is pulled down by gravity. The height of that curve, for a given range, depends upon the velocity of the bullet.

Thus, no trajectory can be flat, because no curve is flat! The curve will be less with a bullet of high velocity, and higher with the slower bullet, if both are sighted to shoot at center at 100 yards (or any given distance). Thus the advantage of higher velocity with lower trajectory, is it extends the range at which one can hit game without making a close guess as to the distance, or allowance for the drop of the bullet.

Suppose, for instance, that you are hunting with a rifle such as the old .45-70, which has a lower velocity than the average big game outfit. For many years this rifle was the favorite with moose hunters in Maine. Usually this sort of hunting is in heavy cover, so that even seventy-five yards seems like a long range.

Your guide says, "Don't bother holding high — just hold where you want the bullet to go." He has the idea that most of your shots will be at short range.

But the days slip by, and no moose, so you start hunting the more open country, along the lakes and flat shore line. About this time, and close to the last day of your hunting, a large moose steps out on the margin of the lake. There he stands clearly outlined against sky and water, as fair a mark as you have ever seen. But this particular moose is a long way off, and just how far off is not an easy matter for city-trained eyes to determine.

Your guide moves the canoe close into the shore, where you can take advantage of a convenient log for your rest. You say to yourself, he must be at least three hundred yards away, but the guide says around two hundred.

Still, you set your sights for what you think is correct for a longer shot. The moose is so far away that he does not wind you. There is no hurry, and you aim as you never aimed before, then squeeze the trigger carefully. A complete miss. Your moose has long since departed back into the heavy cover. And you wonder just what was wrong. Nothing more than this matter of trajectory.

Your guide was correct when he said that most moose hunting is at close range, or about nine shots out of ten are at close range, but for your one chance of the day he was mistaken. And you simply overestimated the range by some one hundred yards or so and your bullet that was aimed for three hundred yards went over the moose.

Now, if this shooter had used a more modern rifle, like the .30-06 or the .270 Winchester, and had been a little closer in his estimate of the range, he might have returned home with a fine trophy.

No rifle ever shoots swift for one man and slow for another. The trajectory of any bullet is pre-determined when the cartridge for that particular rifle is loaded. One can no more alter it by anecdotes of fluke shots than he can by pulling harder on the trigger.

Trajectory is something that every sportsman should understand. To do so one must pay attention to a few figures. The trouble is that those commonly printed in catalog tables do not tell the facts that a hunter most needs to know.

This midway rise of a bullet over certain ranges may have some value in comparing rifles, but very little in actual hunting. Very few will ever make the mistake of fifty percent in judging the distance. I would say that trajectory tables, to be of practical use to the average sportsman, should show the height of bullet curve every fifty yards or so from muzzle out to the range it is sighted for. Also the drop below line of aim, at similar intervals, for some distance beyond that range.

In chuck hunting, I've found that with a rifle that gives the 55-grain .22 caliber bullet a muzzle velocity of from 3,600 to 3,700 foot seconds, the best results are with the rifle sighted in to shoot about one half inch high at two hundred yards.

Most of my chucks are killed at a range of from two hundred to three hundred yards. Long ago I passed up the close easy shots, for no one can ever expect to be a good long-range shot unless he does *only* long-range shooting. I killed my first chuck way back in 1890. I have always been fortunate to live in an area that offered plenty of hunting. Here in the Mohawk Valley, it is a simple matter, most any evening, to bag from a dozen to twenty chucks before it is too dark to hunt.

During the last thirty years I have given considerable time to long-range crow shooting. Chuck hunting is easy compared to this sport. I have made a study of crow shooting. Wonder if my readers know that the crow is about the only bird that will sit facing the wind, if a heavy wind is blowing.

The next time you are out hunting and see a hawk or an owl sitting way out on a limb, in the wind, note well through your scope that the tiny feathers on the bird's back will sort of curl up in the wind. You will never see this with a crow. A crow faces the wind, and if you remember this fact it will help you on the long shots to correct for windage. Out where the crow is sitting the wind will blow from the direction in which the crow is facing, so you make proper allowance.

For long-range crow shooting you want a rifle that will keep its shots under an inch at two hundred yards. I use my regular chuck hunting gun. For years I used the Lyman Super Targetspot scope, in 15X, with a tiny dot on cross hairs. In recent years I have used the Leupold scope in ten power, with tapered cross hairs. I can see better later in the day with this ten power scope than with one of greater power. One cannot shoot any better than he can see.

While working in Rome, New York, between 1905 and 1915, I spent about all of my spare time chuck hunting, and I kept a careful tally of all shots and kills. Today I enjoy looking over these old records. These old record books show that my average for each of those ten years was around 350 chucks. But some years it was nearly four hundred. I had the whole Mohawk Valley as a hunting ground, from Rome up to Westernville, and toward Boonville, New York. This is still fine chuck country.

I have continued this hunting up to the present time, but in recent years my score is only around from 75 to 150. Today I do not start hunting so early in the spring. Nor do I try and kill every chuck that I see. My shooting is confined to the longer shots from 150 yards and on. One can easily kill off too many chucks, so that you later have poor hunting.

About the hardest shot one can get at a chuck is when it is sitting up near the burrow, out at two hundred to three hundred yards, with a crosswind blowing. I usually sit and wait for the chucks to start feeding again; then you have the whole length of the chuck as your target. One can usually know within an inch in elevation of where the bullet is going at that range, and by having the whole length of the chuck as your target, if you misjudge the windage, you still have a dead woodchuck. You can watch the direction of the wind by checking the way the grass blows near the chuck, but it takes a good scope to get all the details.

One learns long-range shooting only by a lot of practice. There are no short cuts. When one has mastered long-range chuck shooting, it is time to take up long-range crow shooting. This is my specialty, and I enjoy crow shooting with the rifle. It affords the very best practice for long-range varmint shooting.

This rather long letter started out as a treatise on the matter of trajectory, and moose hunting. Somewhere along the line it changed over to chucks. Having hunted these animals all my life, when I get started on the subject I hardly know when to call a halt!

Yours truly,<br>
Harvey A. Donaldson

Yours truly No. 36

# Ramblings on the Past

October 25, 1971

Friend Neal:

I have been asked to write more about some of the chuck rifles we used back in the old days, soon after 1900. These old rifles used cast lead bullets, but they were very accurate. Very soon after 1900 I placed an order with the J. Stevens Arms and Tool Company of Chicopee Falls, Mass., for one of their single-shot rifles, the Stevens Ideal Range rifle No. 45. This rifle had the long 28-inch heavy barrel, chambered for the .28-30 Stevens cartridge, and it had double set triggers.

At about this time Harry Pope was working for the Stevens Company, so I ordered one of his breech-loading barrels. This barrel could be used with fixed ammunition, with the bullet fired from the case, or it could be loaded with the cast bullet seated in the breech with a bullet seater, and then the loaded case with a greased wad on top placed in the chamber. This rifle was mounted with a Smith telescope, in ten power. At this time the above outfit was about the most accurate rifle available. I used if for years in chuck shooting as well as in two hundred-yard offhand shooting.

The .28-30 cartridge, along with the .22-15-60 and the .25-25 Stevens Straight were designed by my old friend, Chas. H. Herrick, who lived in Boston. His nickname was "Crimp" and he was one of the most expert riflemen and chuck shooters in the country. The last time I saw Crimp was at the Walnut Hill Matches, held near Woburn, Mass. on July 17, 1938. Harry Pope was also at this match along with Lucian Cary and another old-time rifleman, Phil E. Brooks.

This old .28-30 was quite a cartridge. It was made by U.M.C. and the cases would last forever. The empty case was two and one-half inches long, with a long straight taper. I still own this fine outfit along with several hundred new .28-30 cases. The .22-15-60 was a good case for squirrel hunting. The barrel would foul badly if used with black powder, but when we used the white Du Pont smokeless rifle powder, we got better results. All three of these cases are museum pieces today.

While the .28-30 was quite a popular cartridge, for some reason the long slim .25-25 Stevens was never used as much as the more popular .25-20 Single Shot case, with its 86-grain bullet.

About the time that Pope was working for the Stevens company, a man named Smith was making his telescopes in the same Stevens factory. They were fairly good scopes for the time, but not as good as the Sidel scopes. Sidel had his shop on Race Street in Philadelphia and he made about the best scopes one could obtain. I had one in twenty power that I used for years in chuck hunting. Today I would pay ten times what it cost to have it back again.

Old Harry Pope never got along very well with the scopemaker Smith, as I remember it. It seems that Pope had made up a target rifle for my old friend Chas. Rowland of Boulder, Colo. After testing the new rifle out carefully, Rowland returned it to the factory, in Chicopee Falls, to have Pope check it over. This rifle was mounted with one of Smith's scopes, in ten power, and it was not shooting properly.

Upon close examination it was found that the trouble was in the Smith scope, and not the rifle. It seems the ring holding the crosswires was loose. When Pope found out about this he was one wild man. It seems he went after Smith with a machinist's hammer and actually chased Smith right out of the factory. It was several days before Pope cooled down enough for Smith to get back to work. But from that time on Pope would have nothing to do with the Smith scope. He used Sidel scopes, same as my own. Pope only worked for the Stevens company a couple of years. There was some trouble when the company tried to put the Pope barrels on a production line basis. Old Harry would not stand for that. He told the company that if they wanted to market his barrels they would be made as he had always made them — one at a time.

There was plenty of activity out in California with the offhand Schuetzen rifles, so they managed to coax Harry to move out to San Francisco, where he set up a new shop. This was an unfortunate move on Pope's part, for the day he was to open shop in April, 1906, was the day of the San Francisco earthquake.

In my files I have data from several letters written about Pope soon after 1900 that would make interesting reading. One incident that occurred while he was working for the Stevens company I might as well tell about at this time. It seems that Pope had a one hundred-yard range only a short distance out of town. This distance was obtained by shooting across a small pond, with the targets placed under an apple tree. This pond was very shallow, hardly more than a foot deep. Pope had a bench set up and it was here that he tested out his rifles before they were shipped to the customer.

Well, after one hectic day at his shop, he had to test out a muzzle loading rifle, for shipment, and it was getting late in the day. He soon got set up for shooting, but in his hurry, etc., he was more or less upset. On the very first shot he fired, he shot the false muzzle right off the barrel of his rifle. It went out over the water a short distance and dropped in the water on a line with the apple tree. What to do next? The new rifle was of no use without the false muzzle. Old Harry soon had that all figured out. He called over a couple of small boys who were playing near the pond, had them roll up their pants legs and walk out in the shallow water, on a line with the apple tree, and feel around in the mud with their bare feet, until they soon located the missing false muzzle.

The false muzzle was in no way damaged, so all was well. As Harry told me this story he said it was just another of the many things that happened while he was working for Stevens. I have many more stories about Pope that I would be glad to tell about in later letters to the *Handloader*. There have been many stories published about Pope, but many of the more interesting things that he used to tell about have never been put in print.

In another letter I would be glad to tell about Pope's shop in Jersey City, N.J. This was a famous gathering place for the most famous riflemen this country has ever seen — men like John Hessian, Larry Nuesslein, Sam Clark, Paul Landrock, John Kaufman, J.C. Lippincott, and a host of others.

I have a number of Pope's bullet lubricators that he used to furnish with his moulds. They were used with what we used to call the Leopold lubricant. This lubricant was invented by a brother of Chas. Herrick. It seems that this brother was a chemist, and he and Charley worked out the formula. The lubricant was used in stick form, with Pope's lubricator.

Leopold was a station agent for some railroad, down in Pennsylvania. He lived on the second floor of the railroad station, so he had his home rent free, as well as his lights and his heat, but as his salary was only around $30.00 a month, he had little money to spend experimenting. So the Herrick brothers felt sorry for him and they named their lubricant after Leopold.

Back in the days when we were shooting cast lead bullets the lubricant we used was very important. At times we even used a certain lubricant that was correct for the weather conditions, either hot or cold. Even to this day when shooting cast bullets the proper lubricant to use is of the greatest importance. Very few of the modern-day riflemen shooting cast bullets know about the fine lubricants we had available back in the old days of black powder rifles. This man Leopold was quite a character; I still have in my files a lot of his letters. He liked to shoot but he was so busy with railroad matters that it left him little time for his guns. I used to keep him well supplied with primers.

When I think about it, times sure have changed. We used to buy our primers, either Winchester or Remington, for $1.50 per 1,000. I usually bought 10,000 at a time. The U.M.C. primers were about the best, back in the old days of shooting. I still have some of these old primers around.

In my next letter I will have more to say about the old master, Harry M. Pope.

Yours truly,
Harvey A. Donaldson

## Another New Case

**November 5, 1971**

Friend Neal,

Have had no word from you in one hell of a while. How come? I have prepared a "letter" for the next issue of *Handloader*, and will send it along in a few days. I figured it was time I got busy in this letter writing.

I have designed another new case for bench rest shooting that is *better* than my old .219 Don-Wasp. My friend, Ronnie Czarnota, has been helping me in my testing. When these tests are completed you may receive an article for the *Handloader* from Mr. Czarnota.

I am busy, as usual. Have done some deer hunting since our season opened but have seen nothing but does, so far. Weather has been too warm. We will have to have some heavy frosts before we can do any serious hunting. Dave seems to be doing well in his bench rest shooting. If he wants a tack driver, and I don't mean maybe, he had better get a new rifle chambered for my new case. Records have been made out on the West Coast, as I gave some of my friends out that way the data last spring.

Sincerely yours,
Harve

## 'Yours truly' Ideas

**November 11, 1971**

Dear Harve,

I don't know where time goes. It's been a heck of a spell since I last wrote to you. Neal tells me you've been out deer hunting this fall, so evidently you are feeling well and that's what we like to hear.

I'm anxious to hear more about your new bench rest cartridge. I'm going to be making up a heavy varmint rifle in the near future and just might consider yours. Can you tell me more about it?

In your last letter to Neal you indicated you'd like some ideas for future "Yours truly" letters. I think you could write several columns on your experiences with old cartridges that are no longer available. Some of these could be in old target calibers — for instance the .25-25 Stevens or the old .32 Ideal — or maybe some of the no-longer-available hunting cartridges. Chances are you did a lot of shooting with the Winchester single-shot rifle, and I know that this Hi-Wall was chambered for most of those old cartridges.

Hope your deer hunting is successful this fall. Neal and I are getting ready to attend the Winchester and Remington seminars in Texas and Arkansas next week so we'll be out of the office for a few days. These fall months always put us behind in our work.

Very cordially,
Dave

## Quarter-Inch Groups

**November 13, 1971**

Dear Dave,

I was so pleased to have your letter of the 11th. Getting *any* mail from you is quite an event.

I see no reason you cannot own a rifle chambered for my new .224 Don-Ace case. This case is really something, if I do say so myself. You can read all about the design in the December issue of *Precision Shooting*, and I will see that you get a copy. First off, contact my friend George M. Fullmer. George is tooled up to chamber a barrel. Reamer was made by Keith Francis of Talent, Oregon. The RCBS outfit carries both the case forming dies as well as the loading dies.

Considerable testing has been done with my rifle. The barrel was made by Clyde Hart, who also fitted the barrel to a Remington 40X action. It weighs 1½ pounds.

We have made so many quarter-inch hundred-yard groups that we are getting to expect them right along. So far I have tried 4320, 4064, 4895, and 3031 powders. Actually at this time I cannot say which powder is the best, they all shoot so well. With 30 grains of 3031 and the Sierra 55-grain bullet, we get a velocity of 3,700 fps, and this load gave as good accuracy as any we have tried. I use 30 grains of each of the above named powders, and these loads fill the case right up under the bullet with no air space. I planned it this way. I like 4064 powder for this case myself. While the velocity is less, it still really shoots.

A higher velocity with *equal* accuracy, and it sure looks as if we are getting just that. This is what I have been trying for all along.

My .224 Don-Ace and 6mm Don-Ace are made from the .225 Winchester cartridge, and it seems to last forever. Cases are easy to form. It calls for the 30-degree shoulder. Fullmer can send you a drawing.

Soon as I get this deer hunting out of my system, I will send Neal several letters along the lines you have mentioned.

Sincerely yours,
Harve

## Articles on Pope?

**December 1, 1971**

Dear Dave,

I plan to do several articles for *Handloader* for the coming year that have to do with that famous old barrel maker Harry M. Pope. Mister, I have enough data on Pope to write a book. There are few men living today that knew Pope, personally, and I happen to be one of them.

First I would like to do an article about Pope when he worked for Stevens soon after 1900. Then later more data when he had his shop in Jersey City.

Getting cold out this way tonight, down around zero, as I write. Will be looking for word from you soon.

Sincerely yours,
Harve

## Need 'Fresh' Stuff

**December 7, 1971**

Dear Harvey,

I've sure been hearing a lot about your new cartridge, and Jim Carmichel showed me the sample you sent him. When I can afford it, I will have a bench gun made up for your new baby, hopefully sometime next year.

I don't want to brag, but I had two groups at the Varmint Nationals that went a quarter-inch MOA at two hundred yards. This was in the Sporter Matches and I was shooting a 6x47 with a Remington action, A&M barrel and Brown fiberglass stock. My one hundred and two hundred-yard aggregate barely missed a world record. I really think that fiberglass stocks will give the boys something to think about in the next few years.

Your letter mentioned the desire to write several articles on Harry Pope. I guess you know that a lot has been written on Pope in the last decade, and most of it just a rehash of previous stuff that was written about him. A couple of young writers have simply taken stuff from the Ray Smith book on Pope barrels. I don't know why some editors buy this rehashed material.

Anyway, I realize you knew Pope personally and you probably have some "fresh" material — stuff that's never been in print before. This, I'm sure, would interest our readers. If I were you, however, I would keep this in one article — two at the most. As I'm sure you know, our audience wants a lot of "meat" in their reading diet and you are certainly in a position to give them some.

Very cordially,
Dave

## Lost Every Cent

**December 16, 1971**

Dear Dave,

The data I have in mind has never been published before, and the anecdotes and stuff on the old-timer Harry Pope would make interesting reading in the *Handloader*. I knew Pope from around 1900 up until he died.

His old letters tell about the trouble he had when he was working for Stevens and they tried to get him to produce his barrels on a production basis. Unless this data is shown now, it will be lost forever.

Pope lost his shop in the earthquake in San Francisco way back in 1906. It was Chas. Rowland who sent Pope the money to get back East after this experience, since Pope lost every cent he had at that time. Why not tell your readers about this?

Mister, I know all about that good shooting that you are doing. You are making it *tough* for Jim and Neal to keep up with you. You see I keep up on the bench rest shooting scores.

I sort of had the idea that the fiberglass stock idea had more to offer than some shooters knew about. The fellows on the West Coast are doing O.K. with my new case, but in 6mm caliber. You might want to try that. Best wishes for a Merry Christmas to you and Neal.

Sincerely,
Harve

Yours truly No. 37

# A Visit to Pope's Shop

**December 20, 1971**

Friend Neal:

 In this letter I would like to take my readers along while we pay a visit to the gun shop of Harry Pope, which was located, if memory serves me correctly, at 18 Morris Street in Jersey City. The shop was on the third floor of a loft building, and it was reached by an outside stairway at the rear of the building. From the shop one could look out on the Hudson River and see the Statue of Liberty.

 A long line shaft hung from the ceiling of the shop from which belts were connected to the drill press, milling machine, and several lathes. The shop was so filled with boxes and cartons full of stuff that one could hardly find room to walk around. Seldom did anyone look over the old gunsmith's shoulder while he was working, for there was little room to stand.

 His work bench ran along the side of the room by the windows, and it was about as cluttered up as the rest of the shop. The windows were well covered with an accumulation of dust and dirt. It was Harry's practice to use these dirty windows as sort of a record book. When he wanted to jot down some data he would walk over to a window, and write down with a stub of a pencil on the glass, whatever he wanted to remember. Before long these windows were completely covered with data of all sorts — phone numbers, the names and addresses of many customers, specifications of various barrels, formulas for working out mechanical problems, etc. I will have more to say about these dirty windows a little later in this letter.

 Old Harry was a great one to smoke cigarettes. He would roll his own with fine-cut tobacco, from a bag of Bull Durham. His method was to hold the cigarette exactly in the middle of his mouth where it would remain, at times long after it had gone out, while he was working at the lathe or bench. His gray mustache was stained in the middle of his mouth, where it was discolored from his cigarettes.

 A number of his close friends would often visit him in the shop. He would stop work and visit no matter how busy he might be. He worked long hours, very often long into the night on some particular job that had to be finished. He would bring his lunch with him and eat it when he got around to it. His friends were always trying to play a joke on the old-timer, but it was very seldom that they got away with it. One day Sam Clark was visiting Pope, during the season when a window or so was open, and Sam had his shirt sleeves rolled up. A big Jersey mosquito flew in the window and landed on Sam's arm.

Now, I hardly know if my readers know it or not, but if a mosquito should land on your arm, and sink his "bill" in your flesh, if you simply hold your breath, he cannot withdraw his bill. So, when this particular mosquito landed on Sam's arm, he held his breath and walked over near where Pope was working, and went through the motions of rubbing the mosquito on the back.

Old Harry looked up in amazement, sort of shook his head, and kept on working. Sam then spoke up and said, "Pope, you sure have some very friendly mosquitos over here in New Jersey." And the mosquito flew away.

John Hessian and Larry Nuesslein, as well as many other expert riflemen, were always welcome visitors in Pope's shop. At times, if the door at the foot of the stairs was locked, and a window in his shop was open, one had to stand down on the walk and holler "Hey, Pope," and he would stick his head out the window to see who was calling, and then come down and let them in. A stranger might have quite a time calling him, if he were busy.

One day, a new customer did manage to get up into Pope's shop. This customer wanted to place an order for a target rifle barrel. But this was hardly a simple matter. When Pope made one of his fine barrels he was *quite sure* that it was going to one who knew how to use it. He said that there were so many fine riflemen around the country still waiting for one of his barrels that he was going to know just who bought his barrels.

So . . . it was hard for a new customer, unknown to Pope, to even place an order for a new barrel. In this instance, after some time was spent, back and forth, in trying to determine if the new customer was even able to place an order, it was necessary for Pope to leave the shop for a few moments. While this visitor was waiting for Pope's return, he must have looked up at the dirty windows and decided he would do Pope a good turn by washing them. So he got a cloth and some water in a basin, and went at it.

My readers can well imagine the surprise that came over Pope when he had returned to the shop. He was sure one wild gunsmith. His years of records, customers' names and addresses, phone numbers, etc., were completely wiped out. It is hardly necessary for me to relate that this particular customer got out of the shop, a soon as he found out just what he had done, and that his order for a new Pope barrel was never filled.

*(Editor's Note — I mentioned this story to Charles Pope, Harry Pope's son, and he said he remembered the incident well: "Boy, was Pop mad." Charles said that it wasn't just the missing data and phone numbers that upset him; the grime on the windows diffused the bright sunlight and cut down the glare. — Neal Knox)*

I have in my files many letters that I have received from Pope down through the years, and many of them are very interesting. He suffered quite a severe loss when his shop was destroyed by an earthquake in San Francisco, in April of 1906. He lost just about everything and was stranded there. Our old friend Charles Rowland sent money to Pope that made it possible for Pope to return East after the big fire.

The last time I saw Pope was on July 17, 1938. This was at the Walnut Hill

Range in Woburn, Massachusetts. We were both attending a rifle match. Pope came to this match with Lucian Cary.

We sure had a fine visit and had a chance to talk over the early days of Schuetzen shooting from around 1900 up to 1920, or so. Pope had a wonderful memory, and he told me many things that happened back in the early days, which was quite a while before I took up Schuetzen shooting. Paul Landrock, of Union City, New Jersey, was also at that match in Woburn back in 1938. At that time Landrock was about the most expert off-hand shooter in the country.

If my readers are interested I might be able to look up more data about Pope, from some of his letters, which would fill many letters to the *Handloader*. I am sorry that this is such a short letter. The fact is I have misplaced some of the notes I had set aside with more data about Pope, so I had to write strictly from memory. Will try to do better next time.

Yours truly,
Harvey Donaldson

## Needs Fired Case

**December 21, 1971**

Dear Harve,

Just got a note from Fred Huntington. I had asked him about dies for the .224 and 6mm Donaldson Ace. He sent me a set of .224, but said he had no information on the 6mm. He'd like to have a fired case. Would you be able to send him one?

Season's Greetings!
Dave

## Good Ol' Fred

**December 25, 1971**

Dear Dave,

I have already given my buddy Fred Huntington all the necessary data on the 6mm Don-Ace. Fred is a good friend of long standing. I was able to help him when he started making bullet swages before he got into the loading tool business, and he never forgot it.

Later, when this Christmas business is over, I will send you some fired cases for your collection, and I will make one up in 6mm. You can get the reamers from Keith Francis. He makes the best reamers I have seen.

Sincerely yours,
Harve

Yours truly No. 38

# Shooting A Pope Rifle

**January 9, 1972**

Friend Neal,

Recently I have been getting many inquiries about the use of the old Pope muzzle loading rifles. One fellow wanted to know just why the bullet seating rod that came with his rifle was such a loose fit in the barrel. Another asked what the two pins that were placed on each side of the barrel, near the muzzle, were used for, and so it goes question after question — far more than I can personally answer. At this late day very often a shooter will pick up one of these old muzzle loading rifles with many of the most important items missing.

Back in the old days, soon after 1900, any data required as to the use and care of these fine old rifles was easily obtained. But today most of the old-timers who used these rifles have long since passed away, and evidently a lot of this important information has passed along with them.

One can look in vain for any data on these old rifles in any of the books published on shooting. But worst of all, if you do locate such a book you will find that it usually was written by someone who had at one time attended one of the old matches, but only as a spectator, and not a contestant. Most of the reading matter in such a book will be found full of errors, with no real information.

First off, let's take up this matter of the loose fit of the bullet seating rod, which pushed the bullet down the barrel after it had been seated in the false muzzle. Pope had a good reason for making these seating rods with a rather loose fit in the barrel. In some of the old rifles that had been fired maybe 50,000 rounds or so the bore would be worn down enough that the bullet as seated from the muzzle might be drawn partly up the barrel, after it had been seated properly, by the suction afforded by a tight-fitting rod. This would of course result in a ringed barrel, which would destroy it for any more shooting. One will often find an old Pope barrel that has been ringed in this manner, and its new owner wonders why his fine old rifle will not shoot properly.

Sometimes today one will find an old Pope rifle that will not hole the bullet in the breech, just ahead of the cartridge. To overcome such a situation is a simple matter. One should make up a dummy cartridge of the same size as the barrel, the

.32-40 case for instance. Fit a tight rod into this case, with the end sticking out about a sixteenth of an inch. Place this in the breech of the barrel after the rifle has been placed in position on the shooting bench.

Then push the bullet down carefully 'til it touches the dummy case seated in the breech. Next take out the dummy case and insert a loaded cartridge and you are still in business. I remember well how Pope told me one time to never place a loaded case into the chamber of one of his rifles, until after I had looked to see if the seated bullet was in its proper place. This was good sound advice. One gets into the habit of doing this after a while.

Now we take up this matter of the little pins on each side of the barrel near the muzzle. These pins were made to hold the mechanical bullet seater in position. All of my Pope muzzle loading rifles used this mechanical bullet seater except the first rifle Pope made for me soon after 1900, to use the .28-30 Stevens cartridge. This fine little cartridge was designed by my old buddy Charles Herrick. I still have several hundred of these old cases; most of them have never been fired.

To have all the bullets seated into the barrel with the same amount of pressure, Pope designed the mechanical bullet seater. This was a device that was attached to the muzzle of the rifle after the bullet had been placed in the false muzzle.

One hook on each side of the starter hooked over the small pins placed in the barrel, locking it in position. Then you placed one hand on each lever and pulled down. This would start the bullet into the barrel with very little effort.

Next you removed the starter, and after placing the rifle on top of the shooting bench, the bullet was pushed down into the barrel with the bullet seating rod. This rod was then removed very carefully. Next you looked to see if the bullet was seated properly, and the loaded cartridge with a greased wad on top was placed in the chamber. Loading one of Pope's fine barrels was more or less of a ritual, back in the old days. One had plenty of time so no necessary operation was neglected or hurried.

One reason for placing the rifle on the shooting bench, before the bullet was pushed down the barrel and seated into position, was to prevent the bullet dropping down into the chamber if the throat was worn so much as to not hold the bullet in position.

All of the moulds Pope made to cast the bullets for these M/L rifles were made to cast the tapered bullet. The last three or four bands on the bullet were larger than on the front of the bullet. That is one reason why the modern day shooter runs into trouble if he picks up a M/L Pope rifle without the mould, and tries to get results with a modern bullet having bands all of the same size. Also, this modern shooter casts his bullets too hard. They should be from around one tin to thirty of lead, or not softer than one to thirty-five. A mild primer also works best with these rifles and I still have plenty of these old primers on hand, together with the old Schuetzen powder. There is still so much more to be written about Pope's fine old muzzle loading rifles, and so little time left to write about it, that it will require several more letters to cover only part of it properly.

When I sit down and think about the old days of rifle shooting, it does not seem so long ago. But again when I think about my many old shooting friends who have passed away, it does seem a long time ago. As far as I can learn I am about the only one left who remembers about the old days of rifle shooting. I have been shooting for over eighty years, but the best part of all is that I am still able to shoot a rifle.

While I receive many inquiries on shooting matters I have as yet to receive word from anyone who took part in the shooting during the early part of this century. If any of the old-timers who remember those days are still around, I would sure be pleased to hear from them.

When I stop to think it over I do not believe I have ever seen in print, in any book on shooting matters, some of the data I have shown in this letter. There is so much more to be said that I hardly know just where to start.

Yours truly,
Harvey A. Donaldson

## Hunting Wolves

**January 9, 1972**

Friend Neal,

I have just time for a short note. I had word from Dave that I was behind in my "letters" to *Handloader,* so here's another. I started this column early this morning but right after that a friend called and we went out hunting. We have some eighteen inches of snow on the fields. I have been hunting brush wolves, as we call them. This is done by driving slow over the back roads out of the valley, and watching the fields on either side of the road. These wolves travel in packs of six or more, and we can see them easily on the snow.

We shoot them at long range with a rifle. A couple were killed last week, but today it clouded up and snow is in the air so the wolves must be laying low for a day or so. Anyway, I had a good hunt; it's always good to get out in the weather.

You may be surprised to learn we have these wolves in New York State. Some time ago, when we had a hard winter, the St. Lawrence River froze solid, so these wolves came down from Canada, and they have been here ever since. Many are killed during the deer season.

No word from you in one hell of a while.

Sincerely yours,
Harve

## How's the Rifle Coming?

**January 12, 1972**

Dear Dave,

How are you coming along with your new rifle for my new case? Who will you have do the work on this rifle? What barrel will you use? Will you use the 6mm or my .224 case?

Last Monday I mailed another "letter" to Neal, so I should be one ahead.

About every Sunday I am out hunting the brush wolves. A week ago today a friend killed a big one. Best regards to Neal.

Yours truly,
Harve

## Atkinson & Marquart

### January 18, 1972

Dear Harve,

Just received your letter of January 12. It will be several months before I am able to start on a new rifle. Have to accumulate the cash first. Chances are Atkinson & Marquart will do the work, and make the barrel. We now have five bench rest barrels by A & M and all have been winning matches lately. My wife recently took the Grand Aggregate and the 200-yard Aggregate in a registered shoot at Casa Grande, Arizona. She was shooting a heavy varmint with A & M barrel, in .222 Remington.

Glad to hear you are feeling well. Good shooting this spring!

Cordially,
Dave

## We Walked 1,000 Yards

### February 7, 1972

Dear Dave,

I did a lot of testing of the .224 Don-Ace back in October, and you should see some of these targets. I have one in particular — it shows only five shots at one hundred yards and it measures around .300. But wait 'til you hear how it was made. If you think it is easy, try it some time.

I had a fellow with me who is a bench rest shooter, and one who has the idea he is plenty *hot*. But when he had finished his shooting, he wasn't so sure.

I put up two targets, one for each of us. Then we each fired *one shot*. We left the rifles on the sand bags and walked up to the target, to mark the shot. Thus we covered two hundred yards walking. Well, we did this five times, thus we walked 1,000 yards.

After it was all over, I had a group that measured, as I mentioned, .300. His group was over an inch. I have done this same stunt many times to train myself to get into position on the bench. I touch *only* the trigger. I position the rifle on the sand bags, and fire the first shot. After walking back to the bench I sight rifle in again and fire another shot.

Mister, make no mistake about this, it is the *best practice* I know to get you into shooting position for every shot. Some time have our buddy Neal try this out.

I find that a lot of shooters put more pressure on the stock than is necessary. When you can shoot with *no pressure* you sure have it made. Of course, your sand bags have to be right, and one has more trouble with a rifle that has a lot of recoil.

You are doing O.K., and I see Mrs. Wolfe is doing all right herself. I never knew it to fail, if a man teaches his wife to shoot, the time will soon come when she will beat him. And the same goes for fishing. If you teach that wife of yours to fish, she will beat you every time. But, more power to her, and I sure am pleased to learn she has taken up shooting.

I will be 89 in April, but I don't feel that old. I am feeling O.K. and I am as active as ever.

Will be looking for word from you soon.

Sincerely yours,
Harve

*Another "rare" photo of Harvey, rare in the fact that there were no notations on the back. This was found in one of the boxes of letters dated in the late 1960's.*

# 89 Years 'Young'

**February 10, 1972**

Dear Harve,

Just received your two-page letter and thoroughly enjoyed it. I see what you mean about that small group and the conditions under which it was shot. I've done the same thing — that is, getting up from the bench between shots. However, it was simply that I wanted to shoot each shot from a completely cold barrel. Anyway, that's mighty good shooting and I envy you that fine gun.

So you'll be 89 years young in April. I hope I'm as active as you are when I reach 60. Sitting behind a desk all week certainly isn't good for one's health.

Tomorrow I leave for the *cold* Midwest. There's a National Sporting Goods Show in Chicago and I have to attend and see all the manufacturers. I'll be very happy to get back to the nice warm Southwest.

Thanks again for the nice letter and I hope your crow shooting is good next month.

Fond best regards,
Dave

# Favorable Comment

**May 4, 1972**

Dear Dave,

I'm busy as the devil so only have time for a note. My friend Ronald Czarnota will very soon mail you an article on the .224 Don-Ace cartridge for publication in one of your magazines. I wonder if this data might be shown in both *Rifle* and *Handloader?* Our bench rest shooting starts at Johnstown in June. I figure the *Rifle* will be out in June, and some of my friends read the *Rifle* but not the *Handloader*.

There will be some targets shown with this article. Sorry we were so slow in getting all this data together.

You should have Clyde Hart make up your next rifle for this new case. He can make a barrel with the twist same as my own. My new rifle will even shoot factory 55-grain Sierra bullets like a bench rest job, and no fooling.

I am getting considerable favorable comment on my data about Harry Pope. They should write to you and not to me, for I am too busy to answer so many letters.

Best regards to Neal and I'll write him the first chance I get.

Sincerely yours,
Harve

# Visit to Pope's Son

**May 10, 1972**

Dear Harve,

Dave is running around the Midwest right now, so I'll answer your recent letter. I am looking forward to seeing the material on the .224 Don-Ace, but whether we can use Czarnota's article depends upon the quality of the manuscript and his photos, of course. It's already too late to get the story in the July-August, for that magazine is going to the printers today.

Did I tell you that I spent three days with Charlie Pope (Harry's son) over Easter? It was surely interesting. We may do a reprint of Harry M.'s copy of *The Bullet's Flight,* with his annotations and comments, which are written on about one hundred pages. I don't know when this would come out, but we will be sure to send you a copy.

Best regards,
Neal

Yours truly No. 39

# Loads for .225 Winchester

May 15, 1972

Friend Neal,

In the May-June 1972 issue of the *Handloader*, Ken Waters has given us a full and comprehensive coverage of the handloading of the .225 Winchester. In this letter I would like to give my experience and the methods I use in handloading the .225 Winchester case. When I first heard that Winchester was bringing out this particular case, I managed to obtain a few of the empties. My first thought was that here was a case that was made to order for 4064 powder with the 55-grain semi-pointed bullet. I have never seen fit to change this opinion.

I sent some of these early sample cases down to G.R. Douglas, together with a Remington 722 action with a 40X trigger. He fitted this action with one of his stainless steel barrels in medium sporter weight, 26 inches long, with a fifteen-inch twist. The only change in the case design was that I wanted a chamber with the case neck having a 30-degree shoulder.

When the rifle arrived I found it had a fairly close chamber. I own several accurate varmint rifles that I use in crow and chuck hunting, but none of them will equal the accuracy I get from this rifle. It is the only chuck rifle I ever saw that will equal the results I get from my most accurate bench rest rifles.

In loading for this particular case I would say that one should not use a faster powder than 3031. As I am interested in accuracy more than anything else, I stay well away from maximum loads. This following load was worked out for a .225 Winchester rifle with the 14-inch twist.

With the 50-grain bullets I found that a load of 29 grains of 3031 gave the best results. So then I set my powder measure to throw 29 grains of 3031. The measure is then set at this bulk weight, and locked. Next I fill the measure with 4064 powder, and using this same bulk measure, I find that it weighs 30 grains. This load I use with the 55-grain semi-pointed bullet. This combination of powder and bullet has given me the best accuracy in a fourteen-inch twist Winchester barrel. Next I fill up the measure with 4320 powder, for use with the 60-grain bullet. Having the same bulk measure as before, we find that this load weighs 31 grains.

All I do with my method is to use the same bulk measure or the same volume of powder with each load. As the weight of bullet is increased I simply turn to a slower burning powder. For the fifteen-inch twist rifle I use one more grain.

In my system I have no trouble from pressure; I have found it to be simple, safe, and sure. It can be used with most any of the medium capacity of rifle cases.

For my long-range crow and chuck hunting, I am getting the very best results in several of my .224 varmint rifles with the use of the semi-pointed 55-grain bullet. The lighter weight bullets are O.K. for short range, but when you want to reach way out yonder, use the 55-grain bullet. I believe this bullet has a better balance than does another bullet with the sharp point. A younger shooter will usually select a light bullet with the sharp point, but he may find out, when he knows the score, that this 55-grain bullet will carry a lot better from two hundred yards up to four hundred yards than a lighter spitzer. My targets have proved this beyond a doubt.

There is another thing I would bring to the attention of the younger handloader. He will find for the medium capacity cartridges that he will get the best results with the use of 4064 powder. In fact it is probably the most useful powder we have. If my reader will turn to most any handbook on reloading he may find that in most every instance with the medium capacity cases, he will get a higher velocity with the use of 4064 powder, where an equal amount of powder is used.

I have several friends who use the Model 70 Winchester rifle chambered for the regular .225 cartridge. Each and every one of these fellows uses his rifle in chuck hunting, and each claims he has the most accurate chuck rifle in the country.

On checking up on this matter, I also found that with the use of this rifle with factory ammunition, one does get outstanding accuracy. When you can put five shots into a half-inch at one hundred yards with a factory rifle and ammunition, you own a fine shooting outfit.

All in all I would say that this factory .225 Winchester rifle and cartridge is about the best outfit available for a super varmint rifle. Today our factories are turning out a very superior product, even better than what we had back in the old days of rifle shooting.

Yours truly,<br>Harvey A. Donaldson

*Editor's Note — When using Harvey's method, using an equal volume of slower burning powder for heavier bullets, bear in mind that the differences in powder burning rates often do not match the differences in bullet weight. For this reason, check the manuals to be sure you're within safe limits for any charge with any powder. Harvey's 31.0/4320/60 load is beyond maximum for some rifles. In some instances powder volume does appear to have a relationship to accuracy, even with different type powders — so long as the loads are safe. For instance, when Hodgdon BL-C(1) became scarce, many .222 and .222½ bench shooters substituted an equal volume of RL-7 with excellent results. Whatever volume of BL-C had done best, usually did best with the RL-7. — Neal Knox*

## Footnote Agrees

**May 15, 1972**

Dear Neal,

Right now I want to rush my enclosed "letter" which I hope you can get in next issue of *Handloader*. Busy answering a lot of mail. A lot of fellows have written in telling me how much they like my stuff on Harry Pope. Glad you were able to meet his son.

Note how well my data on Pope agrees on your own, as per your footnote in last *Handloader*. I sure wish I could visit with old Harry's son.

Yours truly,
Harve


## Has Plenty To Learn

**May 25, 1972**

Friend Neal,

Ken Waters did a good job on his data for the .225 Winchester case. But I don't see just why he tried so many powders to find out what was best. I would say Ken has plenty to learn. Of course, he's not 89 years 'young.' All he requires is more experience.

No doubt about it, this .225 Winchester case and rifle combination are hard to beat.

I very seldom hear from you any more, so get busy and write more often. Is Dave back on the job? Tell him to drop me a line.

Best regards,
Harve


## Old-Time Riflemen Not in Hall of Fame

**May 27, 1972**

Friend Neal,

I note the announcement of the *Rifle* Bench Rest Hall of Fame. Where are the names of those shooters who were making and breaking bench rest records before your committee took charge?

Off hand, I could mention the names of many bench rest shooters who, while no longer active, deserve proper mention in this Hall of Fame business. Or does your organization take note of *only* those who are shooting in this year of 1972?

Most of these riflemen I could mention were not only making records, but they were active members who had considerable to do with the success of our present day bench rest shooting. Those were the days when it required all the help it could get. And I might mention we got no help from any of those shown in the *Rifle*. The trouble now seems to be that those now in charge of bench rest shooting know very little as to what has happened in the past. With the possible exception of Paul Gottschall, all of the names shown are present-day riflemen.

What about Sam Clark, Jr., Charles Hankins, Doc Garcelon, Al Marciante, Croff Hollidge, Ferris Pindell, Col. Whelen, Gerald Southard, Ray Biehler, Clyde Hart, Bob Hart, Lyle G. Heap, Frank Hubbard, Harry Jackman, Bill Purcell, John Collins, Charles Kingsley, Gene Beecher, Alex Hoyer, Larry Nuesslein, Clyde Yockey, H.B. Reagan, Dan Huffnail, L.E. Wilson — and many more I might mention? They are only a few names that come to mind. Down through the years each and every one contributed a lot to bench rest. You may be hearing from some of the older riflemen.

Best regards,
Harve

## Honorary Members
## In Hall of Fame

**June 13, 1972**

Dear Harvey,

Dave and I just got back from the Varmint & Sporter Nationals in Tulsa. We didn't exactly set the world on fire — there were record number of sporter (135) and light varmint shooters (140-something) and more than 150 heavy varmint shooters — and the competition was fierce.

In one heavy varmint match Dave shot a .166, and I beat him with a .161, and another fellow beat us both with a .153 — and conditions weren't all that good either. Dave and my wife both placed in the three-gun Top Twenty, and Dave was in the light varmint Top Twenty. All I managed to come out of it with was a fourth place at 100 yards in the sporter. Oh well, there's always next year.

I appreciated your comments about the Hall of Fame, and frankly I expected such comments — but we set it up on the basis of shooting achievements, going all the way back to the first National Championships, and these were the only ones who qualified on that basis. However, because you are quite correct in that many others have contributed greatly to the game without having won that many championships, we have a provision for honorary members of the Hall of Fame — based on their contributions and upon the recommendations of other shooters. I will keep your letter handy so the committee may consider each of the names you mentioned and, I should add, you, yourself.

Best regards,
Neal

## For Future Reference

**July 5, 1972**

Friend Neal,

Just ran across some old data on the .30-30 Winchester that you can file away for future reference. When the first Model 94 rifles in .30-30 caliber were made, they had a ten-inch twist. I had one of these rifles way back in 1898. After 1900, or around the time the old Pyro powder was discontinued and the more modern powders were available, Winchester changed the twist to one turn in twelve inches.

This not only cut down on the pressure but increased the velocity. When the .32 Winchester Special rifles were made, for some reason or other, twist was one turn in sixteen inches — same as in the .32-40 Winchester rifles. This gave the same weight of bullet as was used in the .30-30 a higher velocity, but again cut down on pressure. And perhaps this was the reason deer hunters of that time favored the .32 Special over the older .30-30.

No matter what the reason, for a long time, 'til more modern rifles were available, the .32 Special caliber in the 94 Winchester was *the* deer rifle for our New York State deer hunters.

It might also interest you to know that back around 1915, Remington Arms Company made their rifles in .30-30, .30-40, .303 British, 7.65, and 7mm, all with the twist of one turn in nine inches. I was working for Remington at that time as an inspector. Remington made some good rifles, as you know.

In 1915 Winchester made their .30-30 and .303 British rifles with the twelve-inch twist, but they used one turn in ten inches for the .30-40 Krag rifle.

Best regards,
Harve

## Barrels Glued In

**July 12, 1972**

Dear Harve,

I have been using 3031 powder with 80-grain bullets in the 6mm Remington and getting excellent results. I tried 4064, then 4320, and couldn't beat the very good (3/4-inch) accuracy of the Remington factory ammo with Power-Lokt bullets. So I asked Mike Walker about it and he suggested 34 to 36 grains of 3031, which is the Remington test load. It worked!

I talked to Jim Stekl quite a bit at Tulsa. He was using a 40XB-BR with the barrel glued to the stock for about five inches forward of the receiver ring, with no bedding material under the action. Selby Wright has used this same system for a couple of years, but hasn't talked about it. In fact when I mentioned it to him at Akron he asked "How did you know that?" I told him it was a reporter's business to know things. Anyway, Selby won the 200 and Heavy Varmint aggregate at the Speer Matches, and Frank Jezioro used another gun glued together by Jim to win the 100-yard Heavy Varmint. I'll bet by next year we see a lot of glued-together guns.

Best regards,
Neal

## Lost Thirty Pounds

**July 17, 1972**

Dear Neal,

So you talked with Jim Stekl at Tulsa. He is what the boys call a professional shooter. He works for Remington here in Ilion, under Mike Walker and has been helping Mike bring out that special rifle for bench rest shooting.

It would not surprise me if the glued-to-stock idea wasn't Walker's. A couple of fellows showed up at Johnstown in June with actions glued to the stock; they were among the top shooters, too. But they were trying to *keep it quiet*. Word sure gets around.

I note that Ed Shilen is stepping out with a very accurate varmint rifle. This may be worthwhile to look over. As I said some while ago, things are getting *tougher* all the time in this bench rest shooting game.

What concerns me right now is that I have been sick for the last six weeks or so. My main trouble seems to be from loss of appetite. My doctor says it is nothing that a few pills won't cure, but it will take me some time to get back into shape. My heart condition is O.K. and blood count normal, but I have lost over thirty pounds in weight over the last few months. This has been coming on gradually.

About all I do is sit around the house and take it easy. I feel sort of listless, with no ambition for anything. When I tell you I have done no shooting for months you will know *I am sick*.

I don't even feel like driving my car. I have lost so much weight that it has weakened me, more or less. Have not even had enough ambition to try any trout fishing. Spending most of my time just sitting around the house reading. So, this may bother my writing, as well. Right now, the way I feel it would be too much effort to dig up any stuff. I can't seem to concentrate on anything.

Best regards,
Harve

## New Shilen Action

**July 25, 1972**

Dear Harvey,

I am sorry to hear that you haven't been feeling up to par. Right after I wrote my last letter I discovered the column you had sent in, so we're in good shape. Maybe you'll get a little energy before long and feel like doing some writing as well as shooting. Sure hope so.

I have one of Shilen's new actions on a heavy varmint rifle, but haven't had time to shoot it — been too busy here in the office, trying to get ready to go to New Orleans. I'm making some bullets for the shoot, but don't know when I'm going to have a chance to finish them up. Dave isn't going; he's been snowed under trying to get a new magazine under way.

Hope you get to feeling better soon.

Best personal regards,
Neal

## Think This Over!

**September 6, 1972**

Friend Neal,

I read your Editor's Note to my last letter in *Handloader*. If you read this letter of mine carefully you will see that I mentioned that *my rifle* has the fifteen-inch twist, not fourteen-inch. How come you lost track of this when you wrote that my loads may be beyond maximum for some rifles?

In *my rifle* my loads are O.K. with no trouble with pressure. Mister, my loads are for *my rifles,* and most anyone who reads my letter should understand this matter. My rifle chambered for the .225 Winchester case *(with fifteen-inch twist barrel)* is the most accurate chuck outfit I have ever seen. With the 55-grain Sierra semi-pointed bullets and 31 grains of 4064, I get a velocity of 3,700. You can't do this with any .22-250 rifle.

In my Husqvarna 7x57 rifle, the barrel has the twelve-inch twist. The loads I use in this rifle are nearly on a par with the .270 Winchester. This slower twist, by the way, will even handle the long 175-grain bullet way out and beyond any range one would use in deer hunting. What it might do out at 1,000 yards doesn't interest me.

And I get results with these loads. Maybe about now you will understand why my rifles have this slower twist. Simply because in my own experimenting I have found that a slower twist is *best.* Maybe twenty years from now some other shooter will come up with a better idea.

In the meantime, you fellows will keep on shooting a rifle made to the regular factory standards. No one but a damn fool would use a 1,000-yard rifle for two hundred-yard shooting, and even two hundred yards is way beyond normal hunting range.

Think this over a little!

Sincerely yours,
Harve

## Feels 'Chewed Out'

**September 12, 1972**

Dear Harve,

Apparently you're feeling better — good enough to chew me out. I didn't overlook the fact that your rifle has the slower twist, which will allow a heavier charge. But I didn't want the readers to make load substitutions on the basis of volume without checking the manuals. As you well know, some of the IMR powders are very close in burning rate, but sometimes there is a considerable jump in bullet weight, so if someone didn't take proper precautions he could wreck a rifle. I know that you know this, but some of the readers undoubtedly don't, which is the reason I added the editor's note.

We have a project in the works — it's been hanging fire for months due to lack of time to work on it — to build a 7mm using a shortened .308 case. We want the cartridge to be "just right" for up to three hundred yards for bench shooting, and up to three hundred meters for International matches. Naturally, we'll put a somewhat slower twist on it, but haven't yet decided just how slow. We plan to use the long 168-grain boattail, and I've been thinking about a thirteen-twist; since your 7x57 (which has about the same capacity) will stabilize the 175 in a twelve-inch, the thirteen-inch twist might do it. What do you think?

Best regards,
Neal

## *Your Idea Is My Idea*

**September 18, 1972**

Friend Neal,

Have just received yours of the 12th which will be answered at once. First off, where is my check for the last *Handloader?*

You fellows out in Prescott are getting smart for you are on the right track when working on a case design in 7mm for three-hundred-meter shooting. I have used a case about what you have in mind for several years, only mine is in .270 caliber.

You can't go wrong with a rifle in 7mm for today we have many fine bullets in that caliber, and your idea of working out a case for three-hundred-meter shooting is my idea exactly. If I were you I would select the thirteen-inch twist. That long 168-grain bullet may not work out so good with a slower twist. Use the 30-degree shoulder on your new case and you can use heavier loads in that thirteen-inch twist barrel.

Leave the .308 case the full length, but just change the shoulder angle and neck down to 7mm.

Keep me posted as to how the new rifle works out. In a day or so I will get busy on a letter for the next *Handloader*.

Sincerely yours,
Harve

View of Harvey's loading bench in fall of 1977. By this time his shop had been rummaged by several collectors; all the old tools, powder measures, moulds and most supplies were gone.

Yours truly No. 40

# *Ideas on Handloading*

**September 21, 1972**

Friend Neal,

Recently I have had requests to write about the tools I use for my handloading operations. My handloading started back around 1900 through correspondence with Harry Pope, Dr. Mann, and Niedner. From Niedner I got not only handloading data but drawings and information from which I made up a small arbor press loading tool, which is still in use on my loading table. At that time Niedner had his shop in Malden, Massachusetts, and he was busy doing experimental machine work for Dr. Mann.

Niedner made the first neck sizing dies and straight line bullet seaters which I used with this arbor press. Since then I have made my own dies. My first loading operations were for the .28-30 Stevens and .32-40 Marlin. I used black powder and cast lead bullets. Today my loading operations are confined to the .225 Winchester case, .22-250 Remington, .250-3000, .270 Winchester, 7x57 Mauser, and the .308 Winchester, though I have dies and shell holders for about anything you might mention.

I must have a dozen or more different powder measures — made by the old Ideal Tool Company, the Lyman Company, and RCBS. My oldest powder measure is one made by the Ideal Company that bears a patent date of August 1892. This old measure will still throw as uniform bulk powder charges as any measure I own. My favorite powder measure is the RCBS. It is easily adjusted and convenient to use. Besides the arbor press I have some dozen or more loading presses: a Lyman Spartan, as well as their turret head press, a heavy duty Pacific press and the regular and heavy duty RCBS presses. I believe I use my RCBS tools more than any of the others.

I use the arbor press tool for seating primers, because it gives a better feel. They are seated properly with no great amount of pressure. I never use the regular loading presses for seating primers. And, speaking of primers, I know several handloaders who spend plenty of time weighing powder charges, but sort of fall down when it comes to the selection of primers. They will use anything handy, regardless of the type of primer.

Selection of primers is more important than meets the eye. For a great many years I have used only Winchester primers. Today most of my cases are primed with the No. 120 Winchester primer. I have little use for magnum primers. I also use only Winchester brass in loading my cartridges. I find it is a good idea when you find something that is good, to stick with it.

I use Du Pont powders, either 3031, 4064, 4320, or 4350. If one will look in the books on handloading he will find that for the amount of powder used in most any load, 4064 will give a higher velocity than most any other. I use more 4064 in my own loading operations than any other powder.

In most of my resizing of case necks, (sizing about one-third of the neck) I use straight-line neck-sizing dies in the arbor press. On some cases I use conventional 7/8x14 dies in my RCBS presses. If I have any full length case resizing to do, it is done under a powerful heavy screw press in the dies made for that purpose. It is a poor plan to do any more case resizing than necessary. A fired case will fit the chamber of your rifle a lot better than any other case, so I don't go for full length sizing of any case after it has been fired in a particular gun.

If one will try and keep his fired cases clean he will have no trouble from sticking cases. As I use only the one brand of rifle cases I have no trouble in getting the cases mixed up. I see little sense in having my loading operations more complicated than necessary.

One can load cases as required at any time. If they are loaded and standing on a shelf you may have to draw the loads. I know some fellows who are all the time drawing loads and then loading them up again with some other bullet. They may be having a wonderful time but it is not my idea of handloading.

I keep my loaded ammunition in the original boxes with all loading data marked on a sticker on the outside of the box. In deer hunting I only carry two or three 7x57 cases loaded with the 175-grain round nose Hornady bullets. These cases have the primers marked with a blue pencil, and I usually carry them in my left hand rear pants pocket. My regular deer loads have the round nose Hornady 154-grain bullets. I keep these in my hunting coat pocket, so they never get mixed up.

I continue to be amazed at the performance we get today from factory-made rifles. One can step into a gun shop and buy right over the counter one that will shoot a lot better than most shooters can hold. These rifles are held to a closer tolerance, evidently, than was possible only a few years ago. Factory ammunition is also better than it used to be.

Recently I have seen a factory Winchester rifle in .225 Winchester caliber, that with good handloads would shoot into better than a half inch at one hundred yards; I've seen the same thing with a Model 700 Remington in .22-250 caliber. It never used to be that way. I have a very accurate Remington Model 700 chambered for the .22-250 case and a Ruger Model 77 chambered for the same cartridge. Both rifles have close chambers. I figured that I would have to keep my fired cases separate, but I sure was amazed when I found that a case fired in the Ruger was a perfect fit in the Remington, and the other way around as well.

It wasn't like that in the old days. Back when the Winchester Model 54 came out I had one in .220 Swift caliber. I had to do plenty on that stock before the rifle would shoot properly. We can buy factory bullets in most calibers that are more accurate than our best handloads used to be. Things are sure picking up in this rifle shooting business. I sort of wonder if our bench rest shooting has had something to do with this improvement in guns and ammunition.

As this letter will not appear until the November-December issue of *Handloader*, I want to wish my readers a very Merry Christmas and Happy New Year. I am looking forward to the hunting season that will soon arrive. Our summer here in the Mohawk Valley has been one with plenty of rain, so we should have a pleasant fall.

Yours truly,<br>H.A. Donaldson

## Doesn't Make Sense

**Date Unknown**

It is wonderful what we read in certain gun articles. I have noted well in a particular magazine that a gunsmith, who evidently has quite a following, has found that it is possible to add some 200 feet per second to a cartridge (his .222½ design) by adding only .098 inch to the length of the .222 Remington case. This makes the case half way between the length of the regular Remington .222 and the .222 Magnum. We read that this makes a better case than the .222 Remington which, because of several good .222 Remington rifles I have used, will take a bit of doing.

Now if we are to believe that .098 of an inch will add 200 feet velocity, will twice that length, or .196, which is the same length as the .222 Magnum now in use, add another 200 feet to the velocity? So why not use the regular .222 Remington Magnum case *as is*, and call it a day.

From my own experience with a rifle chambered for the .222 Remington Magnum, it has what it takes to make a good varmint rifle. One can use a number of powders with this larger case, as well as several different weights of bullets, and I can see very little difference in accuracy. It allows more leeway from the handloading viewpoint.

I wish I could understand why, when a really good cartridge is produced, the factory that makes the rifles soon takes them off the market. Winchester took away the .220 Swift and the .358 Winchester, and now I hear Remington will chamber some of their rifles for the .223 instead of the .222 Magnum. It sure doesn't make sense, to my own way of thinking.

H.A. Donaldson

# 'Left the Range Forever'

**November 14, 1972**

Friends:

Our friend Harvey Donaldson "left the range forever" on November 6, 1972. He was 89 years old.

Harvey was perhaps the last of the old-time Schuetzen shooters, having learned to shoot and compete in the style and with the equipment of the last century. Yet unlike so many who refused to adapt to the new-fangled high-velocity cartridges, Harve was one of the first to experiment with, design, and use them. Over the years, he tried many wildcats and played a part in the development of several now-famous cartridges; but while Harve wanted velocity, he also demanded accuracy. And his most famous case design, the .219 Donaldson Wasp, was for years the standard among bench rest competitors — a few are still in use. Harve never quit shooting or experimenting — an article on his latest design, the .224 Donaldson Ace, appeared in the November-December 1972 *Rifle*.

Harvey's fascination with accuracy caused him to organize, in 1947, the Eastern Bench Rest Shooters Association, of which he was the first president and Col. Townsend Whelen was vice president. Four years later the organization became the National Bench Rest Shooters Association. In appreciation, NBRSA subsequently made Harvey an Honorary Life Member and gave him a gold membership card.

Harvey's *Handloader* column began with the first issue, in 1966, and was the outgrowth of personal letters to Publisher Dave Wolfe. With that first published letter, Dave commented that he'd eat his typewriter if Harvey's columns didn't become one of the most popular features in the magazine. And Dave was right.

Harvey's interesting, informative, often controversial reminiscences made his letters "must reading" for virtually every *Handloader* reader — for whether or not you agreed with him, you had to listen to what he had to say, for Ol' Harve had busted more caps than most of us will ever see.

Rather than attempt to summarize his life, I'll let Harvey do it himself, in his own inimitable way. The following personal letter, received a year or so ago, gives an intimate glimpse of the life of a man who spent the better part of a century shooting with, and often collaborating with, the most advanced gun buffs of their times. Harvey A. Donaldson was the last of them. He will be sorely missed; he cannot be replaced. — Neal Knox

Friend Neal,

You wrote recently asking how I got started in this matter of rifle shooting, so I will try and explain. One might say that this all came about naturally, as I was taught rifle shooting at around the age of seven years by my mother. Of course I also had a shooting uncle, who was one of Berdan's Sharpshooters in the Civil War and this also helped. I have often thought that this country would be a lot better off today if there were more mothers like mine. Before she was married, my mother was a school teacher, so when the time came for me to attend school, I was already able to read and write.

When my mother was only 15 years old or so, her brother, my shooting uncle, taught her how to shoot a rifle offhand. Very soon she got so expert that she could beat him. I have heard my uncle say that at about the time she got married back in 1868, she was the best rifle shot in this part of the country. She and her brother used to attend many turkey matches. I still own the fine old heavy muzzle loading rifle that my mother used in these turkey shoots, held at forty and even eighty rods from the rest. I also have the 18 gauge muzzle loading shotgun that she used in bird shooting, along with the wad cutter that made the felt wads used in that old gun.

I started to school at the age of seven years, and I believe my mother got the idea if I was able to go to school, it was time that I learned to shoot a rifle. As I remember it now, one of the first rifles I used was a .22 Long Rifle Stevens Expert. Since this was a rather heavy rifle for a kid to use, I shot it at first from a prone position, mostly to get used to the trigger and sight picture. Very soon I had to learn to shoot offhand, and I have practiced offhand shooting ever since. I had to learn the hip rest position, and the rather heavy barrel was a help in slowing down the swing. This was around 1890, so to date I have been shooting for over 80 years, but best of all, I am still shooting.

While attending the local school, I hunted woodchucks and crows in my spare time, and along about 1898 I attended the Peekskill Military Academy at Peekskill, N.Y. Then after 1900 I attended the Albany Business College in Albany, N.Y., where I took up the subject of bookkeeping, as I was always interested in any subject that called for accuracy. I did some bookkeeping over the years, but liked making accurate things even better. So after business school I learned the woodworking trade, and made wood patterns for the Rome Brass and Copper Company. Then during World War I, I worked for the Remington Arms Company as a small arms inspector and taught manual training in the high school at night. I decided to learn the tool-making trade, and that's what I still do.

I started driving a car in 1900, and back a few years General Motors gave me a write-up in *Corvette Magazine* stating that I was the oldest sports car driver in the

U.S.A. Well, I am still driving a sports car, and my driving license doesn't run out 'til I am over 90. It is time enough then to call it a day.

At the turn of the century, I was also interested in Schuetzen or offhand 200-yard shooting. I got my first real offhand rifle, a .28-30 caliber which had a breech-seated bullet barrel from Harry Pope. This fine rifle was on the Stevens-Schuetzen action. With this outfit I started shooting, which I followed up 'til around 1925. Later I had a very fine Ballard rifle with one of Pope's muzzle loading barrels with his mechanical ball starter. This was in .32-40 caliber. This was soon followed by rifle after rifle until the time I left off Schuetzen shooting around 1928 or '30. At this time I was living in Little Falls, New York, and spent most of my time hunting crows and woodchucks. There was no one interested in Schuetzen shooting, and that was the only reason I gave up this sport.

About 1903 I met Harry Pope in person. He was in his prime at that time, and the most consistent shooter I have ever known. We were good friends from then up until the time he passed away. The last time I visited with old Harry was in July of 1938 when we both attended the Schuetzen matches then held on the old Walnut Hill Range near Woburn, Mass. He came to this match with Lucian Cary. My old friend John Kaufman, and Paul Landrock, L.L. Heath, Louis B. Cooperman, John W. Cole, and his wife Susie, were also in attendance. While visiting with old Harry, I took a long .32-40 bullet out of my pocket and handed it to him. He gave me one startled look and then said, "Where in hell did you get that bullet?" When I told him I cast it in one of his moulds, he said, "That is impossible."

Then he explained. He said he had only made up three moulds to make that particular bullet. One for Charles Rowland, one for John D. Kelley, and one for himself. When I told him I got the mould along with one of his fine rifles from the family of Mr. Kelley, he said that explained matters. He also said that Rowland had damaged the mould that was sent to him, and that his mould, along with the cherry that cut the mould, was lost in the San Francisco fire of April, 1906. Harry told me to take good care of that mould as it was the only one in the world, and, he said, it was the most accurate bullet he had ever used. Then he said some day that mould would be worth a thousand dollars. This fine mould is in mint condition and I still own it. The mould casts a long .32-40 caliber of bullet of nearly 200 grains weight.

It must have been around 1905 or '06 when I first met Dr. Mann, Charles Newton, and A.O. Niedner, who was then living in Malden, Mass. I got some fine swages from Niedner, and about then my own metal-case bullet-making started, and I am still making fine bullets today, but now I use swages by Fred Huntington and Biehler & Astles.

I was for a time more or less associated with both Dr. Mann and Niedner as I had designed a metal case bullet in .224 caliber, as well as a cartridge in the same caliber that we called the .22 Krag, which I used in a single-shot Winchester rifle. At first we made a short bullet in .22 caliber from the .22 Short case, with plenty of lead exposed on the tip. Later we used the .22 caliber Long Rifle hulls, which made better bullets. Friend Niedner made up a fine Schuetzen offhand rifle for me soon after this to take my .224 Krag case.

Soon after this, maybe 1909 or so, we attended a Schuetzen match held at Union Hill, N.J. I used that .224 rifle and caused quite a stir, as all the other rifles were in .32-40 or .38-55 caliber. Niedner said my three-shot target was a world record at the time. I was shooting on the German ring target, offhand at two hundred yards. The possible was 75 and my score was 74. Two shots were in the center ring, which measured less than one and one-half inches, and the other shot was a quarter-inch or so out.

I had several things going for me in this match. First, I had a very accurate rifle with which I had done considerable offhand practice, but the most important thing was the higher velocity of the 60-grain .224 caliber bullet that I used. It reached the target a whole lot faster than the other bullets used in that match; there was no recoil. This was about the first time such a small caliber Schuetzen rifle was ever used in offhand two hundred-yard shooting. Some of this data was shown at one time in the NRA's magazine.

I can still see well enough to put five shots into a quarter inch or less at one hundred yards from bench rest, but when I sit down and try to shoot a long string of shots at one time, the target seems to fade out, which is to be expected at my age, but this does not bother me in any chuck shooting.

I will be 89 in April, but I don't feel that old. Years don't seem to bother me very much. I am feeling OK and I am as active as ever. When snow conditions are good, I do considerable fox hunting on snow shoes. If you want to follow me all day on snow shoes, you had better be in good condition. I have done this all my life, so why stop now as long as I am able to keep going. I can walk and hunt all day without getting tired, but I have always been a good walker. I am only five feet, seven inches tall, and I weigh 150 pounds. Now this may show you why I am still so active, for when I was married at 21 years, I weighed 148 pounds.

All my life I have learned about shooting matters from my long association and personal contact with about the best riflemen this country has ever produced. But all this comes with a touch of sadness when I recall that most of my friends have left the range forever. Some may still be with us, but most of the old-timers have long since passed away.

Some of my friends wonder why I don't retire and take it easy. Well, the reason is that I have been plenty active my whole life, and I am still able to get around as well as ever. So I continue to work in the local machine shop, as I like the work, and I was never one to sit around and do nothing. I mean to keep on working and shooting as long as I am able; after that is plenty of time to take it easy.

Yours truly,<br>
H.A. Donaldson

*Early photo (not dated) of Harve during motorcycling days.*

Camping trip on Jessup River in 1913. Scenes on next two pages were from this same trip. Harvey failed to identify photographers on the early pictures found in his shop.

*Notations found with the photos on these two pages indicate they were taken in the 1920's.*

Next three photos show Harvey with his favorite hunting dog, Ace, for which he named several cartridges. Noted on photo above: "My dog Lemonas Ace, Born, May 14, 1927 — died in 1939, Little Falls, New York."

*Harvey with one of the thousands of woodchucks he hunted over several generations. It is believed this photo was taken during World War II.*

Portrait of Donaldson, taken in his shop in the mid-40's.

One of Jean Streeter's pictures of Harve during her interview in the summer of 1968. Her biographical article appeared in the January-February 1969 Handloader.

*This old barn was converted into a print shop, operated by Harvey's brother, and Harve's shop on the second floor. Windows were broken and the roof leaked badly when these photos by Dr. Roger Wolfe were taken in 1977. At right is the Donaldson house, next door to the barn.*

As you climb the stairs to Harvey's shop, the sign "Anglers Roost" greets you at the door, an obvious reference to the old experimenter's love for fishing and the out-of-doors.

*Light was extremely poor inside Harvey's shop when this 1977 photo was taken by Dr. Roger Wolfe, but the disarray caused by various collectors can readily be seen.*

*Harvey A. Donaldson, designer of the .219 Donaldson and more than a dozen lesser-known cartridges, relaxes while recalling another era of shooting.*

# Harvey A. Donaldson

## The Case Designer, The Shooter, The Experimenter, The Man

### By JEAN STREETER

(Reprinted from *Handloader*
January-February 1969)

When Harvey A. Donaldson was a young man, his 'shooting uncle' gave him a piece of advice which could be followed today. "Boy, if you want to learn about shooting, go to the man who knows how to shoot."

If cut from this page those words wouldn't quite fill a .219 Donaldson case, but they define a lifetime of learning and teaching.

We dare say there are few, if any, serious shooters today who have not heard of Harvey — a man who "knows how to shoot." On his letterhead he lists himself as a firearms consultant and designer and originator of the 2-R Don., .22 Krag, .25 Krag, .219 Don., .220 Don. Ace, 6mm Don. Ace, 6.5mm Don. Ace, .250 Don. Ace, .250 Don., .270 Don. Ace, .270 Don. International, and the .300 Don. Ace.

Bench rest competitors know Donaldson personally, for he has been a familiar figure at matches from the very beginning of the organized centerfire sport. But for the thousands of readers who would like to know more about him, we interviewed "Harve" at his home in Fultonville, New York, and offer this bit of background on a truly interesting gun enthusiast.

"My family, generations ago, migrated from the Highlands of Scotland to the Albany area of New York. Later they moved to Washington County and settled in the Scottish community of Argyle. Many of my ancestors are buried in the colonial cemetery nearby."

The Highland warriors carried their fighting ability to this country and the defense of their new land. During the French and Indian War, two of Harvey's relatives fought at Ticonderoga with the Black Watch. A half dozen fought in the Revolution. One, John Barkley, who served as mayor of Albany, fought in the Battle of Oriskany and his name is inscribed on the battle monument. Three ancestors fought in the War of 1812 and five uncles served in the Civil War.

"My shooting uncle, A.B. Jones, was a member of the Berdan Regiment of Sharpshooters in the Civil War. He was my mother's older brother, and he taught my mother how to shoot a rifle and a shotgun. He told me once that she could shoot better than he could. Guess that's where I got my love for shooting. It was this same uncle who started me shooting when I was under eight years old.

"My mother used a muzzle loader. If you didn't know how to cast bullets you didn't know how to shoot. When I was a boy my mother taught me how to mould bullets over the kitchen stove. I've still got some bullets that my mother cast."

Charles A. Donaldson, Harvey's father, was not a shooter, though. He ran a hotel and drugstore in Fultonville.

Harvey's years span a fair portion of history. Born on April 6, 1883, in Fultonville, he has lived his whole life in the Mohawk Valley within sight of the Mohawk River. But this has not enclosed him. Harvey has traveled the breadth of the United States and his interests encompass the globe.

After learning the basics in reading and writing from his mother, Harvey went to the public school in Fultonville. During the Spanish American War he attended the Peekskill Military Academy where he finished his rudimentary education. Around 1900 he studied banking and bookkeeping at Albany Business College.

Harvey enjoyed athletics, participating in football, basketball and tennis. At eighteen he could run 100 yards in eleven seconds. Now, at 85, he can still give you a run for your money.

After business college Harvey started work in a woodworking plant in Fultonville, learning the woodworking trade — stair building, wood carving and cabinet work.

In 1905 he married May Galbraith and moved to Rome, New York, where he worked in a wood pattern shop making patterns for the Rome Brass and Copper Company.

During World War I Harvey lived in Little Falls and commuted by trolley to the Remington Arms Company in Ilion where he worked as a small arms inspector. Nights he taught manual training in the high school.

Following the end of war he worked a short time as a bookkeeper and then hired on as a cabinetmaker for a local woodworking concern. He also studied the machinist trade and learned toolmaking.

He returned to Fultonville in 1935. About twenty-five years ago the Fultonville Machine and Tool Company was founded and "Harve" hired on as its first machinist. Today, he is the oldest employee in years of service as well as age, and he still puts in his eight and ten-hour days. As he says, "I'm not exaggerating — but I don't know what it means to get tired."

When Harvey sits back in his comfortable old chair, legs crossed, the ever present cigar in his mouth (more chewed than smoked), then it's time to listen. Maybe he'll tell of canoeing up the Erie Canal and down the Mohawk River, or shooting deer and 'chucks, or finding Indian relics in the surrounding countryside.

"In 1900 I bought my first automobile, a Stanley Steamer. At that time registration for license cost $2.00. There were less than a thousand cars in all of New York State. That Stanley Steamer! Top speed was twenty-five miles an hour — downhill.

"You'd come to a hill, hold the brake with your foot and get up about 300 pounds of steam, hoping the boiler — mounted right on the seat — wouldn't blow up and send you sky high. Then, over the top of the hill you'd go. It steered with a lever and you sat on the right side."

Harvey has owned a Stutz Bearcat, National Marmon, Mercer, Apperson Jack Rabbit, Simplex, and Scripps-Booth, among others. In recent years he drove a Corvette and an article in the Corvette Magazine of 1961 lists him as the oldest sports car driver, not only in years but in years of experience driving sports cars.

For almost fifteen years he rode a motorcycle in hill climbs and road races and bears the scars from many spills. One, at over eighty m.p.h., gave him a fractured skull and burned his leather jacket and the World War I leather flying helmet that he was wearing.

There isn't much that doesn't interest

"Harve." But it is as a shooter, the originator of the .219 Donaldson, the man some call the father of bench rest shooting and a man who willingly shares his vast shooting knowledge, that Harvey A. Donaldson is best known.

His shooting started with a Stevens Expert Model .22 and an old muzzle loading rifle. By the time he was a teenager he was using heavier muzzle loaders and going to shooting matches.

"About the time that I was fifteen years old, around the time the Spanish American War started, I used to accompany my uncle in the fall when he went to turkey shoots, and I shot a big rifle at those shoots. We used to shoot prone with the gun laid on the ground over rests, shooting at forty rods (220 yards), at the head of a turkey. The body of the turkey was usually protected by a pile of railroad ties. The turkey was fastened by the foot back of those railroad ties and all you could see was his head and part of the neck. The guns were muzzle loaders, no breech loaders, and they had peep sights — aperture rear and pinhead front.

"The trick was to hold that pinhead on the turkey's head at the time he was looking over the top. Sometimes you'd pull the trigger and by the time the bullet got there, the turkey had moved his head. We paid twenty-five cents a shot and the man who hit the turkey got the bird. That's the kind of turkey shoots that we had in those days."

Harvey read his uncle's copies of *Shooting and Fishing*, which developed his intense interest in Schuetzen shooting. His first Pope rifle was made in 1903. The more he used the rifle, the more he questioned many things and searched for more information than the magazines offered. Then it was that he received his uncle's sage advice. "Boy, if you want to learn anything about shooting, go to the man who knows how to shoot."

Transportation was primitive then, so Harvey went to the experts the only way he could — via Uncle Sam's postal delivery service.

"I got to know many good fellows through correspondence. In my readings I would find these different people who knew shooting — Pope, Mann, Niedner, etc. So I'd write to them and in the old days they would always give you a good answer. That's one reason I've always tried to repay what I learned by answering letters. It gets rough at times. I answer letters every week from people that I never heard of," and Harvey voices his only complaint, "and half of them don't even send a stamp."

Learning by correspondence was one thing. Shooting was another.

"It took a lot of practice. You had to

*Some of Donaldson's bullet moulds are hung on the rafters of his shop.*

This well known group of bench shooters, photographed at the 1949 or 1950 matches, includes, from left, M.D. (Bud) Waite, NRA; Warren Page, shooting editor of Field & Stream; Col. Townsend Whelen; Fred Huntington, president of RCBS; Samuel Clark, Jr.; Al Barr, NRA; and gun writer Lucian Cary.

shoot all the time. You had to eat and sleep and dream shooting. There isn't one man in a hundred thousand today that can devote all that time to practice.

"I lived three miles from Little Falls, and when I came home at night, my gun was right back of the kitchen door. The range was just outside. I'd get my gun and go out and shoot. I'd shoot night after night after night. Fired thousands of shots.

"Now, bench rest shooters don't do that. They go out and practice shoot, but about the time a guy gets the right load, he's worn his barrel out. You couldn't do that with a Pope rifle. Those lead bullets didn't hurt the barrel at all. Some of them were fired many thousands of rounds and they still shoot."

Harvey frequently compares rifle shooting to playing golf. Just as the golfer maintains a certain hold and stance, so the offhand shooter must do also.

"The way you hold a rifle is a habit. Just like the way a man hangs onto a golf club. He does it the same every time. You never want to bend your body. You want to stand natural, with the weight between the two feet. When you bring the gun up you want to be in your natural position.

"Suppose the hold is higher or lower than the target. Moving or bending your body to get on mark will throw you all off. So you adjust your palm rest. It's got a screw and a stop on it so you can raise it up and down. This brings you back into your natural position. After years of getting that natural position, don't ever let anything disturb it, because it'll spoil your shooting."

Harvey's words, while dealing with Schuezten shooting, and still valid for today's shooters. Whether it is a palm rest or sling that is used to position the rifle in offhand shooting, or the adjustable front rest of the bench rester, the shooter should still maintain his natural position that's comfortable for himself.

Schuetzen shooting seems to be a favorite topic with Harvey, understandable when a person realizes that he is about the last of that clan. The lessons learned through the years were the foundation for the various case experiments for which Harvey Donaldson is well known. It was a necessity to experiment, to find a proper load for the rifle.

"The Schuetzen is the most temperamental rifle ever built. You use a different lubricant in the summer than in cold weather. It'll shoot better between five o'clock in the afternoon and dark than it will between seven o'clock and noon. It might take several months to work up a load, and then you weren't sure it was the best.

"Some guns will use bullets hardened 1 to 25. Another rifle made by the same man with the same tools might need a 1 to 30 mixture. Maybe this rifle will work better with a heavy cylinder oil and vaseline mixture, and another rifle will shoot better with another combination — beeswax, carnauba wax and a little bit of rosin as a binder."

After 1900 Harvey started attending Schuetzen matches at Walnut Hill Range in Woburn, Massachusetts, and at Union Hill, New Jersey. Correspondence changed to personal contact and Harvey met, shot and worked with Harry Pope, Dr. Mann, Niedner and Charles Newton.

He started designing cases around 1910 and made metal cased bullets in Niedner swages. He credits all his early information about bullet making and experience in case design to Dr. Mann and Niedner. The only wildcat cases at that time were Niedner's, who designed the first .25-06. Harvey had a rifle chambered for that wildcat and had to make his own bullets with a hand swage.

About 1933 Harvey decided that the .22-3000 Lovell cartridge would give better results if changed slightly to accept additional powder and have better burning ability. The resulting 2-R Don. was successful. But never content, he kept trying for something better.

By 1939 he had switched from the Lovell design through the .22 Niedner Magnum and the .25 Remington Rimless to the .219 Winchester Zipper, looking for a good basic design upon which to build a cartridge of longer effective range, flatter trajectory and greater accuracy. The result was the renowned .219 Donaldson, also called the .219 Wasp.

The cartridge rapidly gained supporters and grew in popularity. Custom rifle makers across the country fitted and chambered barrels for the Donaldson cartridge. As bench rest shooting came into vogue, the .219 Don. played a vital part.

Modern bench rest shooting is but a series of refinements over the technique used by the old-time 40-rod shooters who rested their muzzle loading rifles across a log. Up until the 1940's, experimenters were vitually the only ones who set up any type of bench to help them in testing for accuracy. Reports of these tests circulated and hunters and shooters wanted to know more, to learn how to make their rifles and loads more accurate.

Hearing that a Northwestern group, the Puget Sound Sniper's Congress, had been holding a type of bench rest match since 1944, Harvey arranged for a similar shoot in Machias, New York, in early 1947. Then he and others in the Pine Tree Rifle Club arranged a large invitational shoot at their range in Johnstown, New York, over the Labor Day weekend, 1947.

The Eastern Benchrest Shooter's Assn. was formed at that time. Harvey was elected president, Colonel Townsend Whelen, vice president, Samuel Clark, Jr., executive officer and Frank E. Hubbard, secretary and treasurer.

The excellent shooting at the 1947 matches caused national interest in bench rest shooting. By 1950 bench resting was national in scope and correspondence between various clubs was carried on, culminating in the organization of the National Bench Rest Shooter's Assn. in 1951 with five regions, covering the United States and Canada.

Harvey had designed a target for the 1947 matches and with minor changes, it is the target now used officially in all bench rest shoots. For several years he donated a trophy, an added item to spark competitive instincts. For all his organizational work, publicity to get the movement going and his tremendous willingness to help other shooters, Harvey earned the title of Father of Bench Rest Shooting.

He quit competitive offhand shooting after a lot of his old friends and shooting partners passed away. "When the competition dies off, what are you going to do?" He stopped shooting bench rest when he began having trouble seeing the target. He still shoots and sights in rifles for others, but his ability to sight a target all day has failed.

Ever the experimenter, his name is attached to more than 10 cartridges. Through the years, when he has needed a tool or an adaptation of commercial ones, Harvey has invented and made what was required. His shop is filled with strange little gadgets, seen nowhere else, that he had made to fill a purpose or put into reality an idea.

What does the future hold for the 85-year-old man who doesn't know what it means to be tired? "I'm still working at case design. Why, you know, I've got in my mind right now an idea . . ."

*The glorious clutter of Donaldson's shop, where he can find about anything he may need, is the envy of his visitors.*